SAVE THE HUMANS

SAVE THE HUMANS

ROB STEWART

with **Evan Rosser**

RANDOM HOUSE CANADA

PUBLISHED BY RANDOM HOUSE CANADA

Copyright © 2012 Sharkwater Productions Inc.

www.randomhouse.ca

Random House Canada and colophon are registered trademarks.

Library and Archives Canada Cataloguing in Publication

Stewart, Rob, 1979–
Save the humans / Rob Stewart.

Issued also in electronic format.

ISBN 978-0-307-36007-6

1. Stewart, Rob, 1979–. 2. Environmentalists—Biography. 3. Political activists—
Biography. 4. Environmentalism.5. Green movement. I. Title.

GE56.S74A3 2012   333.72092   C2011-905282-2

All interior photos courtesy of Rob Stewart and the Stewart family.

Text design by Andrew Roberts

Cover photos: Richard Sibbald

Printed and bound in the United States of America

10 9 8 7 6 5 4 3 2 1

To my parents, my sister, Nana,
and everyone with a vision of a better world.

Contents

Introduction

The Revolution to Save Humanity

As a kid, when I wasn't outside catching frogs, snakes, fish and lizards, I spent a lot of time imagining the animals I might eventually encounter, and even more time fantasizing about the things I wished I could have as pets. Ideally, I wanted a dragon. Thirty-five to seventy-five feet long, covered in impenetrable scales, capable of breathing white-hot streams of fire, tame for no one but me, badass as hell—as a dragon obviously would be. Hours spent dreaming about what it would be like didn't get me any closer to owning one. A dinosaur would have been almost as cool but despite the fact they'd once walked the earth, the relative availability of a T. Rex or velociraptor was about equal to that of a dragon. When it came to real animals, the closest I could get in all of my imaginings to hunting alongside a dinosaur or riding on the back of a dragon was swimming with sharks.

When I was a kid, people knew very little about sharks. I read book after book and learned all the facts I could: approximate sizes of the different kinds of sharks, what experts thought they ate and where certain species could occasionally be found. The

There just aren't that many T. Rexes around, so I had to make do with what I had.

experts got most of their information from yanking sharks onto shore and studying their anatomy. But even the experts didn't know where sharks spent most of the year, how long they lived or where they mated.

The mystery that surrounded much of their lives leant itself to daydreaming—the details were mine to shade in. But the basic facts were irrefutable: like dragons, sharks were unbeatable predators, and like dinosaurs they ruled an entire world. It was an underworld we couldn't see and didn't understand, and they ruled it so well they terrified people. Friends, relatives, teachers and television all preached that we needed to fear the ocean because there were these creatures in it that got to decide what lived and died and they would rip any trespassers to pieces. The fact that everyone was afraid of sharks made them seem cooler to me. The cute and cuddly already had advocates and aficionados. Everybody loved pandas, elephants and tigers. They were spoken for. I gravitated towards anything weird, different or dark. From the moment I knew sharks existed, I loved them.

As I got older and my knowledge of sharks deepened, my fascination with them did as well. Sharks were the first creatures on the planet to develop jaws, more than 400 million years ago. People call them primitive eating machines, but there's nothing primitive about them. Sharks have two more senses than human beings. Like all fish, they have a lateral line that runs along their bodies and allows them to form a sensory impression of all of the movement that occurs around them: a full 360-degree picture or feeling or some kind of sense of their environment at all times. More amazing is sharks' ability to detect electromagnetic fields. At first, I didn't know what an electromagnetic field was or what it meant that sharks could sense one, but it was clear to me that nothing could compete since nothing perceives the world the way sharks do. When I finally understood what that meant, my respect grew. Everything we perceive as matter—trees, ice cream, mountains—is actually energy, moving at a speed and arranged in such a way that makes it a tree or an ice cream cone or a mountain. That's an idea that most of us can only grasp abstractly, but sharks feel it. They can feel the energy emitted by every living thing on the planet (and some dead things too).

How can an animal like that exist? An animal with two entire senses we can't even imagine; an animal that can keep replacing its teeth if they get broken or lost throughout its life, and that can birth genetic clones of itself in hard times. The level of sophistication is mind-blowing. Even individual shark scales are made of tiny little teeth called dermal denticles. As a shark passes through the water, each denticle creates a tiny vortex. Taken as a whole, all of these vortices create a slipstream around the shark's body, allowing it to move through the water with less friction than any other animal. They are the most hydrodynamic things the planet has ever seen.

Sharks evolved a form and a function that has seen them survive five major extinctions that wiped most life from the planet. Pretty much everything else has changed. Dinosaurs became birds and uncountable numbers of species have come and gone. Through it all, sharks have moved beneath the surface of the oceans, ruling the most important ecosystem on the planet. They've shaped the evolution of life in the oceans and, just like that, they've shaped all of life on earth.

For an animal born into a world of sharks to survive, it had to be shark-tested—its appearance, defence mechanisms, feeding habits, mating behaviours. As the top predator in the oceans, sharks drove evolution. Schooling behaviours, communication, camouflage and mimicry, poison—I think a lot of these things were adaptations to avoid sharks. Their rule of the oceans was challenged only briefly by ocean-going reptiles who were unfit to survive the mass extinctions. Ever since I first saw a picture of a shark, I've believed they are the most perfect animals on the planet.

And then, when I was about nine years old, I met one.

Under water, even the best free divers seem clumsy and ridiculously out of place, and then you see a shark—the thing you've been taught your whole life is going to rip you to shreds. You freeze. Its power is unbelievable. It swims without seeming to move any part of its body, barely using its tail for propulsion. It's so beautiful you forget to feel afraid. It makes eye contact. Its eyes are just like yours, big and round and open, and you watch it scanning you, figuring out what you are. It's like an alien, sensing you with two faculties you know nothing about, but there's something so familiar about it, too, as it contemplates you and considers its next move. Then its tail springs to life—one hard swoop and it's gone. Without its overpowering presence, your awe starts to dissipate and you realize *It didn't eat me . . . I don't have to be afraid anymore!*

That first experience changed everything for me. It showed me

Shark catch and release.

that sharks weren't menacing predators of people and that our fear of them might be unjustified, manufactured out of a few stories of attacks and passed along to keep us from swimming out too far. After I saw that shark, I started to wonder what other beautiful things there were in the world that I was missing out on because someone had persuaded me they sucked or taught me to fear them.

Sharks are awesome. I grew up studying sharks, zoology and evolution with a sense of awe, and then, when I became a wildlife photographer in my late teens and early twenties, I uncovered something horrible. Because of us, and our attitude to them, in the last three decades we've lost more than 90 percent of the world's sharks.

We're losing sharks to legal and illegal fishing and unsustainable fishing practices; we're losing them as bycatch, the accidental victims of "targeted" fishing for other species; we're losing them to pollution, particularly to the accumulation of heavy metals and plastic products in our oceans; we're losing them to recreational fishing; and we're losing them as climate change and carbon emissions raise the temperature and acidity of the oceans, blanching reefs and destroying marine habitats.

The counterpoint to my first awe-filled encounter with a shark was the first time I witnessed the horror and destruction caused to sharks by illegal longlining. Longlining is a method of mass fishing in which a boat lays out a single high-tensile line up to 60 kilometres long with as many as sixteen thousand baited hooks hanging from it. The catch it yields is indiscriminate and can include a variety of large fish, sea birds and turtles. Sharks unfortunate enough to get hooked are often dragged onto a fishing boat still alive and struggling. On deck, their fins are cut

After its fins are removed, the shark is simply pushed back into the ocean to slowly die.

off and they are thrown back overboard still writhing, to sink and suffocate in the ocean.

After first seeing finning in the waters around the Galapagos Islands, I knew I had to do something to save sharks. I first tried to use my pictures to educate the public and encourage donations toward a patrol boat in the Galapagos Islands. After a year of championing the plight of sharks, I'd raised $1,300 in donations. A pitiful and disheartening number that made me realize I needed to change my approach, and instead attempt to show people why I loved these creatures so that they would become as outraged as I was. In 2002, at the age of 22, I teamed up with the Sea Shepherd Conservation Society, a "radical" marine wildlife conservation organization, and set sail to Central and South America to make a movie about sharks. Along the way I helped battle illegal fishing boats, ran from the Taiwanese mafia and the Costa Rican authorities, dove in the most shark-filled waters on earth and almost lost my life twice. *Sharkwater*, the documentary feature I shot during that trip, had its North American theatrical release in 2007 and went on to receive thirty-five international awards, inspire more than a dozen conservation groups and change government policy around the world. When the film was released, only sixteen countries had active bans on shark finning. Today, that number is more than ninety and still climbing. The success of both the film and the advocacy work it sparked taught me a valuable lesson: People want to do good, but they need to be informed in order to do it. When they watched *Sharkwater* it was as if they were witnessing some of the atrocities committed against sharks firsthand. People were more than capable of taking it from there.

The threats to shark populations that I focused on in the film are the result of the multi-billion-dollar global shark fin industry. Shark fin is an ingredient in shark fin soup, used for texture and prestige, not flavour. In parts of Asia, it is also ground into powder for use in assorted pills, supplements and tonics. Shark cartilage is mistakenly thought to have curative powers—particularly for cancer patients—because sharks are resistant to certain parasites.

As daunting as it seemed, I knew early on that I had to find a way to get *Sharkwater* released in China, the country that is by far the biggest consumer of shark fin. It was also the country where *Sharkwater* had the greatest potential for good. If audiences there could see it, they could launch a significant attack against shark finning and make a serious dent in the practices that are killing sharks.

It took three years of effort but with the help of the conservation groups Wildaid, EcoVision Asia and the Bharti Charitable Foundation, in April 2010 I finally found myself boarding a plane to attend the film's Hong Kong premiere. EcoVision had negotiated a month-long engagement with a chain of IMAX theatres and had arranged for Lisa S., a popular Hong Kong-based model and actress,

Lisa S. and me at the Hong Kong premiere of *Sharkwater*.

to attend the premiere, which was being held at a theatre on the seventh floor of a giant mall in downtown Hong Kong.

Walking out of the elevator, I was blown away by how many people had come out. We had been expecting some representatives of the Hong Kong press, but reporters had come over from mainland China as well. My handlers found and introduced me to Lisa S. and then set about assembling an impromptu press conference in the theatre lobby. As reporters crowded around Lisa and me, all I could think to myself was, *wow, people really care about sharks!*

Lisa and I were each handed as many microphones as we could hold. Each one bore a logo, cut out of cardboard and attached to its handle, declaring its station affiliation with candy-coloured anime enthusiasm. I ended up with both hands full. Then the questions started.

"Lisa, when will you be getting married?"

"Lisa, Lisa, where is your husband today?"

"Lisa, how was your vacation?"

"Lisa, are you thinking about having kids soon?"

Lisa S., it turned out, was the hottest thing going. Born in America, she had moved to Hong Kong to model and ended up marrying Daniel Wu, one of China's biggest movie stars. They are Hong Kong's version of Brad Pitt and Angelina Jolie. As the press conference progressed I made myself useful by holding all my microphones in front of her. None of the media there gave a shit about the movie or me. Lisa kept saying, "And this is Rob Stewart. He made a documentary called *Sharkwater*." But only a few of the reporters were interested.

Then Lisa S. took off to meet her husband, and the film played for the first time in China. The IMAX theatre was full, with around 750 people watching *Sharkwater* on the biggest screen it had ever played on. When it was over, I got up on a small stage for a Q&A session with the audience; I didn't know what to expect, but it turned out the people who had turned out were concerned and connected, and had been drawn to the screening by our press and publicity over the preceding weeks. A few questions in, a young woman raised her hand. Audibly nervous, she began by citing a UN report based on a study from Dalhousie University in Halifax that predicted the collapse of every fishery on the planet by 2048. "What's the point in stopping finning," she asked, "if the sharks—if *all* the fish—will be gone anyway?"

Her question stopped me dead. I had to think for a moment about how to even reply. "I think it's going to take public pressure," I finally answered. "It's going to take people mounting up against these atrocities to turn anything around. Yeah, every fish could be gone by the year 2048 if we continue business as usual. But if you tell your friends what's going on, if you talk about this and make it an important issue for yourself, your family and your friends, then everything can be turned around." She nodded, seemingly satisfied, and handed off the microphone.

The trouble was that I wasn't convinced. *Sharkwater* was the embodiment of my desire to do something to save the animal I love the most. It represented almost ten years of my life and making it had taken more from me than I thought was there to give in the first place. I believed it was the absolute pinnacle of what I was capable of at the time, and in the years since it had first been released, it'd seemed like it might be enough. But there was nothing in *Sharkwater* that could answer her question in any way that satisfied me.

Were we really headed for a future with no fish? Part of me already knew we were and accepted the UN report as further evidence. If *Sharkwater* wasn't enough, what could I do to save sharks? If saving sharks wasn't enough, what could I do to save the oceans? I couldn't get that question out of my head for weeks after I left Hong Kong. Eventually, I just embraced it and let the pursuit of an answer push me farther in my thinking about conservation, humanity and the world than I ever thought I could go.

We are currently facing the greatest challenge ever put before humanity. Carbon emissions, deforestation, ocean acidification, climate change, soil erosion, desertification, mass extinctions, pollution, overpopulation, food scarcity—these are just some of the problems we haven't come close to adequately addressing. Scientists estimate that at our current western levels of global resource consumption, we would need six earths to sustain us. If trends continue, by 2048, when every single fishery and most of the rainforest is predicted to be gone, there will be nine billion people on the planet. Forty to fifty percent will not have access to enough safe drinking water, and twenty percent won't have enough food. Affordable oil and energy will be a thing of the past and millions will have been displaced by rising sea levels, desertification and agricultural failure. The environmental movement is no longer about hugging trees and saving pandas; it's a fight for basic human survival.

We have to save the humans. That's the goal that has been absorbing me since the Hong Kong premiere of *Sharkwater*, both in the pages of this book and in the new documentary feature I've been shooting, which I'm calling *REvolution*. Whenever people ask me what my next project is about, I tell them it's about how humans are going to survive the next hundred years. The two most common responses I get? "We're not going to" and "Yeah right, good luck."

Everyone seems to know that we're in deep, deep trouble, but very few of us are doing anything about it. Instead of taking matters into our own hands, we're gambling on the hope that someone will invent a solution to all of these problems. That's not a bet we should be staking the human race and the entire natural world on. We have far too much to lose.

My hope for this book is that it will persuade you of two things. The first is that we can't put off our responsibility to the planet any longer. The science is clear on that point. It screams, "DO SOMETHING."

The second is that to have any chance of a future we need all hands on deck. Instead of banking on a select few scientific minds, governments and non-governmental organizations to save us, we need united communities and every brain on earth pumping at full capacity to come up with answers, inventions and initiatives.

That's the real point. That's the point of stopping shark finning, the point of recycling, the point of lobbying for measures to reduce carbon emissions, the point of every single action we take to help the environment. The crises confronting us are so big, interconnected and intimidating, each of us must find an issue we care passionately about and simply attack it. Considered as individual efforts, such a scattershot approach may seem insignificant, but taken together I believe it's our best hope for survival and evolution as a species.

The fight is not going to be an easy one, but as I hope to prove in the first parts of this book—which tell the story of how I became an environmental activist—the place to be isn't on the couch. We need to be out on the front lines.

The plus side? Fighting for something greater than ourselves will call out our greatest heroes; it has the potential to unite humanity to a degree never before seen in our history. It will also give our ailing societies a purpose other than consumption and push us toward the next step in human evolution. In a way, I think this crisis is exactly what we need right now.

If my own experience is anything to go on, I bet you will find it fun to join the fight. Trying to save sharks has taken me all over the world on crazy adventures with amazing people. Activism has given me the kind of life I dreamed of as a little kid, a life that's never boring, a life of total engagement. And the same fun, the same adventure, the same sorts of challenges, the same purpose? They're all sitting there waiting for *you*.

There is no better feeling than waking up in the morning knowing that you're going to battle to save something you love, and that there are awesome people out there working hard, too, to help you do it.

The revolution to save humanity has already begun. All that's missing is you.

PART ONE

CHILDHOOD

Chapter One

Out Catching Frogs

Before school, before toys, before play dates, before candy, before books, before cartoons, before music, before girls, before games, before babysitters, before trips, before friends, before fighting with my sister, before anything, there were animals.

When I was born, we already had pets and as soon as I was mobile I started looking for more of them. There might be a new pet hiding in the grass or under a rock in the backyard. Past the backyard there was a field that wasn't yet a subdivision and down the street there was a ravine. There might be pets in the field or in the ravine or in any of the streams and ponds that snaked and dotted it. There were definitely pets at the grocery store. They floated in tanks or sat, packed in ice, waiting to be taken home to join the ones we already had. Eventually, I discovered that there were pets in the waters of the Caribbean, in the mangrove swamps and ditches and on the beaches of Florida, in the lakes and woods of northern Ontario, orphaned at veterinary offices or at the Humane Society, in the seizures department of an international airport and waiting for me to buy them in bait shops and pet stores.

There were so many animals out there that to have even the slimmest chance of meeting and getting to know all of them, I would have to be chasing, catching and studying them constantly. If I stopped for a second I might miss one. And what if the one I missed was really cool?

My mom loved cats and fostered them for the Toronto Humane Society. At any given time our house could have as many as ten of them in it. We bottle-fed orphaned kittens, and gave a temporary home to older ones that ripped around our house and up the curtains. Inevitably we'd bond with at least one of our foster kittens and wouldn't be able to give it up, and Pusser, Munroe, Sniff, Spike, Paddington and Miskit all became permanent residents. My dad was allergic to cats, and spent much of my childhood on allergy medication so our family could have cats.

From the time I was born, we always had a fish tank in the house. At first they were small, but as our family's passion for fish grew, so did the tanks. I can't remember the family room without the 110-gallon version that became my favorite microcosm of all things awesome and predatory, but it arrived after I did, in 1982 I think, when I was two. It sat three feet off the ground, next to the couch, the perfect height for me and the cats to watch its occupants in wonder. I would park myself in front of the tank, and cat after cat would sashay over to join me. I'd sit there until someone carted me away.

I found the fish tank fascinating, and the cats—my fellow observers—much less so. There's nothing mysterious about cats, no challenge when you're trying to understand them. I liked them well enough, but they let you pick them up and get a good look. The fish were much harder to figure out. Why were they fish? How did they move like that, flying through the water with so little effort? How did their eyes work? What did they eat? How did they breathe? Even with them confined in a couple cubic feet of tank, it was hard to get a good look. They rarely held still. They often hid behind waving fern-like seaweed or inside rocky caverns;

some of them were so tiny you had to look as hard as you could to make them out in any detail; and there were dozens of them. The population of the tank changed over time as well, evolving from a handful of goldfish into much more diverse and exotic species.

Even as it got more elaborate, though, the fish tank was for when I was stuck inside in the winter or when I couldn't get one of my parents to take me on an adventure. As soon as I could walk, I wanted to be outside catching dragons, or at least butterflies and grasshoppers, and lifting logs or overturning stones in case there was a toad underneath.

About a kilometre from our house in north Toronto, there was a park and ravine where my mom would take me walking, searching for critters in the grassy fields, among the trees, in the bogs and along the banks of the Don River. My first clear memory of catching something bigger than a frog, toad or tiny lizard is set in that park with my mom in early summer. I was three and we were taking our usual route when I spotted a garter snake just off the path and went for it. It darted into thicker underbrush before I could get to it, but I thought it might still be nearby, so my mom and I combed the side of the path trying to scare it into the open. We had no luck and eventually she dragged me home, but the next day on the same stretch of path, we came across the snake again. I resisted the urge to rush it this time. Instead, at my mom's direction, I crept towards it, trying not to startle it. Again, it escaped into the thicker brush, but much more slowly, and I was able to get a sense of the direction it had slithered off in.

We met that snake on the same path every day for a week. With each encounter and with my mom's help, I got a little closer to catching it and I learned a little more about it — how it moved, what startled it the most, what I could do to coax it into sticking around a bit longer than it should. After seven days of trying, I finally caught it with my bare hands and got it into the bucket (my mom always carried one in case I found a pet and needed to bring it home without dropping or hurting it). When I got the snake to our house, I put it in an empty fish tank. I fed it goldfish, as well as frogs, grasshoppers and crickets I caught in the back field, and I gradually landscaped the cage into snake heaven. I kept that garter snake for the whole summer, letting it go so it could hibernate for the winter.

On weekends if I was lucky my dad would take me, and occasionally friends of mine who felt like tagging along, to an area of swampy marsh behind York University to catch frogs. We'd spend hours tromping around, diving into muddy little ponds, and we'd come back looking like the first half of a Tide commercial. In those early, unsophisticated days of frog-catching, all I had was a flimsy green rectangular plastic pet store net about 8 inches across, with a short handle. To catch anything with it I had to get within a couple of feet and really commit, diving fully extended and smashing the net down as quickly as possible. The net was so wimpy that often the force of bringing it down would cause the handle to bend and the frog would escape. To make sure of a capture I had to get the frog from the net to my hand as soon as possible. Then I could get a close look at it and decide whether, based on its size and colouring, it was cool enough to keep.

Keepers went into one of several plastic reptile containers that had pre-punched breathing holes in their lids, and were made by a company called Hagen. I tried not to go anywhere without at least two or three Hagen containers. To keep up with the influx of amphibians, we put a 35-gallon fish tank in the backyard, which, like the tank for my garter snake, I landscaped into a paradise for its inhabitants. In the height of the summer, it would usually be home to ten to twelve frogs, unless I'd managed to catch a giant bullfrog, in which case that frog ruled.

The best frogging spot was a quarry behind my great-uncle Bob's cottage in Muskoka. We would go up to stay at his cottage for a few days every summer, usually over a long weekend. (My parents eventually bought a place of their own next to it, but that didn't happen until I was sixteen and a lot less interested in frogs.)

As a kid I lived to encounter animals, like this fresh-water turtle. I still do.

The quarry was partly abandoned and slowly giving itself back to the forest that surrounded it. A big part of that gradual untaming was the quarry's frog pond. It was thirty feet in diameter and deep enough that it took a good breath to dive down and come up with a handful of muck from its muddy bottom. It was *full* of frogs—leopard frogs, which were small and pastel green with perfect black spots; common frogs, mottled different shades of green and black; and many dark, forest-green bullfrogs with bright yellow bellies. All these frogs in turn attracted snapping turtles, herons and all manner of other wildlife. The water was always cool and clear at the beginning of the season, and the shallows near the banks full of uncountable numbers of tadpoles, which would scatter into deeper waters as you approached.

In years when we were really lucky, there would be one frog in the pond that was such a genetic freak, so much bigger than the others, that we crowned it the king bullfrog. We're talking a 4-pound frog from the Jurassic, a gigantasaurus frog the size of a small dinner plate. My dad was always my frog-catching buddy growing up. Going to the quarry with him was a ritual, and in the years when there was a king to hunt, catching that frog became our number one priority.

The thing about the king bullfrog was that for it to get that big in the first place, it had to be the most wily and elusive frog of them all. Catching the king was a feat. Sometimes I'd spot him early in the day. I'd lunge and miss and he'd slip beneath the surface and never reappear. My dad and I would sit on the bank of the pond or walk around its edge in the shallower water for hours, waiting with our nets. When it started to get dark, Dad would make me follow him back to Uncle Bob's so we wouldn't miss dinner. I would've stayed all night.

Not only was the king crafty, we were also shamefully underequipped for the hunt. Even in later years, when I was a regular at pet stores and my dad and I had a heap of experience with heavy-duty fishing gear, we always went frogging with those same dinky green plastic nets, which we lashed to the end of a 10- to 12-foot pole to add much needed reach. We had little chance of getting to the king before he escaped, and even if we had caught him, the mouth of the net barely fit around his body. What we should've done, and what I'll do when I have kids, is go to a serious commercial fishing supplier and get strong, metal nets with extendable handles. That would be the best tool for the job.

But my dad and I never got past the pet store nets, so we had to improvise. Using two long poles and a length of netting, we designed the ultimate frog-catching apparatus. We strung the net between the two poles, kind of like a portable stretcher. With one of us on each end to spread the poles apart, we could position the net above the gigantasaurus and catch him by bringing the poles down and then together to close the net. It was still open at the both ends, but he'd have to swim at least a couple of feet to get free before we lifted him out of the water.

After we invented that setup, we only failed to catch the king bullfrog once. In the years we were successful, I'd pack the king up and take him home. He usually fit exactly into the small Hagen container. His bulbous sides would squish against its walls, his bum would press against the back and his nose would kiss the lid. It sounds a bit claustrophobic, but for long distance travel you had to keep the king in a small container. He was so big that if you gave him enough room to jump, or even just to gather his legs under him, he'd blow the lid off anything you put him in. Before we realized that it was better for the king to ride snug and alone, on a few trips home from Muskoka he blasted open the communal frog container, unleashing dozens of leaping frogs into the family car. (I still remember my older sister, Alex, screaming.) We could have duct-taped the lid of a large container closed, but then you risked him hurting himself bashing against the lid.

I always kept the king until the end of the summer. When it was time to let him go, my dad and I would make a special trip to set all the frogs free. If Dad had the time, we'd haul the king back up to Muskoka and set him free at Uncle Bob's, but usually we just took him and all the frogs to the swamplands behind York University or to a camping area called Bayview Glen, a short drive from my parents' place. We'd find a good spot and dump all the containers at once. Then we'd stand and watch our own little army of frogs hop into the water, and disappear.

The supermarket was my earliest pet store. When I was brought along grocery shopping, I often spotted cool-looking creatures in the seafood section of the store from my perch on our cart. Whatever my mom and dad had planned for dinner went right out the window if I got fixated, so the rest of my family ended up eating a fair amount of crustaceans. (I refused to eat any of them.)

Lobsters were the best, because they were still alive when we got them home. Crabs were cool, too, but we rarely found a live one in the supermarket. Alive was better than dead, but I was never squeamish about checking out something dead. Dead was better than nothing.

If I managed to talk my parents into a new dinner menu, I would block off all the doors to the kitchen and make little pens on the linoleum tile. I'd put the lobsters or whatever into the pens and see where they went. I'd pick them up and look at them. If they were dead, I tried to figure out how they would've moved and recreated the motion with my hands.

Sometimes I lucked out and got something really cool like a bulldozer, a lobster that has plow-like arms instead of claws, which it uses to shift sand around as it looks for food. It was a lot easier to win the supermarket argument if I was pushing for an animal I'd never seen before. My enthusiasm always trumped my parents' second thoughts about eating weird crustaceans.

It seems like it should have been a little traumatic—"Yes, you can make a new friend and play with it, until it's time for the rest of us to eat it"—but it never was. I understood that it was my pet for a bit and then they had to eat it. Having it for dinner was part of the responsibility that came with taking it home in the first place. But as a kid I never ever ate seafood. Fish were friends not food.

My first mammalian pets were a pair of rats named R.A. and T. My sister, Alex, had successfully petitioned for guinea pigs. I tried hanging out with the guinea pigs for awhile, but they were too cute—too fuzzy and turd-shaped and boring—for me. I needed something with a bit more edge. Eventually I was drawn to rats.

R.A. and T. turned out to be a male and a female and they ended up having about sixteen babies every three weeks for almost the entire six years I owned them. My dad and I would take the litters to the giant PJ's Pets outlet—the first big box pet store in our neighbourhood. The first time we brought a box of babies in, we were directed to the woman in charge of the store's reptile department. She agreed to take the whole box, with a twisted, Cruella De Vil glint in her eye, but my dad and I refused. We found a guy from one of the fuzzy departments to take them instead. He gave us his word that they'd be sold as pets and the reptile woman wouldn't get a single one. He became our go-to guy when we were dropping off a litter of R.A. and T.s.

I eventually lost R.A. and T. to cancer. The chance that R.A. and T. were siblings was high, and the chance that their parents had been siblings was pretty high as well, and it may have made them susceptible. R.A. was the first to get a tumor and we took him to a veterinary clinic where he had an expensive operation. Unfortunately, the cancer eventually returned, and we couldn't save him. When T. got sick, my parents and I decided that an operation that cost hundreds of dollars to save a rat that cost a few dollars was too much—especially when it was likely not going to work. It was an early cost-benefit analysis of life and love.

The rats were the first and last of my fuzzy pets. Instead I started catching, buying and trading snakes, lizards, fish and amphibians. I'd always had a compulsion to collect and categorize things, which probably underlay my need to not just see and interact with animals, but to have them all to myself and to constantly strive for bigger and more exotic specimens.

When I was really little I collected both screwdrivers and light bulbs with a serious passion. My dad was a fairly disorganized guy when it came to his tools, and he never seemed able to find the screwdriver he needed when he had a job to do, which usually led to him heading out to buy a totally new set. He'd finish whatever he was doing and soon the new set of screwdrivers would join all the sets that had come before it, littered haphazardly around the basement. My first organizational impulses were acted out on those screwdrivers. I'd gather them up and arrange them in groups according to size and type.

For the most part, the screwdriver collection didn't get me in too much trouble. But once when I was in junior kindergarten, I completely unscrewed the bannister of our circular staircase while my parents were at work. That night, my mom noticed a pile of screws on my nightstand as she was putting me to bed. She asked me where they'd come from and I told her. After she'd tucked me in, she gathered up the screws and went to inspect the staircase. In the whole bannister there were only two screws that I hadn't managed to get out; they were driven in at odd angles and I hadn't been strong enough. If someone had put any serious weight on the bannister, it could've been a really nasty scene. Instead, it just worked out badly for the nanny who had been watching me. She'd spent the whole time I was at work on the bannister on the phone to friends back home in Britain, and as a result she wasn't around for much longer. After that incident, I was encouraged to screw things back together before I finished playing with them.

The light bulb collection was the more serious obsession of the two.

Before I could walk, I was after light bulbs. Once I was moving around upright someone had to keep an eye on me at all times. I was a good climber as a kid—I could climb palm trees and find my way up walls. When I was three, my mom came home from work and found me swinging one-handed from the dining room chandelier, trying to unscrew the bulbs. The same thing happened in restaurants, malls and on other family outings. I have a memory of my Nana yanking me by the legs as I'm desperately clinging to a chandelier swinging over a room of stunned diners. The lightbulbs I was after were spectacular, huge, perfectly round and frosted, with globes bigger than any I'd ever seen. Light bulbs were everywhere, and the bigger, weirder looking ones never stood a chance against me. I kept my collection in my bedroom closet, the loose bulbs in a giant wicker basket and the boxed ones on a top shelf. I stopped collecting light bulbs when I was about eight, but I still have a bit of a thing for them. If I see a wicked light bulb, I still have to fight a bit of an urge to unscrew it and take it home.

My collection lit my parents' house for years after I'd given it up. The last of the light bulbs, a red one, went the Christmas I turned sixteen.

I didn't always feel connected to my friends as I was growing up, though my parents maintain that I was popular. According to them, our basement was always full of neighbourhood kids and classmates staging elaborate battles with my collection of Masters of the Universe toys and creating forts out of couches and old boxes. It's probably true that there were always other kids around, but there's a big difference between being surrounded by people and truly connecting with them.

My world and the passions that kept it spinning were built around animals, nature and exploration. Though I made meaningful connections with other kids, some of which have survived into my adult life, I only ever found one childhood friend who was as obsessed with animals as I was, Mike Steinman. Mike and I would spend hours catching and studying frogs and reptiles. But he lived about an hour away in Newmarket and I couldn't see him regularly. By and large, my childhood friendships weren't as deep as I wanted them to be because I couldn't fully share an essential part of who I was. Instead, it sometimes felt that friends were a bit of a distraction keeping me from further discoveries.

Around the time I came along, my parents, Sandy and Brian, were founding and building two enterprises: a publishing and promotions company that operated in the film industry, and another promotional company that arranged the giveaways and prizes in cereal boxes. They regularly went on trips to international toy fairs or to tour the facilities of toy manufacturers. They'd come back with stuff that wasn't even out yet—action figure prototypes, Tony the Tiger plush dolls from twenty different factories all competing for their business, that sort of thing. Our house was always full of the newest and coolest toys.

I liked having a lot of toys (what kid wouldn't?), but I never got too hung up on them. They were fun, but nothing to obsess over. Still, other kids thought I was spoiled. My dad liked fast cars and he often dropped me off in the morning. Getting out of a sports car every day kind of cemented my image as a spoiled rich kid.

To add to the picture here, I also got teased for being chubby. I remember an incident involving some rockets we built in class when I was in grade five—tiny models about 18 to 24 inches long, powered by a charge of gunpowder that would launch them thousands of feet into the air. After each rocket was launched, the kids all had to run to collect the spent rocket from when it fell in the field. I had been running after rockets all day, it felt like, and hadn't yet managed to be the first to get to one, so I decided to take off before the next one hit the ground to get a head start on the other children. I was right under it and things were looking good; I had my arms up to catch the rocket when it slipped through my hands and bashed me in the forehead, knocking me out. I don't remember the half hour after that, but I ended up with a dent in my forehead that you can detect in two whole years of school pictures.

The teasing was all pretty standard stuff. I wasn't coming home in tears every night and I've heard tons of stories from people who got it a lot worse than I ever did. But in public school other kids just seemed petty and cruel to me. Of the ones who weren't outright hostile, few showed an interest in going out to catch frogs and snakes, and the ones who did definitely weren't as interested as I was.

Animals were never cruel, never evil. The closer I got to them, the better they were to me. A picture of a snake in a magazine only gave me a general sense of it. But if I caught it and picked it up, I could see the heat-sensing pits in its face, see what its tongue looked like, find out whether its pupils were vertical or horizontal and whether its camouflaging continued even inside its eyes (if the snake was heavily patterned, it almost always had eyes with a similar camouflaged pattern). I needed time with it—at least five to ten minutes, inches from its face. I needed to get it home and into a cage, so I could really study it.

I found the initial rush of information—as I noticed physical traits I had never seen and didn't understand the function of— intoxicating. The better I got to know these animals and the more I understood about them, the more I wanted to know. I needed to touch them, smell them, talk to them, feed them, examine and interact with them in every possible way. I can still remember facts and figures about every animal I encountered as a kid. How big they get, what kind of cage they need, what temperature range and habitat they live in, what they eat. I never had to write anything down. I think I partitioned off a section of my brain completely for animals—physical and behavioural statistics and observations. Once I'd studied an animal, really gotten to know it inside and out and added it to my mental catalogue, I was always fine with letting it go. Seeing an animal for a flash in nature without learning anything about it was never enough for me.

Each animal I encountered presented an entirely new set of features and behaviours. Each had a different mouth, ate or moved differently, responded to me differently. I became completely obsessed with discovering all of these differences, and wondered why they existed. Beyond the wider peculiarities of species and subspecies, I realized that every animal had its own individual personality and face. The generalities I had been taught—that all dogs are loyal, that snakes are slimy and dangerous, that anything fuzzy is lovable—were bullshit. The more time I spent with animals, the more I realized how much people sold them short because they had never experienced them firsthand.

The more misunderstood and demonized an animal was, the more I came to appreciate it. On one hand I felt that I could relate because I was misunderstood and a bit of an outsider myself, but

I also recognized just how much these animals were being over-looked. On the basis of a completely arbitrary consensus that furry and cute were the two most important qualities an animal could possess, most people had chosen to ignore so much beauty and so many miraculous adaptations. I wasn't going to do that. I was going to learn everything there was to know about these creatures and if no one else wanted anything to do with them all the better— I'd have them all to myself.

Chapter Two

Chain Moray Eels Teach Me a Valuable Lesson

Every year over the Christmas holidays, my parents would take my sister and me on vacation. Usually, we stuck around in Canada to celebrate my birthday on December 28 and then we jumped on a plane and welcomed the new year on an island in the Caribbean. I couldn't bring along a tank or cage big enough to hold anything for any length of time, but I always travelled with my Hagen containers and a net for lizards and snakes. To this day, my parents get a kick out of telling people about pulling up to a resort hotel with a beautiful, koi-filled fountain out front and taking their eyes off me for a second to unpack the taxi only to see me diving into the fountain to catch the fish.

Those trips were also my introduction to the ocean. Early in the morning when the tide was still out, my dad would help me get my sneakers on and we would haul my nets and containers and a bucket or two borrowed from the resort down to the water. In the ambient wash of light just before sunrise, we would load all of the gear onto a little inflatable raft my parents had bought me. My dad would perch me on top of everything, or on his shoulders if the dinghy was too full, and then swim out into the ocean pulling the boat. We'd find a stretch of reef left uncovered by the tide and I would hop off and walk along it looking for crabs and turning over rocks and checking to see if anything was hanging out in the tidal pools. Walking the reef brought me into contact with creatures from another world. The tiniest hints of movement could lead me to animals I'd only ever seen in my imagination, and some I couldn't even find there.

As I got a little older, we brought snorkels and masks with us, and I would do my best to catch darting, brightly coloured fish. It was basically impossible—I couldn't catch anything under water— but the ocean itself was the thrill. I was always a strong swimmer and could hold my breath for ages, having learned in my parents' pool. In the warm, clear water of the Caribbean, I felt like I could fly. I could meet a million different species. I didn't have to take parts of the ocean away with me—I could become a part of the ocean myself.

Dad, Alex and me on the beach in Sanibel.

Even from a distance, the creatures I encountered under water were the most beautiful and mesmerizing things I'd ever seen. If I held very still they would sort of follow suit, slowing to a gentle glide and letting me get a pretty good look, but if I tried to move closer they would take off. They were terrified of me. My mom taught me the best way I could get them to overcome their fear: bribery. We fed them. Slowly working up their courage, they would inch toward my hand and eventually take whatever I was offering. When nothing bad happened to them, the response was immediate. I could be trusted; we had an understanding. We might not be friends yet, but we were definitely business partners. We had made a deal.

When I was six or seven, my parents took us to a resort called Round Hill, near Montego Bay in Jamaica. Round Hill was made up of a collection of small villas, each with its own kitchen, tucked up against a single white sand beach. It didn't have a restaurant or a bar. On the beach there was always a small number of local people selling crafts and offering to braid your hair. One woman painted pictures and elaborate designs on your fingernails, and she taught me how to paint my nails and helped me cut the bristles of small paintbrushes into different shapes to get different effects.

All these local people hung out on a jetty that stretched out from one side of the beach. It was the point of departure for catamarans and boat tours. Wading in from the beach I could never find any cool animals—people are about the only things that like to hang out on or near white sand beaches—but the jetty stretched out past the shallows and its tip was teeming with chain moray eels. Chain morays can grow to be nearly 5 feet long, but they're usually half that size. These ones were babies for the most part, as big around as my finger. They hid in crevices in the rocks of the jetty and rendered my snorkel useless by refusing to come near the surface.

Free-diving off the dock, I'd hold my breath until my neck felt hot and I started to get tunnel vision, trying to catch the glint of their eyes as they hid from me, then have to return to the surface.

The chain morays were some of the shyest creatures I'd ever come across in the ocean, but I was confident I could coax them out with food. I spent day after day pulling barnacles off the rocks at the end of the jetty. With a smaller rock I smashed them open and dove down with both hands full of their soft insides. I held out my offerings to the holes in the rock and the chain morays poked their heads out ever so slightly to investigate.

Morays will almost never entirely leave their hiding places, except at night. Getting them to poke their heads out for food during the day is a serious accomplishment. They were the cutest things in the world. Mostly black, their heads and bodies were covered with a mesh of pale yellow lines that roughly resembled a chain-link fence, hence the name. They seemed to have a golden incandescence that shone so powerfully from somewhere inside their bodies it had begun bursting out through their skin.

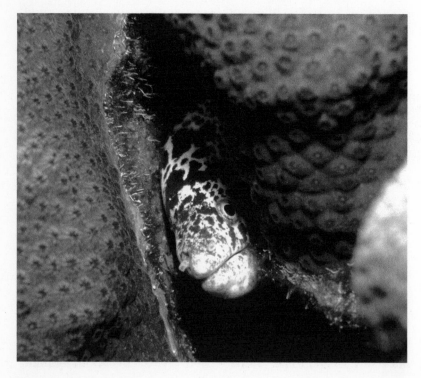

Chain moray eels are extremely shy.

The Jamaica trip was special because I'd had the foresight to bring a bubbler with me—a small water aerator that could be clipped onto the edge of a fish tank or bucket to oxygenate the water so the fish could breathe. After I excitedly recounted my discovery of the chain morays over dinner the first day, my parents went out and found a big bucket for me. Feeding the chain morays allowed me to get a pretty good look at them, but I could only watch them for as long as I could go without air. I needed more time, and to get it I'd have to catch one. A local Rasta I'd befriended, who seemed to spend all his time fishing unsuccessfully off the side of the jetty, lent me a hook and a short spool of line. I smashed open a barnacle and baited my hook and then dove down to catch an eel. Since I'd already been feeding them and we'd developed a pretty good rapport, it didn't take long to find a taker.

He was a little guy, 2 feet long. Too small to muscle his way past the others for the first round of barnacle I'd offered from my hand, he wasn't going to miss the second. When I let the hook and line unfurl, he lunged immediately, grabbed the morsel and started retreating into his hole. Then I pulled on the line to set the hook. It seemed like he started writhing before he had even fully bitten down. His fear and pain ran up my arm in waves and he writhed in frantic endless overlapping knots. I felt the weight of my betrayal and it made me nauseous—every time he jerked at the line trying to get free, I was sure I was going to be sick. I kicked for the surface as hard as I could to get away from what I'd done. But as I rose through the water I kept the line clutched in my hand; I didn't—or couldn't—let go of it.

I was already crying when I broke the surface. As my lungs took in air, my sobs turned into screams. The moray was still struggling in pain on the end of the line. My arm was burning. I clawed my way up the side of the jetty and onto the dock and the Rasta who had lent me the fishing line ran over to see what was wrong. He must've thought I was hurt. He held me by the shoulders and checked me over and then took the line from my hand, keeping me tucked under his arm. The pain didn't ease. He freed the eel I'd hurt and threw it back into the water and then turned to comfort me.

"Breathe," he instructed. "Just breathe. It's okay." I remember how I concentrated on following the strong, slow rhythm of his breathing. The sobs came less frequently. Eventually they stopped entirely. I was calm again, but it wasn't okay. I had hurt an animal that trusted me. It had opened itself up to me and I'd used its vulnerability to try to get what I wanted from it.

I went to find my parents on the beach. For the rest of the trip I stayed close to them and left the jetty and the eels alone. I couldn't take the guilt of facing what I'd done.

Chapter Three

Ninety Percent of the Time I Would Have Been Fine

In 1987, my parents bought a condo in Florida, on the first floor of a two-storey townhouse in a complex on Sanibel Island in the Gulf of Mexico. It had a small screened-in porch and my older sister, Alex, and I each got our own rooms.

We'd been to Sanibel before . . . The first time we went I was three or four years old and my Nana on my dad's side came with us. I remember spending a lot of the trip looking for shells on the beach with her. Sanibel Island is one of the premiere shelling destinations in the world—the island itself is made of shells crushed to bits over some monumental period of time—and Nana was a pretty avid shell hunter. She had a magical, encyclopedic knowledge of shells and she taught me their names, what had lived in them and which were the rarest. If there was still something alive inside, we'd figure out if the shell was worth killing over or if we should just leave it alone. She kept me occupied while my parents lay on the beach. My parents always seemed to want to spend most of their trip just lying on the beach, chilling out. I could never figure out why you'd go somewhere and just lie down. Why wouldn't you want to run around and see things and collect stuff and figure it all out? I'm only starting to understand chilling out now.

Other than shelling with my grandma, the only thing I remember from that first trip was almost catching a diamondback rattlesnake. Having been warned to stay away from rattlesnakes by my parents, I was nervous and I took a second too long to think before diving for it. I brought the net down too hard and a bit late, and the rim of it landed across the snake's back. I was scared I'd hurt it. When the snake didn't try to fight its way out of the net, I picked it up by the tail to check if I'd accidentally killed it. Just as I realized the snake was still alive, I heard my dad screaming. He got to me, still screaming, before either the snake or I could react. He must have been powered by one of those rushes of adrenaline that allow housewives to act like superheroes when their children are trapped under cars or swept away in rivers. He grabbed me, threw me over his shoulder and started running, trying to get me away from the

Mom, me, Alex and Nana in Sanibel.

snake, but I still had it. As he ran, the snake whipped limply behind us until I couldn't hang onto it anymore and it slipped out of my hand. Nobody got bitten, but I was upset with my dad for days for preventing me from getting the snake back to our hotel room and into a cage. He probably wasn't too pleased with me either. (Did I mention that my dad has a snake phobia?)

We visited Sanibel twice a year after we got the condo. On one of those trips I got my first chance to check out the J.N. "Ding" Darling National Wildlife Refuge, a huge swath of undeveloped mangrove ecosystem that must cover a good 30 or 40 percent of the island. My family went by canoe through a section of the reserve called Tarpon Bay. All around us mangrove trees rose from the water on huge islands of roots that were themselves a thriving ecosystem. Small crabs scurried over the trees and the water below us was teeming with mullet, plant-eating fish with a fondness for hurling themselves out of the water and through the air. They grow to be about a foot and a half long. As we paddled, we saw dozens of these fish shooting 4 or 5 feet in the air. Tarpon Bay was also a great place for spotting dolphins and even the occasional alligator, but I can't remember if we saw any of either on that first canoe trip.

We also explored Ding Darling on foot. At one point on the trail, I noticed a water snake in the swamp beside us. You can't catch a water snake with a net, as they figure their way out of it too quickly, so I dove into the swamp and grabbed the snake with my hands. I was holding it up in triumph when my parents both jumped in after me and pulled me out of the water. Apparently while I was focused on catching the snake, a bunch of alligators had been making their way towards me.

That kind of moment was a bit of a theme running through my childhood—the rattlesnake, the alligators. I would get sucked in by an opportunity and go a bit too far, and my parents would always be there, trying to pull me back to safety or to reality. The alligator situation I'm not sure I had under control, but I was definitely fine with the rattlesnake. I'd say that 90 percent of the times they pulled me back, picked me up and carried me away, I would've been fine. They didn't see it that way, though.

I managed to talk my parents into getting me a couple of small cages for the condo as soon as we moved in. Not enough equipment to house all the animals I wanted to catch, but it was a start. On each successive trip I would negotiate for more, adding another tank, net, filter or cage. I kept them all on the condo's screened-in porch and it didn't take me long to fill the space; plastic portable cages for lizards and snakes, bait buckets for fish and bait, a cast net to catch anything close to shore, and a couple of fishing rods for fishing from shore. The largest tank I had was a 2-foot by 1-foot by 18-inch glass fish tank.

I started with anoles, little brown or green lizards five or six inches long that were everywhere on the island. The anoles hung out all over the condo complex, warming themselves in the sun, so I didn't have to go very far to catch them. I'd rip around all day with my net and a Hagen container. When it was full, I'd take it back to the condo and go through a selection process, keeping only the biggest and most unique-looking anoles. Unexceptional specimens got returned to the wild. I'd study the keepers at night or when it was raining and I couldn't go outside to catch other stuff. When we had to go home to Toronto, I'd usually set them free, though one time I did smuggle some back on the plane inside an oversized bulk box of Starburst candies.

Anoles were so abundant I got bored with them pretty quickly, even though they were the largest wild lizards you could find on Sanibel at the time. Instead, I went looking for snakes, which in Florida could get to be five or six feet long, but were far more elusive. While the island was a pretty benign place on the whole, there was always a chance I'd come across something cool and poisonous, like another rattler or a coral snake. Coral snakes were supposed to be all over the island. Their venom is super toxic, easily strong enough to kill a full-grown person, and they're beautiful with really bright yellow, red and black stripes running around them in rings down the length of their bodies. I spent my whole childhood on Sanibel looking for a coral snake and never found one. They were sort of like Polkaroo for me.

The first year's visits to the Sanibel condo set the pattern for our future trips. We'd spend the week Alex and I got off for March school break there and we'd always manage two more weeks in the summer. We hoped to make it down more often than that, but those were the guaranteed trips. The rest of the year my parents rented the place out, so the cages, tanks and fishing stuff would be packed away with my dad's golf clubs in the storage closet. Because we rented it when we weren't there, we kept the decor as impersonal as possible. We didn't hang family photos and we brought all our mementos back to Toronto with us. It was like staying in a hotel. The only time the place ever felt like ours was when I had all my tanks and cages full of creatures and arranged on the screened-in porch.

In the summer of our second year, I found an indigo snake hiding in the shrubs around one of the neighbouring condos. It was about 5 feet long and jet-black. No species of snake on earth is blacker than the indigo snake. This one was so black it shimmered and I could see shades of blue and purple playing across its skin. All I had with me was a dinky plastic pet store net and a small bucket. I couldn't catch such a large snake with them, but I managed to make enough noise trying that one of the gardeners came over to help me. I had the snake trapped against the screen porch of the neighbouring condo, but it was too fast and smart for me to coerce into the cage and too big to catch in my net. The gardener took the bucket from me and held it steady while I used my net to coax the snake inside. Then I carted it back to my parents' condo where we deposited it into the biggest cage I had. I watched that snake for days, but the cage was too small for it, so it just lay still looking depressed, and I let it go.

The only other indigo snake I've encountered was one I spotted on the PR tour for *Sharkwater*. I was driving from the Suwannee

River to Fort Lauderdale, Florida, and I saw an indigo snake on the other side of the highway that had to have been 8 feet long. I skidded to a halt on the soft shoulder and went sprinting after the thing across two lanes of traffic in bare feet. I crashed into the brush where I'd seen him go in, but by that point he was 15 feet on the other side of a barbwire fence. I figured I'd really have to go for it to catch him, but I was in a gun-toting part of Florida so trespassing was out. I still wish I'd jumped the fence.

At night when I was a kid my parents wouldn't allow me out of the condo complex, so I focused on catching geckos and tree frogs. The geckos were nocturnal so I could only track them at night. But geckos are fast and have sticky pads on their feet that enable them to scurry up walls and across ceilings well out of my reach. I had to develop some new techniques. I had a Nerf gun that shot short foam darts with small suction cups on their ends. I modified a dart by attaching a furry foam ball over its suction cup end so it was really cushy. It didn't travel as far or as fast as the unaltered darts but that turned out to be a good thing. I'd stalk the geckos in the parking garages and overhangs under balconies. I'd use my flashlight to surprise them, then shoot the fluffy dart at them, knocking them off the ceiling or wall. Then I'd catch them in my net as they fell. I spent a good chunk of time every night after dinner running around with a flashlight and my gecko dart gun.

The condo complex had these white globe lights that lit up pathways and the sides of buildings, circled the pool and lit the area where the residents dumped their compost. Tree frogs would hang around underneath them and even crawl around on the lights themselves. Eventually, I figured out that during the day you could find the same frogs hiding in the shade behind palm leaves. But like the geckos, they were much more abundant and easier to catch in the dark. I had to catch the tree frogs with my hands because they jumped too fast and far and always leapt out of the net. (Thinking back on it there wasn't a whole lot you could actually catch with those nets.) These tree frogs secrete a toxic mucous that acts as a natural deterrent for predators. If I grabbed one and then later forgot I had tree frog on my hands and touched my eyes, within seconds they would start to burn. Even if I just touched my face, not getting anywhere near my eyes, the stuff would somehow make its way into them. I'd end up screaming, and my parents would have to get me to dunk my face and eyes in ice water. I quickly developed a safety protocol for hunting tree frogs; when you catch one, put it in the bucket or cage then go immediately to the pool and wash your hands.

Bowman's Beach was within walking distance of the condo complex. Anytime my parents went, I tagged along. Once or twice a day, we'd follow the path down to where it dead-ended in a bridge that spanned an estuarial swamp, nicknamed "the Bog," that connected the path to the beach. The Bog was full of crabs, snook — a popular Florida game fish — and even the occasional alligator. I'd watch the crabs running around as we crossed the bridge, but it wasn't until I was old enough to go down to the beach by myself that I started spending a lot of time catching things in the Bog.

On the beach, my parents behaved exactly as they did in the Caribbean: they spread out towels and spent big chunks of the day reading, talking and just laying around doing nothing. Occasionally, one of them would get up and walk down to the water for a swim. I was on their cases constantly to come and catch stuff with me, but for the most part they were content to keep an eye on me from Towel Island.

Snorkelling and free diving were nowhere near as satisfying in Florida as in the Caribbean. There was still the wonderful feeling of flight, so much more overpowering in the ocean than in my parents' pool, but the water of the Gulf off Sanibel was murky and you could only see a few inches in front of your face. In the clear waters of the Caribbean, I didn't have to catch the fish to observe, understand and connect with them. To get a good look at anything

Heaven.

in Florida I had to catch it, and catching stuff in the ocean meant learning how to fish.

My dad had taken me out fishing for bass and sunfish at Uncle Bob's cottage, but my real education in catching big stuff started in Florida with Captain John Fussel. Captain John ran half-day fishing charters up and down the coast of Sanibel and occasionally farther out. He first took my family and me out when I was six, before my parents had bought their place on the island.

Captain John was a redneck Floridian who'd caught and interacted with so many big and awesome animals I'd only ever read about, he was a hero in my books. Right from the start he loved my enthusiasm and seemed to really enjoy taking us out fishing. Any time we got a bite and hauled something in, I made him tell me everything he knew about it. My dad refused to kill anything he wasn't going to eat, so often Captain John's explanations came between laboured breaths as he and my father struggled to land something, then work the hook free so we could toss it back. I'd have a few seconds to get a good look and absorb as much information as I could before they sent our catch crashing back into the water.

On some trips we didn't catch anything. On others we struck gold and caught a tarpon, a huge silver fish up that can weigh as much as 200 pounds. Tarpon are known as a great fighting fish on account of their aerial acrobatics as they fight the hook. We also caught sharks—mostly nurse sharks, as long as eight feet, and some hammerheads. Their size and sharp teeth meant that we could never bring them aboard, and would cut them loose in the water. I never really got a good enough look at them.

Trying to prolong my encounters with these new friends, I always argued with my dad to keep whatever smaller creatures we caught. When we kept something, it would get stored in a little freezer box at the back of the boat and I'd get to study it for as long as I wanted. I'd pore over our catch, taking in every detail. Anytime I noticed something I'd never seen before or couldn't figure out the purpose of, I'd call Captain John over from his cockpit and ask him to explain it to me. We kept silvery-white sea trout most often—my parents must have enjoyed the taste of them.

On one trip with Captain John, we caught a cobia. Cobia are fish most closely related to remoras (the sucker fish that will often tag along on sharks and large marine mammals), but they look a lot like sharks. I was so excited about catching one that I began begging my dad to let us keep it before he and Captain John had even gotten it into the boat.

Cobia are beautiful fish. Their smooth skin is the dark grey-blue of wet beach sand, and they have stripes of white on their flanks and bellies. I guess they don't look very appetizing, though, because my dad really didn't want to take ours home. Since we wouldn't be eating it, he argued, killing it was a totally senseless thing to do. He tried to get me to see the logic of this, but I was well past being open to rational argument. Eventually, he gave in. I could keep it if I really wanted to, he said, but when we got it home, I would be the one who had to gut it, clean it and cut it up for dinner. He was definitely trying to get me to stop and think about what I was asking, and he may also have been trying to gross me out, but I agreed to his terms without a second thought. I figured I'd get the fish home and get a really good look at it before I had to cut it up.

The condo's kitchen had an island in the middle of it and that's where my dad laid the cobia, ready for me on a chopping block. I studied it for awhile. I spread its webbed dorsal spikes, which rise from the spine like a fin and are probably the biggest reason cobia get mistaken for small sharks. I looked into its eyes, wondering if there was any life left in it at all. I got closer and closer, until I could see the way its smooth skin broke into a million tiny scales. When I'd seen everything there was to see, I got a knife. I decided I would cut its head off first and work my way down from there.

I put the knife against the side of its body and pushed, easily working my way through skin and soft tissue but coming to an abrupt halt when I hit the spine. This was a big fish, at least 8 inches in diameter, and its spine was thicker than either of my thumbs. I couldn't find a single knife in the whole kitchen strong or sharp enough to cut through it, no matter how hard I pushed. Using the biggest knife we had, I tried to samurai chop the cobia's head off. I swung the knife hard, and as it crashed to a halt against the impenetrable spine, little bits of cobia flew everywhere. I was in tears by the time I put the knife down, both from what I'd done to this beautiful animal and from the frustration of being in way over my head. I was coated from the waist up in fish bits. There was cobia in my hair and eyebrows, on the ceiling fan, even on the turquoise shell-patterned sofas (forever altering their smell).

Until I had cut it, that cobia had still seemed alive. It was as though it had just been stunned or was lying still waiting for me to finish examining it. It had been so substantial, so slick and shiny with life. Now it was just a pile of mush. My dad took over and showed me I could skip the spine and filet it instead. Then he beer-battered and fried the cobia. I didn't eat a single one of the resulting fish sticks. My desire to possess and study an animal ran so deep I'd acted without thinking about what I was doing; I had campaigned to kill something without really understanding what my decision entailed.

As horrible an experience as it was, I was still too young to fully grasp the difference between alive and dead, between what was good for the planet and what satisfied my curiosity. I did, however, learn the lesson my parents were trying to teach me: If you're going to kill an animal, there's a responsibility that goes along with that. You can't kill it just to look at it—you've got to do something with it. Something that involved gutting, cleaning, cooking and eating it. The process of doing something, I'd learned, was traumatic and gory. It was something I knew I wasn't ready for yet. I hadn't had any earth-shattering revelations about the value of life, but I had definitely learned the lesson. The responsibility wasn't worth it. I never killed anything again just to look at it.

After I'd learned to fish on Captain John's boat, my parents bought me some more serious fishing gear that I kept in Florida— some rods and lures, a landing net with an extendable metal handle and a cast net. Every morning I would wake up around five, gather my gear and head down to the beach. When I got there, I'd wade up to my waist in the ocean and spend the rest of the morning trying to catch the biggest, craziest creatures I could. I fished catch-and-release mostly, but if I caught something really cool, I'd try to haul it—alive—back to my parents' place. Sometimes the creature was too big for my bucket or too heavy for me to lift, or I had no possible way of keeping it alive once I got it back home, and I'd have to let it go.

The cast net, which you throw over a group of fish, was an invaluable tool. If you stretched it out flat on the beach, it was a circle of netting about 10 feet in diameter with weighted edges. You found two opposite points on the circle and held one in each hand, and you held a bunch more of the net under your chin so that it would unfurl properly when you threw it with a twist. When I got good enough, I could cast it onto almost anything I wanted. I used this net to catch small fish to use as bait, to feed the pelicans waiting patiently next to me, and to catch anything awesome that came within range.

Fishing from the beach I caught cobia, ladyfish and sailfin catfish. The sailfin catfish were always a nightmare. They have a giant dorsal spike on their back, which gives them their name. The spikes are poisonous and incredibly sharp, so I always had to use a pair of long barbeque tongs to carefully manoeuvre the catfish off the hook, which was a hassle and stressful and took time away from catching other stuff. Captain John hated sailfin catfish because of the danger they posed anytime you got one in the boat—and because they ate the bait aimed at other more charismatic species. Anytime he caught one, which seemed to happen at least once every charter, he'd beat it to death with a baseball bat, and then unhook it and toss it overboard. My mom and sister came with us on one charter where Captain John pulverized a couple of sailfin catfish and vowed never to come again.

By far the coolest things I caught were baby blacktip sharks. They were the only sharks I ever caught from shore, and only when they were still small—usually about a foot and a half long and not much wider than the business end of a baseball bat—but they were rad. Their bodies were all abrupt angles made of layer upon layer of muscle and nearly every angle seemed to have a corresponding stripe of black or white. They looked like fighter jets. They were small enough that I could grab them and lift them out of the water as they'd wiggle around and try to bite me. I'd work the hook free and then play with them for a bit, maybe flip them upside down. I always had to release them because I couldn't have kept one alive at the condo, though that was my dream. Over my entire Floridian fishing career, I only caught about ten of them, but that was more than enough to justify hauling all my gear down to the beach every day we were on Sanibel.

Chapter Four

In Awe of Specially Designed Oddities

Ever since I was little I've classed animals into distinct categories of coolness. General criteria, like size and feeding habits, largely determine where a given animal ends up on my scale, but even tiny differences in the arrangement of features between animals of the same species can take a creature from "I don't even want to hold it" to "Oh my God, I'd sell my organs to get my hands on it."

Vertical pupils are cooler than circular ones and scales are much more interesting than fur. I want to see some teeth with serious size and shape. Teeth that look like they could do damage, that hint at the animal's predatory strategy. Same goes for claws. The more senses they've got, the better—anything from the heat and movement senses of a snake all the way up to the lateral lines and electromagnetic senses of sharks; the more colourful the better, too, though a predator's cool camouflage tops colour. And the more unique or intimidating their means of moving through their environment, the more I'm obsessed.

Size isn't the most important criterion when judging a species' overall coolness, but when it comes to picking a pet, it's crucial.

The closer in size something is to me, the easier it is to see in real detail. The bigger it is, the easier I can wrap my head around it. If I've got to sit there and look at an anole that's 6 inches long, I've got to press my face right against it to really understand its eyes or its mouth. With something that small there's a lot you can't see properly, meaning there's a lot you can't understand. I did have a set of magnifying glasses as a kid, but I was never that interested in them. I just wanted to see what I could see with my own eyes. With bigger animals my own eyes were enough.

Gila monsters are a 6.5 out of 10 on the coolness scale. On the pro side, they're about 2 feet long, pretty big for lizards; they're venomous; they have big, beaded scales; and they're black and red. But on the con side, they're slow, less predator than scavenger, surviving on a diet mostly made up of eggs and carrion.

How specialized an animal is, how uniquely suited to its environment, is another deciding factor. Green tree pythons are native to Papua New Guinea and northern Australia, and live almost exclusively in trees, barely ever touching the ground. They sit coiled on branches feeling for prey using the heat sensing pits that cover their chins. When something edible comes within striking distance, they lash out, often snatching birds from mid-air. Not only are they extremely specialized and badass hunters, they're also beautiful. They're bright green and have clearly defined heads, a huge aesthetic plus for me (I don't really dig rat snakes or kingsnakes because their heads are basically indistinguishable from their bodies). They are nearly identical to Phoenix, my captive-bred emerald tree boa, who hails from the other side of the world in the Amazon jungle. Despite these two animals having a different evolutionary lineage (boas have live babies, pythons have eggs), they have evolved into beings of nearly identical size, shape, colour and behaviour—adapting to life in the trees producing an example of convergent evolution.

I find animals that are jacks-of-all-trades, like raccoons, admirable but boring. There's a sophistication to specialists. They have carefully designed oddities that set them apart from everything around them. They're also the most fragile of species in the sense that the things they rely on to survive are so specific. Green tree pythons live along a single latitude in Australia and Papua New Guinea. Boelen's pythons, which are without a doubt the coolest snakes on earth, only live in temperate rainforests in the highlands of Papua New Guinea. Specialists are the animals that remind us what an incredible fluke it is that our world exists at all; that the temperature is what it is, that the air we breathe is 21 percent oxygen. They remind us how much damage even the smallest changes to that system can cause and they show us how badly we're screwing things up.

At the pet store, I always bought the coolest, most expensive animal I could afford. I'd study it until I'd learned everything there was to know about it and then I'd trade it in for something even bigger and cooler. As my pets grew in number and size, so did the cages and tanks I housed them in. My pride and joy was our aquarium, 5 feet long, 2 feet tall and 18 inches deep. It sat roughly at eye level—depending on my age—on a specially designed metal aquarium stand. Below it, in a space about the same size, I kept a bunch of smaller tanks and cages, and in the corner of the room I had a tank for my iguanas—two Iggys and a Tony all told, but not simultaneously—that was 3 feet long and about 18 inches both high and deep.

I put a great deal of effort into saving and fundraising to buy inhabitants for that big 5-foot fish tank. I especially focused on predators. There were always oscars, stingrays, catfish, arowanas and crazy plecostomus. Arowanas are a primitive bony-tongue fish that dates back seventy million years. They have huge scales, giant wing-like pectoral fins, a long body shaped like a feather, forked barbels on the lower jaw and an enormous mouth that hinges open to engulf prey. Arowanas can leap so high out of the water they've been known to pluck bugs, frogs and birds out of trees. The red, gold or green Asian version of the species are known as dragon fish, and can fetch tens of thousands of dollars each; in Asia they're thought to both bring luck and protect the home.

Plecos, commonly called sucker fish, are some of my favourite fish. They're catfish, and their mouth acts like a suction cup. If you walk into a pet store and there's a fish stuck to the glass of a tank, it's almost definitely a plecostomus. People used to think that plecos only ate algae, but many are omnivorous and pretty adept hunters. When I first started collecting fish, all I could ever find were regular brown plecos. But as they gained in popularity, mostly due to the fact that they help keep a tank clean, they started to become available in all kinds of sizes and colour combinations. Two of my favourites were blue-eyed plecos, which have black bodies and glowing blue eyes, and royal plecostomus, which have grey bodies with black stripes and bright red eyes.

I would have had a shark, but a saltwater tank is much more expensive and difficult to maintain than a freshwater one, and it would have had to be huge to house a shark. Occasionally I made a go of keeping fish I'd caught in the ocean in my tank on the porch in Florida, but for the most part that didn't end well. Saltwater tanks require huge filtration systems. You need to keep the temperature, salinity and pH right and you can't let nitrates build up in the water from all the fish shit. You also can't feed your fish too much because the food residue builds up as well. It's a delicate ecosystem; the band that sustains life is a narrow one. If I wanted to keep these animals long enough to hang out with them, I had to learn how to keep them alive.

I started with books on the animals I had in my tanks—about fish and what they ate and how they lived in the wild. I got books on aquariums and books solely dedicated to keeping things alive inside them. Then I moved on to my lizards and snakes. The more I read, the longer my pets—both those I'd caught and those I'd bought—survived and the healthier and happier they seemed. Not only that, the books helped me learn things I couldn't pick up through observation. I learned the average measurements of tails, teeth, tongues and bodies; I learned average numbers of young, breeding patterns and the characteristics that made for a desirable mate; I learned the range of territories, migratory patterns and physical stamina. I memorized all these things about all the coolest species and I could recite them like other kids could rhyme off sports statistics and *Simpsons* jokes.

School, for the most part, got in the way of my desire to learn. I couldn't bring my pets to class and I had to read books that covered subjects I wasn't interested in. I spent most of my time lost in my own world, free to do whatever I wanted inside my head. I resented the teachers for forcing me to endure lessons and participate in activities that had nothing to do with animals. I didn't pay attention, I half-assed assignments and just generally made it clear that I was a prisoner, held against my will. None of that made me particularly popular with the staff.

All in all, elementary school was a bit of a nightmare. I was picked on by other kids and got into a lot of fights I didn't instigate, and was sent to the principal's office fairly regularly. Luckily, the principal enjoyed my company. He had a 35-gallon fish tank in his office, full of tiger barbs and neon tetras. I offered him advice on his set-up and ecosystem, told him what he was doing wrong with the fish, and what other tank mates could thrive with them. He liked to hear my tales of the badass creatures I kept at home.

I did my best to keep myself occupied (if only because I had no choice), but it always felt like life was on hold while I was at school. My teachers, my peers and the lessons were a distraction from all the more important things I wanted to be doing. Summer could never come fast enough.

When summer finally did come, I made the most of it. I spent every waking second outside, crashing through the fields and wooded areas in our neighbourhood in hot pursuit of frogs and snakes with one or the other parent or a nanny in hot pursuit of me. It must've been pretty exhausting trying to keep tabs on me. By the time I was ten, my interest in catching and taking home every animal I could hadn't waned. My parents found the solution: nature camp.

Jim Lovisek is an animal handler and trainer for the film and television industry. If you check out his IMDb page, you'll see a list of awesome credits—"snake wrangler," "raccoon trainer" and "live leech wrangler"—from a bunch of movies spread over the last twenty years. When I was a kid, Jim Lovisek was *the* reptile guy in Canada. He toured schools doing assembly presentations with a group of animals and in the summer he ran a nature camp that I attended every single year it catered to my age group.

The camp was based in a classroom at Branksome Hall, an all-girls private school sort of near our house. The classroom itself

Me and Jim Lovisek, and snapping turtle. Lovisek was *the* reptile guy in Canada, and therefore my hero.

was pretty standard—a single large teacher's desk at its head and an orderly series of twenty to thirty smaller desks arranged in rows down the middle. But when Lovisek's camp was on, along with the kids, it was filled with dozens of cages, each occupied by a wild animal that had been rehabilitated from serious injury but couldn't be released for one reason or another.

As cool as the classroom was, we didn't spend much time in it unless it was raining. Mostly, we tromped over the grounds of Branksome Hall—a good portion of which were wooded—catching stuff. I remember wading after Jim chest-deep through a swampy river to try and catch little freshwater fish. We came out completely covered in leeches—a fairly common occurrence at his camp—and had to give up on fishing for awhile to remove them. We also found a shallow frog pond where dozens of baby snapping turtles were hatching on the bank and stumbling around. Jim basically told us to go nuts and I was grabbing snapping turtles with both hands, scooping them into my bucket.

Jim Lovisek was the first adult I'd ever encountered whose job was to catch and play with animals all day. That was pretty revelatory for me. Here was this guy who was basically up to the same stuff as me, but he was an adult and got paid for it and could take home as many pets as he wanted. With Jim I could go after critters my parents had expressly forbade me from trying to catch, like full-grown snappers. With him I caught a snapping turtle 18 inches across. If I had done that up at Uncle Bob's, I would never have been able to bring it back home. At Jim Lovisek's camp, catching stuff wasn't just tolerated, it was the entire curriculum. His camp was exactly what school should have been like.

Chapter Five

Chunk and Satan

I wasn't the only one who had a say in whether or not I got to take on a new pet. If I wanted to keep something, especially something I had never had before, I had to negotiate with my parents. My earliest deals were pretty straightforward affairs. I knew my parents liked it when I read, so I'd offer to read five books if they bought me a $9 lizard. When they agreed, I'd read the five books, all on lizards, and end up with another pet.

As I got older, the pets I wanted required greater investments of time, money and space. The more pets I got, the harder it was to persuade my parents to let me get anything new. At that point negotiating became less about striking a deal and more about manipulating my parents into accepting my terms by any means necessary. When I could, I tried to make my acquisitions seem like their idea. In the era of books for pets, that was a fairly easy thing to do. But there wasn't much hope of persuading them that it was their idea for me to get a 6-foot red-tailed boa constrictor. By the time I was gunning for big lizards and snakes, it was easier to aim for acceptance.

My parents' biggest problem with large reptiles was the idea of feeding them. I talked them into letting me buy Chunk, a 2-foot-long savannah monitor lizard, by telling them that he could survive solely on dog food. That got him in the door and once he was in, we were golden.

Chunk was dog-tame. You could throw him over your shoulder and walk around the house. When you were watching TV, he'd curl up next to you on the couch. Chunk was the best of both worlds: he was a fat, friendly poster-child for big lizards in front of my parents, but when it was just the two of us alone in my bedroom and I tossed a mouse or rat into his cage, Chunk was a seriously bitchin' predator.

A lot of the time I tried to sidestep the negotiation completely by telling my mom and dad I'd already got whatever I was gunning for. "I heard about a deal on a 9-foot python and I couldn't pass it

Chunk, the savannah monitor lizard, dog-tame in
public, but the complete predator too.

up," I'd say. If they didn't seem too, too pissed that I'd just bought a 9-foot python, I'd run out and actually buy one.

I was such a successful negotiator that in grade six, when my parents sold our house and moved us into a slightly bigger one, I was given the room beside my bedroom exclusively to house my pets, and got my own aquarium, an 86-gallon tank that was 4 feet by 18 inches by 18 inches. I set it up at my eye level and underneath it I kept smaller lizards, crabs, stingrays and, for a long time, a giant African bullfrog named Gilbert.

The biggest addition to the reptile room, as it quickly came to be known in our household, was a giant enclosure—6 feet by 4 feet by 4 feet—that I built out of plywood and ⅛-inch thick Plexiglas to house the greatest negotiating coup of my life: Satan.

Of all the lizards you can keep as pets, water monitors are the pinnacle—or they were to me when I was twelve. Native to most of Southeast Asia, they're the second biggest lizards in the world, behind komodo dragons. Owning a komodo dragon would have been even cooler. But seeing as there are only a few hundred of them left on earth it would be nearly impossible to buy one, not to mention irresponsible. Water monitors you could buy in specialty pet stores. They're available, they look almost exactly like komodo dragons and can grow to be seven feet long from nose to tail.

I badly wanted a bigger, more badass version of Chunk. But to tame a water monitor to that extent you have to log serious time with it from the moment it's hatched, holding it every day. Years down the line you'll end up with a 7-foot long, 80 pound lizard that'll let you treat it like a teddy bear, but I wanted to jump the gun. I checked out baby water monitors in the pet store, but they just weren't as cool as the bigger one. So I bought Satan, who was already 3½ feet long. He wasn't Satan yet, though. He had to earn that nickname.

To pick up a water monitor you have to wear giant leather gloves, similar to the ones you see on falconers, because they've got large, strong hands and sharp claws. Even a fairly well-behaved water monitor could rip your arm to shreds just trying to get away from you. Satan was not well behaved. To pick him up, on top of gloves, I always had to put on a few layers of clothing topped by a thick hooded sweatshirt to give his claws something besides my arms and chest to dig into. Decked out in my protective gear, I then had to brace myself for a struggle. Satan would do everything in his power to get out of my arms and run free around my room. He'd bite me and whack me with his tail, which by the time he was fully grown was 3 feet of solid muscle. I've still got scars all over my arms from trying to hold onto him.

In his cage—where he couldn't tear me up, take pieces out of me and shit all over me—Satan was a stunning creature. He was big enough that through ⅛-inch Plexiglas I could still make out all the details of his face: black with beaded grey-black scales that crept from the crown of his head down between his eyes, giving way to smoother swathes streaked yellow-gold beneath his eyes, around his mouth; his tongue, impossibly long, like a split piece of black ribbon; the ridges that arched above both eyes and allowed for a range of expression that most people would never believe possible from a lizard; his teeth, massive, irregular and curving. Watching him hunt was a whole other level of joy. I once put an entire tank of fish into his cage. He dove into it head first and demolished everything inside in a matter of minutes, using his forked tongue to smell for the fish even underwater.

Satan broke out of every enclosure I built for him. He shattered the ⅛-inch Plexiglas, he tore chicken wire, he even separated plywood from a wooden frame. He would rip around both the reptile room and my bedroom, deciding for himself where he should live. He took up residence in a bookshelf for awhile and spent weeks living on the top shelf of my closet. As he moved around the room, he would tip over bookshelves, rip my clothing and sheets and shit everywhere. I was always worried about him breaking into my other tanks and eating the animals. My parents and sister, who had been reluctant guests under normal conditions, completely avoided my rooms for the three years I owned Satan. The only exception was when we had a bunch of family over for Christmas or Thanksgiving and everyone decided to head upstairs and "see all Rob's stuff," though my sister would do her best to avoid the tour even then.

When I was fifteen and started staying out later and occasionally sneaking a few beers with my friends, Satan made slipping back into the house unnoticed nearly impossible. I'd creep up the stairs as quietly as I could, trying not to wake my parents so they wouldn't find out what I'd been up to. Opening my bedroom door, I'd find Satan on the loose. Inevitably, when he registered my presence he'd find it unsettling. He'd turn away from the books or clothes or whatever he'd been flinging around and look at me full on. He'd flicker his tongue once or twice, then begin to cover the ten or twelve feet that separated us. His first tentative steps would turn into a full run, and in the last couple of feet before he hit me, he'd rise up on his hind legs and sprint with his arms flailing. Then he'd grab, shove and attempt to bite me in a display of territorial dominance. Calming him down was impossible, so I'd have to muscle him into the closet and lock him in, trying not to catch a bad scratch or bite. Then I'd have to sit for awhile, letting the adrenaline ebb away, before I could go to sleep. After a few of these episodes, I finally decided he needed a new home.

I tucked Satan into a potato sack and put him in a cooler, then I took him to Port Credit Pets, an exotic pet store in Mississauga, Ontario. The half-hour drive to the store must have traumatized him because when we arrived and I reached into the sack and pulled him out, he lay cradled in my arms like a baby. He just poked his tongue out and looked around. He even let the clerk pet him. For the first time in his life he was tame.

Large water monitors are worth a fair amount of money, owing to their rarity. Unsurprisingly, a tame one is worth a lot more than a vicious smashing bastard. In Satan's case, tame was worth about $250 more than pissed off. So as he sat in my arms playing nice,

I decided not to let the clerk in on any of our unpleasant history. He directed me to put him into a cage that was fronted by two wussy sliding glass doors. I recommended he choose something stronger and went so far as to tell him that Satan had broken out of enclosures before, but the clerk assured me it would be fine. I decided that I didn't want to lose $250, so I put him in the cage and used the profits to buy a red-tailed boa constrictor.

Later I heard that not only had Satan broken out of his cage on his first night at Port Credit Pets, but he'd gotten into a cage full of very expensive geckos from Madagascar, eaten them all and then disappeared. I don't know if they ever found him. I didn't go back to Port Credit Pets for four years after trading in Satan. When I finally did, it seemed best to let sleeping dogs lie.

Chapter Six

Getting Off an Alligator
Is Trickier Than Getting On

Around the time I parted ways with Satan I fell in love with skateboarding. If my parents bought me a skate mag, I'd sit in awe flipping through it over and over for hours. If they bought me a new deck, I'd sleep with it in my bed.

I started to bring a board down to Florida when we went on vacation. On the skateboard I could go farther to catch stuff. I was also bigger and could carry more nets and fishing rods. I had more specialized tools, like snake catchers I'd built with my mom—long sticks with a bit of cord at the end looped through an eye hook, so you could lasso a snake and then pull the cord tight to hold the snake's head against the stick. I also possessed better intel. From years of experience, I knew where I was most likely to find big snakes, alligators and fish. But no matter how much of a catching-stuff machine I made myself, there was nothing better than stone-cold luck.

There's one main highway on Sanibel that runs alongside Ding Darling down the entire length of island. To get anywhere beyond the immediate vicinity of the condo complex, I had to skateboard or bike on a path that ran in a thin ribbon between the highway and the nature reserve. I'd take the path to Ding Darling or cruise into the main town on the island and go to the mall or the movies. When it rained, the sides of the highway would often flood. As it slowly dried out, small pools would be left behind. If you were lucky, you could find something cool in or near one of those pools. The luckiest I ever got in Florida was along the bike path: I found a 5-foot alligator.

I was skateboarding back from town and the alligator was only 3 feet from the edge of the bike path, but I didn't notice it until I was right beside it. It didn't react to me at all as I passed. I let my foot drag along the asphalt and came to a quick stop. I looked back and saw that the alligator still hadn't moved, so I kicked my board into the rough at the side of the path and crept back towards it, keeping low to the ground. I got around behind the alligator and slowly crept towards it. It didn't seem bothered at all, didn't move, didn't seem to know I was there.

When I got close enough, I jumped. As I came down straddling its back, I concentrated on securing its head. I caught its jaws and held them closed with my hands and then I stretched out along its back and laid the side of my face against the top of its head, waiting for it to start thrashing. It didn't. After a few long seconds, I lifted my head and sat up. I didn't really know what to do. I felt its smooth, ridged scales against the sides of my knees; I looked at the top of its head and snout; I leaned back and looked over one shoulder to see its tail, stretching out motionless behind the both of us. I wasn't strong enough to move it, I didn't have a cage I could put it in and I didn't have anything to tie its mouth shut. So I just held it and looked.

I looked and looked, but there was no getting around having to let the thing go. Getting off, I knew, would be trickier than getting on had been. What if I let go, and it turned and snapped at me? If I got my legs free and worked them around the front of it so I could hold its mouth for as long as possible, then I would be way too close to its jaws when I let go.

I slid one leg over its back so I was riding it sidesaddle and I looked some more. Then I let go of its mouth and sprinted away past its tail. I ran like the wind. If it tried to snap at me, I was already gone. I ran 20 feet, and looked over my shoulder. The alligator slid into deeper water and disappeared. I turned around and walked back along the bike path to where my skateboard was waiting for me in the grass, then rode the rest of the way home to the condo.

Not all of my animal interactions were so benign. When I got older and would occasionally bring friends down to Florida, some of the stuff we'd get up to was downright morbid.

You could often see blue crabs swimming around in the Bog, beneath the bridge to Bowman's Beach. One summer, when my friend Tyler was down with us, he and I attached steak knives to the ends of a couple of broomsticks and harpooned crabs. My parents ate our impaled catch—but still.

One time I was fishing for bait with a cast net from my usual spot at Bowman's and saw an entire pack of cownose rays flying up and down in the shallows. I had my cast net with me. As the pack was passing by, I threw my net into the middle of it and caught one. For the first time ever, when the net landed, it started moving away from me. Usually its weighted edges would be enough to bring the small fish I'd caught to the bottom and I'd pull the net in and scoop up my catch. But the ray bolted, flapping like mad inside the net. I managed to drag it to shore but it kept struggling after I got it out of the water and I saw that it had tangled itself in the webbing in a million places. It was making awful, desperate sucking and breathing noises—the sounds of valves and gills and its mouth opening and closing. I panicked, but knew I had to drag the ray farther across the sand to get it to a place where I could untangle it from the net. The noise of its attempts to breathe seemed to get louder as I set about trying to set it free.

I could feel that it was afraid and getting more and more desperate.

It was incredibly difficult to get the net untangled with the ray flapping and whirling its tail. The longer I tried, the more frantic I got. I still remember my panic as I knelt on the beach working at the netting. Weirdly I don't remember how it all turned out. I do remember burying a dead stingray on the beach at some point, but I think that was one I found washed up on shore. I'm not 100 percent sure.

I had another disturbing, yet formative, experience on vacation in Jamaica just after my thirteenth birthday. I had enrolled in a two-week-long marine biology camp at Hofstra University, in Montego Bay. Like Lovisek's camp, the name of the game was catching stuff. It was only the second time in my life that "catch it" was part of the curriculum *and* it was out in the ocean *and* they gave you the right tools for the job. Holy shit, I caught everything. Free diving and snorkeling I caught a torpedo stingray—a soft, tan pancake with a short finned tail capable of delivering a 220-volt electric shock. I caught spotted stingrays and moray eels.

We even caught a Portuguese man o' war. A couple of students held open a garbage bag with sticks, while the rest of us used the handles of our nets to push the man o' war into the bag. You had to be really careful not to let any part of the man o' war touch any part of you, which wasn't too difficult because man o' wars have no means of self-propulsion, they just float along the surface of the ocean wherever the winds and currents take them.

Stingrays were a lot harder to catch. I set up underwater traps made from garbage bags with sticks propping them open and then try to guide the animals into them. They often went for the dark bag as a hiding spot, and the movement of them entering the trap would knock the stick loose and the mouth of the bag would drift closed. I'd swim over and grab the bag, bring the animal back to the boat, and then try to get it back to the lab.

We put everything we caught into an interconnected three-tank system. There were two giant holding tanks, each about 9 feet long, 3 feet wide and ½ feet deep, and in between them was a taller observation tank, a foot long, 9 feet wide and 3 or 4 feet deep, with glass sides so you could see everything in it. The man o' war floated by itself in the glass observation tank.

Somehow the screen on the tank's filter had come loose or got knocked off and the man o' war got sucked into it, chewed up and blended into a million pieces and discharged into both of the holding tanks. This massive, poisonous jellyfish, which isn't actually a jellyfish at all but a siphonophore—an organism made up of millions of tiny, poisonous animals—got blended and spewed onto everything else we'd caught. Nothing survived. We spent the last two days of the camp cleaning the tanks, decked out in heavy elbow-length rubber gloves. We had to dispose of the corpses of my beautiful torpedo ray, spotted rays and moray eels. It was terrible.

I don't think that crab stabbing taught me anything important. My parents wanted them for dinner anyway; I just found a more entertaining way of catching them. As with my chain moray eel encounter in Jamaica, though, the stingray I caught off the beach in Florida was another nausea-inducing lesson in the consequences of acting without thinking. As horrible as it was, that experience helped me realize the impact my decisions could have on the lives of other creatures. My desire to possess and study animals ran so deep, that as a child and even as a teenager, I acted before thinking about what I was doing. My parents had always discouraged my impulsiveness because they were worried it would get me hurt, but now I saw another way in which it was bad: it could hurt the animals I was trying to understand.

I think the guilt and horror that came from some of those experiences went a long way towards developing in me a visceral intolerance to the suffering of animals. It also taught me about the damage people can do when they act without thinking, and about the large disconnect that can exist between the human actions that cause suffering and the suffering itself.

Chapter Seven

A Snake with a Personality Disorder

High school was a million times better than elementary school had been, thanks to a few key changes. One was switching in the tenth grade from private school to a public high school. At Lawrence Park in north Toronto there were girls—painfully absent from my all-boys junior high—and I found a group of friends with whom I felt a genuine connection. I also really got into rugby. I wasn't very fast, but I was strong and comparatively big—like 25 percent bigger than all the other kids—and that made me a pretty unstoppable force on the field. My teammates would hand me the ball and I'd just plow my way down the field.

I made a lot of friends through rugby. Not only was it fun, I found that being good at something that other people actually valued gave my self-confidence a boost. With good people to hang out with and an extracurricular interest that kept me involved at school, I rebelled less and got great grades. I still would have rather been in the woods or hanging out under water, but during the best three academic years of my life I got good enough grades to gain a small scholarship to the University of Western Ontario.

You weren't allowed to bring animals into any of the campus residences at Western, so theoretically I was supposed to leave all of mine at home. But living in a res room without a single lizard or snake was out of the question. In the last few weeks of the summer before I was due at school, I built a reptile cage disguised as a bedside table. Inside it I installed a light and a heater that wouldn't be noticed if the front panel was closed. When I moved in, I brought an amethystine python with me and kept it successfully hidden from my residence advisor for the entire school year. Fortunately, my roommate, Colin, was my best friend from Lawrence Park and didn't mind having a snake around.

I had to leave behind my olive python: two large snakes seemed excessive for a shared res room and the amethystine was the less aggressive of the two. I had scrounged every cent I could to buy both pythons earlier that summer. Amethystines are purple and black and similar to green tree pythons in appearance and behaviour, but they can get to be 25 feet long. The olive python was shipped in from Texas, and when I bought it there were only three others of its kind in all of Canada. It was captive bred by Bob and Tracy Barker who ran one of the most respected python and boa breeding centres in the United States, so I figured it would be okay to buy it sight unseen. Plus, olive pythons have, hands down, the coolest heads in the snake world. The arrangement of scales, the size, shape and coloration of the eyes, and the positioning of the heat-sensing labial pits give them one of the most beautiful and striking faces of all pythons. It cost me $900, which is the most money I've ever spent on a pet (though at the time of this writing I am seriously scheming on how to acquire a pair of Boelen's pythons available in Canada for $10,000).

When the olive arrived, I rushed down to the pet store as fast as I could. I was so excited and anxious that I couldn't stop bouncing up and down on my toes as I waited for the clerk to hand it over to me. I couldn't wait to see that head in real life and know it belonged to *my* olive python. The clerk handed me the snake inside a pillowcase. I opened the bag, and holding it with my left arm, I reached in and grabbed the snake with my right. It was a couple years old and already 4 or 5 feet long, so it was a bit awkward trying to manoeuvre it out of the bag. I let the pillowcase drop and used my left hand to gather up the rest of the snake—that's when it attacked me.

It bit the top of my right forearm first—a quick bite, not that deep—and used it as a leverage point to haul itself up my arm. The next bite was deep into my biceps and that one stuck. It broke off three of its teeth in my flesh as it coiled itself around my arm and started squeezing. That was the relationship we had from that point on: If I went anywhere near the snake, it tried to bite me. It would even strike the glass of its cage as I came near. That olive python was one of the most aggressive snakes ever.

No animal is born nasty, and I don't think that the olive was "mean" so much as it was acting out learned behaviours. When snakes are bred in captivity, they're often kept in boxes similar to Rubbermaid containers until they're sold. The experience is like sensory deprivation, and the snakes learn to associate any movement with food. The containers are opened, a thawed rat is dropped in and the containers are closed. Under those conditions,

My olive python, probably the most aggressive animal I have ever owned.

it wouldn't take too long to see movement and chomp without a second thought. My olive basically had a developmental disorder. But it was beautiful, and I spent hours photographing its head and the patterns in its scales.

In second year university, I got a house off campus with some friends and could bring up any pet I could fit into my room, so the olive and amethystine came with me. But in third year, I studied abroad and had to leave them both at my parents' place.

Though my dad often helped me build cages and capture devices for them, he really doesn't like snakes. He can handle a 5-foot lizard, but any snake beyond a garter gives him the skin shivers. My mom's okay with snakes, but she was not okay with thawing out a frozen rat to feed them. So, despite his fear, whenever I was out of town, my dad fed my snakes.

Fear is always a disadvantage when dealing with animals. It makes you jittery and less confident in your movements, which can spook the animal and cause it to behave as strangely as you do. Fear can also cause you to put off whatever it is you're afraid to do. My snakes had to be fed every ten to fourteen days, but my dad would wait up to three weeks, meaning that his jittery ass would be shakily feeding a really, really hungry snake. In the case of the olive python, a really, really hungry snake that by this point had grown to be 9½ feet long.

The story, as it was told to me, begins with my dad walking into my reptile room with a thawed rat clutched at arm's length in a pair of barbeque tongs. The main door to the reptile room let out on a second-floor mezzanine that circled the house's foyer. The drop to the first floor was protected by a bannister.

Leaving the hallway door open, Dad made his way into the room looking to spot where the olive was in its cage. Figuring the coast was clear, he slid open the glass door, moved to drop the rat and saw the olive python in mid-air as it lunged at his face. He half-tripped, half-ran backwards, dropping the tongs and the rat, and somehow managed to avoid the striking snake's head as it flashed past his face in slow motion like a bullet in *The Matrix*. He stumbled out the door, hit the bannister and went most of the way over it, catching himself upside down just barely shy of a long drop to the marble foyer floor below. Muscling himself back over to the safe side of the bannister, he kicked the door to my reptile room closed and then lay on the hall carpet, trying to catch his breath. When he did, he hollered for my mom.

When Dad had calmed down enough, he and Mom crawled back into the reptile room on their hands and knees, coming in through the door from my room in order to sneak up on the snake. They found the rat on the floor and threw it into the cage, then slid the glass door shut and started making arrangements to donate my olive python to the Ottawa Zoo. By the time I got back from my year abroad, they'd donated the amethystine, too, to a travelling reptile show. My dad's run-in with the olive python was the only time anyone in my family ever came close to being seriously hurt by an animal. Although I try to avoid rubbing this in whenever the story comes up, if he'd fed the snake confidently and on time, it probably never would've happened.

Chapter Eight

I Finally Get to Breathe Under Water

Just as I can't remember a time when I wasn't surrounded by and surrounding myself with animals, scuba diving and the underwater world are obsessions I feel like I was born with. The family room fish tank gave me my first glimpse. I also had Jacques Cousteau videos that I watched over and over as a boy. I think it was from those videos that I realized people could go under water and stay there, that they could breathe under water. As soon as I could, I was going to go under water just like Cousteau.

I would've been scuba diving from the moment I learned to swim, but legally you couldn't start until you turned thirteen. I made do with snorkelling and free diving. The wait was taxing at times. It was sort of like waking up hours before your parents on Christmas morning and having to hold in all of your excitement and expectation until you hear them come downstairs—except with scuba diving it took years to arrive.

By the time I was seven or eight, it was already set in stone that as soon as I was old enough we were going to learn to dive as a family. It didn't take any extra persuasion on my part. My parents are adventurous, awesome people, and seemed to always be down with whatever I wanted to do. They were totally game to try diving, they just needed me as the motivation.

I had just turned twelve the first time we went diving, so technically we didn't wait quite long enough. It was at a sketchy resort operation where they gave you fifteen minutes of instruction in a pool and then threw you out into the ocean, sink or swim. There's no way to express what it was like that first time without using a tired old phrase, but it really was a life-changing experience. The second I could go under water and feel like I never had to surface was like finding out I had a superpower.

That summer, my mom arranged for a dive instructor from the police association to come to our house in Toronto. I was still only twelve, but I was a big kid for my age and no one asked any questions. We did our classroom work at the dinner table and our pool sessions in the backyard. By the end of the weekend the whole

Learning to scuba dive felt like acquiring a superpower.

family had completed the classroom and pool parts of the Professional Association of Diving Instructors' open water diver course. All that was left for us to be scuba-certified was to complete four open-water dives in the ocean!

I was so excited to start diving that I'd memorized the course materials before the dive instructor even showed up. I killed the classroom sessions and did even better in the pool. I've always been really comfortable under water. My parents claim that I have a strange natural density that helps me dive. At five, I could walk on the bottom of our backyard pool down the slope from the shallow end to the deep end, circle the deep end a couple of times and then walk back up the slope until my head broke the surface. By the time I was eleven, I could take a fully inflated basketball and touch it to the drain on the bottom of the deep end, 12 feet under water. My parents used to get me to do it as a party trick. For me it was pretty easy: get the ball underwater by doing a handstand on it, then head to the bottom with big frog kicks. All my dad's friends would talk shit about how easy it was until they got in the pool with the ball and couldn't get anywhere near the bottom. Even the police diver we had in to certify us didn't think I could do it and then, after I did, he spent an hour and a half trying it himself. He eventually said he'd done it, but no one was there to confirm it— we'd all given up and gone inside.

Now that I didn't have to surface in order to breathe, even just tooling around my parents' pool seemed like a whole new world. After the first day, the instructor left all the tanks and equipment in our backyard overnight. When everyone went to sleep, I snuck out, suited up and went back under water. I definitely wasn't supposed to, but the scuba tanks were there; there wasn't a hope in hell of me not using them. I sat on the bottom of the deep end in the dark. Just sat there, breathing under water.

We got our certification through PADI, and planned to complete the four open-water ocean dives on a trip to Key Largo, Florida. Before we left Toronto, my mom arranged for an instructor through a dive centre located near our hotel. By the time we got down to Florida, I think I may have actually been the legally required thirteen years of age.

The PADI Open Water Diver course taught the basic skills you needed to stay alive under water. For the most part you practised in the pool sessions and then proved you had mastered the skills and could perform them somewhere other than in a pool on the open water dives. You learned how to get water out of your mask, how to recover and clear the regulator (the mouthpiece that connects to your air tank) so you could breathe again if it slipped out of your mouth for any reason, how to take off your mask, how to safely and quickly shoot to the surface in shallow water if something went really wrong, how to breathe from your buddy's secondary air source, and how to take off and replace your weight belt and buoyancy control device (BCD) both under water and on the surface. (A BCD is usually a jacket or a vest with inflatable chambers that fill with air from your tank to help you stay neutrally buoyant or move up and down under water in a controlled way.)

I knew how to scuba dive. Finally. For the first time in my life, I wasn't a visitor in the ocean. I could stay down and wait for the underwater world to get accustomed to my presence and spring alive right in front of me. The water in Key Largo was warm and crystal clear. I could see everything! I remember watching groupers. A grouper is a pretty boring, mundane, average-looking creature. If I had passed one in the supermarket, I wouldn't have paid much attention to it. But seeing groupers do their thing under water, I gained a whole new perspective. Looking into their mouths I could see hundreds of these crazy glass-like teeth. Teeth like that, a huge mouth and bulky, muscular body? Looking at one up close and at home in its environment, I realized that no matter how benign it may have seemed, it was actually a devastating predator. Being used to the murky waters off Sanibel on the Gulf Coast, it blew me away that such amazing creatures and beautiful diving conditions could exist in the same state.

Scuba diving gave me a proper appreciation for a lot of animals I'd never really been able to see before. When you're free diving, you can only spend a few minutes underwater, and are limited by how deep you can get and how long you can hold your breath. But when you're scuba diving, you can sit and wait for an animal to get accustomed to you and realize you're not trying to eat it. Previously, big animals were the easiest for me to relate to because you could get a lot more information from a couple quick glimpses of a big animal than a tiny one. Now I could hang out with a 2-inch long goby, thinner than a pencil, and study the markings on its sides, how it moved through the water, what scared it and what it did with its time. Scuba diving allowed me to sit still and watch. If I sat very still in front of a pile of rocks for five minutes, it would eventually spring to life in an astounding way. It was like watching time-lapse footage of a flower blooming. A huge crab would start moving underneath a rock, a goby would peek out from a crevice, one of the other rocks would turn out to be an octopus that changed colour and unfurled itself before gliding away.

Not only was all of this a mind-blowing revelation, it was also exhausting. When my parents and I got back to our hotel room that night we all slept for thirteen or fourteen hours. (My sister couldn't make that trip, so we later went to the Bahamas for her certification.) I've never felt as complete an exhaustion from diving since then. Maybe it was the stress of being under water for the first time or the pressure of being tested by our instructor on a new skill set or all of the above. Maybe my parents also crashed so hard because they were worried about me, which added to their anxiety and wore them down. It could have been the mental fatigue of absorbing so much new and amazing stimulus. Or maybe at long last I'd found my place in the underwater world and I could finally just relax.

After my sister got her open water dives out of the way later that year, family dive trips became a pretty regular thing. We wouldn't go somewhere just to dive, but I always pushed for that to be a part of the trip. The Cayman Islands became a popular choice for Christmas vacation because it has some of the best diving in all of the Caribbean, and my family liked the vibe. The Caymans are positioned on the edge of a continental shelf that drops down thousands of feet. The depth means that the water is clear and circulates more than in other areas—like the Bahamas for example, which sit on sand flats. The Cayman Islands have also been a little less ravaged by the fishing industry and boast some of the best coral in the Caribbean.

The only people I knew who I could go diving with were my parents and sister. If they didn't go, I'd occasionally go out on a dive boat with tourists and be the dive guide's buddy, but I tended to prefer family dives where I was in charge of where we went and what we did. Also, having my family diving with me meant someone always had my back. I could get more lost, go farther, explore more and share it all with them. I was always trying to persuade my parents to take us somewhere we hadn't been before, preferably a place with some crazy wildlife.

I remember cooking dinner for my parents one time when I was sixteen or seventeen. It was a dish of my own invention, chicken with mangoes and salsa and all kinds of crazy stuff on it, and I called it Papua New Guinea Chicken. The whole idea was to encourage them to pick Papua New Guinea for our next vacation because it has some of the coolest reefs in the world. A Caribbean reef could have five hundred to a thousand different species of fish, invertebrates and corals, whereas a reef in Papua New Guinea would have 3,500 different species—including the weirdest and most specialized. I don't remember if the dish was any good, but it definitely didn't get me a trip to Papua New Guinea. I guess I can see my parents' point: it takes three days of flying to get there, compared to four to five hours to get to the Caribbean.

After I got my open water diver certification, I realized there were other levels you could get to within PADI—a lot of them.

Regulations meant I had to stay a junior open water diver until I turned sixteen; I took my Advanced Open Water Diver course on a trip to the Bahamas a week or so after my sixteenth birthday. On that same trip, I got to scuba dive with sharks for the first time in my life.

I'd seen a shark already, that brief glance when I was nine and snorkelling on one of our Christmas vacations. Just as I'd spotted it, it had darted away, frightened off by me, a nine-year-old kid. To that point I'd been fascinated with sharks, but also afraid of them. As soon as I saw that they were even more frightened of me than I was of them, my fear disappeared and it opened up the whole under-water world for me to explore. I expected scuba diving with sharks to be as transformative. I couldn't wait to get in the water.

Through a dive company called Stuart Cove's Dive Bahamas, I booked some time with my own dive instructor and guide. There are specific places dive operators go to find sharks. They are places where sharks always hang out because dive boats always go there to feed them, so their clients can see them—a mutually beneficial relationship. My dive instructor took me to a feeding area for Caribbean reef sharks about a kilometre from shore. There didn't seem to be any markers at all, but before we'd come to a complete stop there were sharks swarming off the back of the boat, expecting to get fed. We got geared up and dove down to 40 feet and then I sat on the bottom and watched my instructor feed the sharks.

They were everywhere. You'd be looking at one and then turn to swim somewhere else and find another shark right beside you. They weren't too interested in me—they wanted the food—but it was exhilarating to be surrounded by fifty sharks. I didn't feel like I was in any real danger, but my whole body was one pulsating charge of adrenaline. I instantly knew I had to do it again; I never wanted to do anything else. It was the best moment of my life to that point, one that changed my entire world. The animal I'd always been fascinated with (and fearful of) turned out to be a beautiful, sophisticated creature.

That dive put me on the path to deciding that scuba diving was what I wanted to do with my life. I figured I'd get the rest of my PADI certifications and then I'd live on a Caribbean island and hang out with sharks. All the divemasters at the resorts seemed to do was take people diving, teach scuba diving, and hang out at the bar. The hardest part of their day was hauling a few tanks over to the boat. That seemed like a pretty sweet deal to me, and so I made a deal with my sister that when she was rolling in millions, and I was destitute but happily living on a beach and diving every day, she'd send me some money once in a while. Not sure what benefited her in the deal, but I got her to agree.

The progression of levels in PADI went Open Water Diver, Advanced Diver, Rescue Diver, Divemaster, Instructor, Master Instructor, IDC Staff Instructor and then Course Director, with some little steps and side courses along the way. Open Water gave you the basic skills and Advanced Diver expanded your range from 60 to 100 feet. After that trip to the Bahamas, I had my Advanced Diver certification, but you had to be eighteen to become a Divemaster. I ended up doing every level from Rescue Diver to IDC Staff Instructor while I was in my first year of university. I was up to the IDC level by the time I was nineteen years old.

Since I got all of my later certifications while I was in university, I spent a lot of time diving in Southwestern Ontario and Northern Michigan. I dove in Lake Erie and Lake Ontario, in rivers and in rock quarries that just happened to hit wellsprings and fill with water. Those dives were quite a bit different from what I'd experienced on vacation. The visibility was often very poor; especially in the rock quarries, you couldn't see much. Sometimes when students or other divers stirred up the sediment, it would envelope you, reducing visibility to near zero and making it difficult to tell which way was up, except for the trail of your bubbles escaping to the surface. There wasn't much life in these places compared to the ocean—a couple pickerel or bass, at best.

The water was usually freezing, which meant diving in heavy-duty wet or dry suits that rendered you fairly immobile.

The Caribbean where I learned to dive is warm and clear, and there are animals and corals to look at in almost every direction—it's another level. Still, I enjoyed the certification process, the exploration of those dark bodies of fresh water, mastering the skills of diving, and hanging around old shipwrecks. The reason I wanted to dive was to hang out in the ocean, and I was happy taking the steps necessary to get there. I approached it all with a ton of enthusiasm. I'm pretty sure I was among the youngest IDC Staff Instructors in Canada, if not the youngest. If someone managed to do those courses faster than I did, I'd be surprised.

I got into photography, too, through diving. I'd always liked cameras—almost in the same way I'd been drawn to light bulbs, screwdrivers, cages and containers. I'd used my parents' cameras to take pictures of some of my reptiles and amphibians. After I got scuba certified, my family and I were in a store that sold dive equipment and they had an underwater camera for sale. It was basically a point-and-shoot inside a plastic housing and it cost a small fortune, but my parents bought it for me.

Catching fish under water is really difficult. They move quickly, you move slowly. They're in their element, and you—even decked out in scuba equipment—decidedly aren't. That's where pictures came in. Under water the camera became part of my arsenal of capture devices.

As my pictures gradually got better, photography began to overwhelm everything else. It wasn't just catch something and watch it degrade or become despondent stuck in a cage. Instead, I got to turn it into art. I could possess an animal without taking away its freedom. It would go on with its life while I took it home and studied every inch of it, noticed for the first time the striations in its eyes or counted the radials on its fins. I could also see things that weren't visible to the human eye. As you dive down, the sunlight that penetrates the water is gradually stripped of its colours, one by one. Red disappears almost immediately, 10 feet or so down; orange and yellow follow at around 30 feet. If you dive farther, you lose green, then blue and finally indigo and violet. Life underwater is no less colourful than life on land but there is just not enough light for the human eye to see it. But with a camera came a flash, and, suddenly, things that had looked black, grey and green turned out to be bright red or yellow or electric blue. Lumps I'd written off as mud and seaweed turned out to be vibrant animals. I became intoxicated by the ability my camera gave me to reveal an underwater world so much more beautiful and complex than it looked to the naked eye. The right picture—taken from the right angle and capturing the right colours or behaviours—could reveal animals in ways that made them as wondrous and fascinating to others as they were to me. Pictures had the power to help people see entire species and ecosystems differently.

I could take my pictures everywhere I went. I could share them with friends and family. And if I got good enough at taking them, maybe I could even make a living that kept me under water but allowed me to do more than lug scuba tanks and visit the same dive spots over and over again. That became the new plan.

Chapter Nine

Paradise Might Be the Galapagos

In the summer between my first and second years of university, my parents' publishing and promotions company, Tribute Entertainment Media, took over *Canadian Wildlife*, the members' magazine of the Canadian Wildlife Federation (CWF), and *Wild*, an offshoot of *Canadian Wildlife* for kids. Before Tribute took over, both magazines had been free of advertising, relying on a tiny budget from donations to the CWF to stay in print. With no money to put towards photo assignments or freelancers, they were both a bit dismal.

Wild became Tribute's first priority. It didn't seem to have any dedicated staff and the CWF had no plan to rescue it. It had been dumped and was going to stay that way unless my parents did something. With no money in the budget to hire staff my parents decided to hand the magazine over to me to see what I could do with it.

Wild was meant for little kids and I had some experience working with kids as a scuba instructor, so I figured I could handle it. I thought that at least I knew the kinds of things that got kids excited. More importantly, I knew that the only thing about wildlife magazines that had ever held my attention were the pictures. I began scouring stock image sites for the best wildlife photos I could find. I pulled anything that caught my eye and began stitching them together in a way that told a story. Once I knew which images I wanted, I had to get permission to use them before they could run in *Wild*. Tribute had given me some money for usage fees and other expenses, but the budget was tiny and I had to haggle like a madman with the photographers and stock agencies to get the pictures I wanted. My first issue ran with a great shot I'd found of a koala on the cover—yes, a fuzzy! I also came up with a new layout and structure for the magazine, with a section called Predators and Prey—my favourite part—that profiled animals and the strategies each used to eat or avoid being eaten, comparing them head-to-head the way a videogame or a fight card might.

I wanted a tiger cover for my second issue of *Wild*, but tiger photos were expensive. If I went ahead and paid for a good one, I would have next to no money left to put the rest of the issue together. In my first year of university, I had started working on a correspondence degree from the New York Institute of Photography. I had a decent camera and knew the basics, and I figured it would be a lot cheaper for me to take the pictures myself. So I went to the Toronto Zoo and got a shot of a Siberian tiger sitting in a pool looking into the lens of my camera. I cropped the image close around the tiger's face so no one could tell the tiger was in a zoo. For the price of a general admission ticket, I had my cover.

As I was wrapping up that second issue, my parents asked me if I wanted to do something with *Canadian Wildlife*. I had been having a blast doing *Wild* but I knew with *Canadian Wildlife* I'd be in over my head. I could get pictures together and write a story about how cool animals were for kids, but adults were another story. My geek-like fascination with animals would be tougher to translate into cool or engaging content for adults . . . On top of that, the

My first professional wildlife photo: a Siberian tiger, for the cover of *Wild*.

summer was coming to an end and I didn't think I could handle putting together one magazine in my spare time, let alone two.

Tribute hired a staff, headed by a great editor named Kendra Toby, to take over both magazines. The staff would overhaul *Canadian Wildlife* and put out *Wild* using the framework I had developed. Despite passing off *Wild*, I was determined to continue taking pictures. The involvement I'd had with photographers and photo agencies showed me that it was possible to make a living taking pictures of animals. I wasn't good enough yet, but just knowing that it was possible was enough for me to decide to do whatever I had to do to become a wildlife photographer.

Having a staff meant having to pay them. In order to make the magazines profitable enough so they could cover the salaries, *Canadian Wildlife* had to start running ads. This wasn't an easy proposition. The magazine's circulation numbers were so low it was hard to sell ad space outright. Working with a few people from Tribute, I came up with a plan to exchange ads for services that could be used to improve the quality of the magazine and attract new readers. I approached a dive shop I'd worked at called Waterline Sports and arranged a contest for some free dive trips. I figured that could get more people to pick up the magazine, but we still needed something that would hold their attention when they did. I started brainstorming a list of places I could turn into really compelling photo stories, which in turn got me thinking about the Galapagos Islands.

The Galapagos are a string of islands in the middle of nowhere, 972 kilometres off the coast of Ecuador in the Pacific Ocean. Famous for inspiring Darwin's theory of evolution and sheltered, to some extent, from human incursions, the islands teem insanely with life. They're one of the only places in the world where hammerhead sharks congregate in schools. I can't remember how old I was when I first learned that fact, but as soon as I did I was pretty much destined to go.

In my spare time at university, I started looking into companies that ran trips in the Galapagos, hoping I'd find someone in the mood to barter. I got in touch with a few dive operators outside of Canada, but *Canadian Wildlife*'s readership was so small no one was interested. The Tribute team and I had had the most success when we'd tried to trade for Canadian products and services. So I narrowed my search and ended up coming across a Toronto-based extreme travel company called Marine Expeditions, run by a guy named Sam Blyth.

At the time, Marine Expeditions ran regular trips to Greenland and the Galapagos Islands, and also occasionally teamed up with another adventure cruise line to spin people down to Antarctica. I sent them our "we'll give you ad space for its equivalent value in trips" offer and managed to trade my way into a trip to Greenland and two separate trips to the Galapagos. I would take off for Greenland in early May after finishing the last of my exams, visit the Galapagos for the first time in June and take the last trip in August.

The beginning of the Greenland trip was chaos. I arrived at Toronto Pearson airport hours early to find the check-in line for my flight already snaking out of its nylon-roped confines. I took my place at the end of it and stood around for awhile, but the line wasn't moving. As word gradually filtered back to us from the front of the line, we discovered the problem: the flight we were trying to catch didn't exist.

The trip was supposed to take us from Churchill, Manitoba, across Hudson's Bay, down the Hudson Strait and across a strip of the Atlantic to Greenland—a serious haul on which we'd get to see walruses, whales and all kinds of other awesome stuff. Unfortunately, Hudson's Bay was still frozen over and there was no way our boat could navigate it. Bowing to the elements, the trip's organizers had decided to skip Hudson's Bay, which was home to most of the wildlife I and everyone else in line wanted to see, and instead fly us from Toronto straight to Labrador where we'd board a boat to take us the rest of the way to Greenland.

As far as I could tell, none of my fellow passengers were notified of this change of plans in advance. Like me, they were disappointed and pissed, and before boarding a plane to Labrador, everyone in line wanted to find someone from Marine Expeditions to unload on. There was a handful of employees running around looking stressed and getting cornered by stressed travellers. I found the closest employee and joined the pack of six or seven people grilling him, all trying to find out as many details about our new itinerary as possible. It was in this scrum of people trying to grind out some answers that I first met Michael Buckley.

I'm not sure how we got talking. He might have walked up to me because I was travelling alone and had a giant camera around my neck. Buckley was about forty-five years old. He had shaggy, mussed-up brown hair, large glasses and eyes that squinted into a glare only he could see. He had a strong jaw and introduced himself boldly, but there was something awkward about him, as though he'd had to talk himself out of his comfort zone in order to say hello. He told me he was a travel writer and I realized I was familiar with his work. He was the real deal, the guy behind a bunch of Lonely Planet and Bradt guides to various parts of Southeast Asia. He'd also written an article on Sarawak, one of the Malaysian states in Borneo, for *Outpost* magazine that was one of the best travel pieces I'd ever read. He'd found an adventure I thought impossible in the modern day—meeting, living with, learning from and travelling with a remote tribe. Even the pictures he'd taken for the Sarawak story were amazing. The cover photo was a giant spider in a web in front of one of the tribesmen's faces, a startling image that really drew readers into the story. I told him I was a fan and we talked for a while in the terminal before splitting up to get checked in and organized for the flight.

Michael Buckley, me and one of our fellow passengers enjoying the boat cruise from Labrador to Greenland. Buckley was the real deal as a travel writer.

In Labrador, we were hustled from the airport onto the boat pretty quickly. The cruise to Greenland was five days of nothing but steely blue water stretching out forever. Gull-like birds would circle the boat in groups every now and then, and the odd whale would spout off in the distance (causing someone to say, "Oh look, that's a sei whale," to everyone within earshot) but that was it for wildlife. Buckley and I and a couple of other people we'd met spent the whole time drinking and shooting the shit.

Buckley was an interesting character with a slightly odd and awkward sense of humor, but I liked him. He took me seriously as a photographer right from the start, and it felt good to be talking the talk with someone who was established. Over drinks we began brainstorming trips we could take together, me shooting the pictures and him writing the story. I told him about the trip I had planned to the Galapagos the following month and he instantly wanted to come along.

Buckley went to Marine Expeditions when he got back to Toronto to propose that he come along with me to write the story. All I'd promised them in exchange for the trips was ad space, so Buckley's offer of a full article was an appealing one and they agreed to comp him as well. As quick as that I had a sort of business partner. Soon after we finished the Greenland trip we met up again in Ecuador.

By now, at thirty-two, I've done so many live-aboard dive trips and adventure cruises that they blend together a little bit. I tend to remember only peak moments, usually sparked by looking at one of my old photographs and thinking about where it was taken and what it took to get it. Maybe the peak experiences are the only parts exciting enough to warrant a mention, but I'm worried that by excluding the space between those highs I'll fail to convey just how captivating these trips are, every moment of them.

The Galapagos are a non-stop sensory overload. Every time you step onto land, you find yourself surrounded by the most amazing bounty of life. None of the animals you come across have much reason to be afraid of you because the Galapagos have never been home to any large land predators. You can walk right up to them, until you're mere inches away. You're watching a couple of blue-footed boobies going through their mating rituals and, in your peripheral vision, waved albatrosses are swooping down to settle in seaside nests and feed their hatchlings. You turn around to see dozens of marine iguanas, sunning themselves on the rocks, trying to get their body heat high enough so then can dive into the cold ocean after the algae that sustains them. Stick your head under water and it's the same story: whale sharks, Galapagos sharks, silky sharks, hammerheads, manta rays, sea lions and fur seals, Mola molas, morays—the list is practically endless. There is so much life that species like moray eels, which normally spend all their time hiding in rocks, swim around free and unafraid. Diving in the Galapagos is like plunging backward through time into ocean ecosystems as they were before people began to exploit them. You see the abundance that exists in a healthy ocean ecosystem and, by extension, you realize the potential for life held dormant or suppressed in almost every other ocean habitat on earth. I can't even come close to describing how exciting a place it is to be. If you'd seen my face the first time I set foot there you'd get the idea.

The two Galapagos trips were thirteen years ago and so close together that it's hard for me to remember what happened when and on which trip. I do remember the first trip I took with Buckley began with a Marine Expeditions cruise around the central Galapagos. It was a blast, but it was also a learning experience. Buckley and I toured the islands in a group of ten to twelve tourists. There were people, cameras and rules in the way everywhere. It was very difficult to take the kind of pictures I wanted to get—ones people hadn't seen before. I also didn't do any diving on that first trip, and decided that there were things I needed to change up the second time around.

The only way to get to the Galapagos that didn't involve at least four or five days at sea was to book a flight with TAME, the airline of the Ecuadorian Air Force (FAE). TAME offered regular flights from Guayaquil, Ecuador's largest city and a major Pacific port, to the tiny Galapagan island of Baltra. On my second trip I took off from Toronto and switched planes in Ecuador's capital, Quito, for the flight to Guayaquil. There I boarded my TAME flight. To call the TAME I encountered an "airline" is probably too generous, though maybe things are different now. Whereas my tickets from Toronto to Quito and Quito to Guayaquil had gotten me a comfortable seat and a mostly edible meal, my TAME ticket got me a hard bench seat on a military personnel carrier. Sitting next to kids in military garb with machine guns, who couldn't have been much older than sixteen, made me feel like I was about to be air-dropped into some jungle conflict I didn't want to know about.

After landing in Baltra, I caught the ferry to the neighbouring island of Santa Cruz, where I overnighted before heading down to the docks to meet up with the cruise the following morning. The boat Marine Expeditions had hired for the trip was a monster, 250 feet long and four floors high, the bastard child of a yacht and one of those Floridian mega-cruise liners. It felt well used but clean. There were about two hundred people on board, with staff accounting for somewhere between a third and half of that number. The basic plan for the trip was to set off from Santa Cruz and do a week-long circuit of the central Galapagos. We'd visit Baltra, North Seymour and the eastern side of Isabela, stopping at a few different places on every island. At each stop we'd go ashore with a guide in groups of ten.

The first trip with Buckley had shown me just how difficult and frustrating it could be trying to take pictures as a tourist. I needed some room to breathe and I needed to not have to worry about setting up a great shot only to have someone walk right through it. I told Marine Expeditions I needed my own guide and I'd pay him out of my own pocket if they found me someone good.

They did. Valerio was an occasional employee of the boat Marine Expeditions had hired for the trip. Born and raised in the Galapagos, he was in his mid-twenties, on the short side of average height and the heavy side of an average build. He had a square face to go with his squat, square body and a smile so big and constant that I imagined him having to ice his cheek muscles when he got back to his cabin every night. His English was good and he was a supremely cool dude. We clicked right away.

Unlike any other place on earth, a guide's ability to locate and point out animals in the Galapagos is pretty meaningless. I would have had to walk the trails blindfolded with my hands over my ears to avoid all the critters lounging, mating, diving and running around me—and even then I might have caught a whiff of something by accident. At each landing, we would disembark and follow a set trail inland, which meandered around and then led us back to the boat. Usually our path was marked on either side with painted rocks that we were supposed to stay in between. Certain trails were even lined with wooden railings, allowing me all of a few feet of leeway in my discovery of the Galapagos. The idea that the guides are there to "guide" you or prevent you from getting lost is a small lie. The real reason the trip organizers send out guides is to prevent legions of tourists from roaming free. Fortunately for me, Valerio was less than passionate about rules and regulations. His willingness to let me stray from the paths was completely invaluable. The only times I could freely walk through a forest or across a field were when Valerio and I were out of sight of the other tour groups. He was the reason why my second Marine Expeditions trip felt like an adventure and not a trip to a breathtaking zoo.

Every island in the Galapagos is home to a range of species, but they each tend to have one that sticks out. It's like every island has a specialty. I always tried to focus on the specialty. I wouldn't bother trying to get a shot of boobies mating on Baltra, for example, because I knew I'd get better ones among the boobies on North Seymour.

Though I had experience shooting wildlife, the sheer amount of time you could spend with a species in the Galapagos presented all kinds of new opportunities. Because the animals didn't run away, I could plan the exact shot I wanted and then try it again and again until I got every detail right. Getting the shot I wanted became a matter of having patience and creativity rather than seizing a fleeting opportunity. Trying to get the right shot of a giant tortoise, I sat in one spot for six hours waiting for it to work up the nerve to peek its head out from its shell. I lost all feeling in my legs from staying still for so long, but when that tortoise finally stuck his head out, he immediately stretched his neck up, and I got a good photograph.

I did a lot of playing around with the relationship between movement and stasis in my pictures—having something in the frame in motion while some other thing stayed put. I got one incredible shot of a marine iguana getting hit by waves. He stayed

The Galapagos giant tortoise.

stone still and I took the picture with a really slow shutter speed. In the shot the marine iguana is tack-sharp, black spiked with tiny hits of white and smeared red and purple over his back, legs and tail. He's clinging to a rock that looks freshly moulded out of lava and all around him is this wild white haze from the moving water. I took it from this gorgeous beach, all white sand and black rock. There are thirty-six frames on a roll of film and I went through ten rolls on that one iguana. I didn't need a million shots of a marine iguana, but because he stayed so still I had the luxury of getting it perfect. And out of those 360 pictures of that marine iguana, one was perfect. The tripod stayed steady, the iguana didn't move and the resulting image sums up an entire species: ancient, primal and looking as though they've just dragged themselves out of some boiling Jurassic stew.

Returning to Santa Cruz at the end of those seven days, I wasn't ready to leave the islands. We'd stopped at a lot of places but had

The marine iguana, which I also shot in the Galapagos on those first trips.

still managed to miss some of the coolest parts of the Galapagos: the West Coast of Isabela and all of Fernandina, which have penguins and the biggest and darkest marine iguanas in unbelievable quantities; and Española, home to waved albatrosses, at the time mating and sitting on eggs—places I wouldn't get to check out until a few years later. Fortunately though, this time I wouldn't have to miss out on Darwin and Wolf islands because I had delayed my return flight for ten days and self-funded a live-aboard dive trip. My decision to extend the trip for the chance to dive with and photograph hammerhead sharks turned out to be the first step toward *Sharkwater*.

Chapter Ten

I See Something I Can't Unsee

The day we were supposed to hit Darwin Island I woke up around five in the morning and quickly realized I had no hope of getting back to sleep. I was aboard the *Galapagos Aggressor I*, a 100-foot live-aboard dive boat that had sailed from Santa Cruz the day after I'd finished the Marine Expeditions circuit. Thirteen other divers were on the *Aggressor* with me, and although we'd only done a couple of test dives and gear checks before settling down for the slow, sixteen-hour trip out to Darwin and Wolf, the trip already felt special.

The test dives had been intentionally low-key affairs. In the murky, freezing cold water of the main islands, the dive guides put us through the motions to make sure we had our weights right and possessed the diving skills we needed to avoid being swept away in the fast, open ocean currents at Darwin and Wolf. Normally, I would've been impatient with the test dive process, seeing it as an unnecessary hassle given my diving resume. This time was different though. I was preparing to go dive at one of the only places in the world where hammerhead sharks are known to congregate. I was going to be in the water with my favourite shark, one of the weirdest, shyest and most perfectly evolved creatures on this planet of billions of elusive and eccentric animals. The test dives were the last few steps, the pause and the deep breath to collect myself.

I might not have been able to get to sleep at all if it hadn't been for the welcome distraction of Hilton Smith. Hilton was the president and CEO of East Bay Company (a Charleston, South Carolina, real estate development firm), and was on a family vacation with his wife and two sons. We hit it off immediately. Over a few drinks and more than a few jokes about Speedos, pissing in wetsuits and other high-minded items and activities, he told me about a foundation he ran that gave a lot of money every year to help protect coral reefs. We kept each other occupied long enough for the excitement and adrenaline of the trip to fade and show us how tired we were. A day of diving will take it out of you and we had several more to prepare for. I turned in that night trying my damnedest to avoid thinking about the fact that I was actually going to wake up at Darwin Island.

Well, maybe not quite at Darwin. At five, we were still a good 30 kilometres from our destination, which meant I had two hours or so left to stare out the window. There wasn't much to look at, just the sun barely peeking over the horizon, washing its dim light over huge swathes of cloudless pale blue sky and fairly calm blue-grey ocean. By nature I'm a patient person, and have spent my lifetime stalking and observing animals. I also tend to find being near large bodies of water soothing. But stuck on that boat, knowing how close I was to swimming with hammerheads, I could barely keep still. I was just sitting there, rocking back and forth a bit in anticipation, when I caught sight of something floating in the water maybe 35 metres from the *Aggressor*. It was a marker—a stripped branch that rose from the water about six feet before dead-ending in a torn black rag. I couldn't for the life of me figure out what it was meant to mark. I was still trying to figure it out when I spotted a second marker and then, a minute or two later, a third.

The Galapagos are, on paper at least, among the best-protected marine reserves on the planet. From conversations I'd had with people in town and aboard the Marine Expeditions cruise, I was aware that illegal fishing did take place, but I'd never seen it myself and the idea had remained abstract to me—maybe a couple of fishermen hauling in a few extra sea cucumbers. In my mind the sheer beauty and abundance of the Galapagos was enough of a wonder that the influx of cash from tourism could actually motivate people to protect it.

But now I was staring at crude black markers, obviously thrown together with whatever materials had come most easily to hand; they gave off an air of raw human purpose that seemed totally at odds with the ocean around me. Little black flags that signalled death, evil and pirates.

I made my way up to the wheelhouse to talk to the crew about the flags. They told me that each of them marked a section of an illegal longline that stretched for dozens of miles.

Longlining came about as an unintended consequence of the push for dolphin-friendly tuna in the 1980s. The best way to net a lot of tuna—a valuable catch for fishing fleets—is to look for a pod of dolphins. Dolphins and tuna both troop around in the open ocean, hunting the animals that live out there, and they end up cooperatively hunting a fair amount of the time. Frightening a school of prey up from deeper waters, the dolphins will circle to keep the school packed densely together while the tuna swim beneath, pinning their prey against the surface until everyone has eaten their fill.

Tuna are nearly impossible to spot from a boat. Dolphins, however, have to surface for air. Spotting a pod of dolphins is an excellent indicator of the location of a large quantity of tuna. Fishing boats used to simply tow a purse net around the dolphins in the hopes of catching the tuna that were likely below them. Pulling the net to the surface, they'd kill a bunch of dolphins but also get heaps of valuable tuna. When the world found out and people began to group together to protest the practice, dolphin-friendly tuna was born. The way to catch tuna without catching dolphins is to lay down longlines because dolphins are too smart to bite on hooks.

Compared to other methods of mass fishing, like trolling, gill-netting or pursing, longlining is one of the more selective. A single high-tensile strength line is run for miles along the surface of the water, usually held afloat by buoys. The line can be monofilament, like fishing line, or something more like rope. Dangling down from the main line at selected intervals and depths (which vary depending on the intended primary catch) are baited hooks. A single longline can stretch for 50 or 60 kilometres and have sixteen thousand or more hooks on it. Those hooks will catch anything interested enough in a bit of easy food. That can mean tuna and other varieties of fish, but also turtles, eels and even albatrosses, who will dive for the bait, become entangled in the line and drown. As much as 75 percent of the catch brought in on a longline is useless bycatch to the fisher.

By the time we were pulling in to Darwin Island, everyone was awake and word of the longlining was making its way around the boat. In addition to the one whose markers I'd spotted from my cabin window, there was a second line in the water. The military was in charge of safe-guarding the island and illegal fishing wasn't considered a big enough problem to warrant dedicating any additional resources. At the time, the Galapagos archipelago, the largest marine reserve on earth, was patrolled by a single Ecuadorian military patrol boat that would take at least sixteen hours to reach us. Longliners from Ecuador, Costa Rica, Taiwan and other parts of the globe would hang around just outside the 40-mile no-take zone that surrounds each of the islands. When they were sure the patrol boat wasn't in the area, they'd dip in, lay the line and retreat outside of the protected waters. Keeping track of the free-floating line via radio transmitter, they'd re-enter the no-take zone to collect their catch. On the radar in the wheelhouse our crew pointed out the two longliners whose work we'd stumbled across inside the no-take zone. As we pulled into Darwin, the two blips beat a hasty retreat.

Once everyone on board had been made aware of the situation, we gathered on the deck to decide what we were going to do about the lines. I was agitating for us to pull them out of the water, but the *Aggressor* was a tourist boat and most of the people on board had paid as much as $5,000 for a week of diving. Pulling in the lines would be hard, grisly work and would cost us at least a full day of diving. The crew put the question to us straight: "Do you want to ignore the lines and go diving or pull them in?"

The decision to pull in the lines was quick and unanimous. Then we scrambled to collect every tool we had on board, every set of dive gloves and every dive knife so we could safely haul in the line

The crew of the *Aggressor* pulling in the longline off the coast of Darwin Island.

and cut free any animals we found. Most of the work was done by the crew, but we all helped.

At that point I had no desire to become an activist. I'd just figured out that I might be able to turn my fascination with the creatures of the sea into a livelihood. I had heard of longlining, but hadn't given it much thought. When you see it in person, though, it's too much to turn away from. You're no longer able to think of it as something that happens out of sight somewhere out in the ocean. When I interviewed him for *Sharkwater*, Mark Butler of the Ecology Action Centre gave me one of the best analogies I've heard for bringing home the devastation of longlining: "Imagine if you went into the forest and laid down some kind of trapline that caught moose, deer, skunks, porcupines, squirrels, dogs. Caught all these species when all you were really after was one or two, or perhaps three or four. But you had all these other species that were caught, were dying, were dead. Clearly it wouldn't last a day. Nobody could put a trapline down for thirty miles and throw away half the animals he or she killed or caught. Nobody would tolerate it for a minute. But it's going on out there [in the oceans] on a massive scale every day."

It's impossible to quantify the suffering of a species, especially as a result of a practice that is so poorly documented, but I believe that longlining has hit no animal as hard as it has hit sharks. At the same time as longlining was dreamed up in response to the cry for dolphin-friendly tuna, China opened itself to large-scale trade with the rest of the world. The brand new demand for shark fin born of China's emergence in world markets, combined with a scarcity of tuna owing to the destruction of tuna populations by mass fishing practices, didn't bode well for sharks. Suddenly, when sharks were caught, instead of being thrown away or cut loose they were killed and finned or finned and thrown back into the water alive to suffocate or be picked apart by other animals. Soon, it became more profitable for fishermen to catch sharks than tuna. Fins were a lot more valuable per pound and didn't require expensive refrigeration systems. You just cut them off and dried them out. Longlining quickly became the best way to tap into a global shark fin market that grew into the billions of dollars.

Over the course of the day, we pulled in more than a hundred dead hammerheads, silkies and Galapagos sharks, as well as a handful of manta rays and some tuna. Most of the sharks had struggled to escape the hook until they were so tangled in the line they could no longer move, at which point they had slowly died. A few, either after tangling themselves up and dying or while still alive, had been torn to pieces by other sharks. It was devastating. But competing against the feelings of futility and despair was an urgent need to help the sharks we found on the line.

I knew, though, that I couldn't do more to help these animals than we were already doing, so I started thinking about what I could do to prevent the same fate from befalling other sharks. Here was this crushing event happening right in front of me and I had all the equipment and skill necessary to document it. I knew that I had a guaranteed space in *Canadian Wildlife* where I could publish the shots. Starting from there, I'd get as many people as possible to pay attention to longlining. I figured that if I could get a few hundred thousand people to read my articles and see my pictures that would change things. Surely people wouldn't stand for this shit once they saw it with their own eyes.

I had borrowed a video camera for the trip. It was a Sony VX1000, which was a decent little camera way back in 2000. I wasn't too interested in film yet and had had no real plans for the camera, but I figured that video evidence of the line might be helpful to the marine park authority. So I handed the VX1000 to Hilton's fifteen-year-old son, Matt, and told him to film everything. I don't really know why I picked him. Maybe he was just the person closest to me when I pulled out the video camera. I just knew I was a photographer not a filmmaker. To document the thing properly I needed to dump the video camera and start

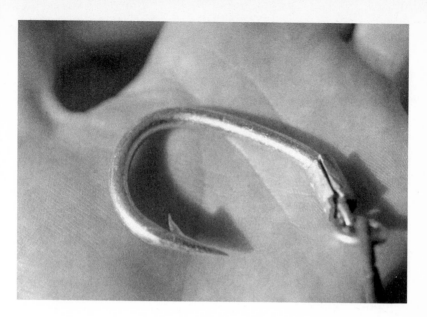

A longlining hook.

taking pictures. (In the end, the footage Matt shot would end up becoming an important, vital part of *Sharkwater*.)

The crew continued to pull in the line. Pretty soon the whole deck was covered in tangled masses of fishing line, filthy cork buoys, radio transmitters and hundreds of evil-looking hooks. While the crew worked, I photographed. I shot everything: people pulling in the line, the reactions of traumatized fellow passengers, the animals we pulled in dead, those we were able to cut free, piles of line, vicious tipped hooks the size of climbing carabiners, seawater rushing the deck and mixing with shark blood.

I ran through every kind of film I had. The truly heart-wrenching stuff, I knew, had to be shot with Ilford SFX, a black and white film that's quite sensitive to infrared light. It makes the blacks in a photo inky and bottomless and gives the greys a silvery, almost liquid cast. I knew that I was photographing something that people wouldn't want to see. I thought that in order to get my pictures published at all, I had to capture images so beautiful that people would want to look at them even if they didn't want to face the reality they depicted. I wanted to create something that people wouldn't be able to turn away from and something that they couldn't unsee.

I shot until the sun set and the light failed me. It'd taken us the whole day to bring in the line, and that night everyone on board was exhausted and not in much of a talking mood.

We had lost a day of diving but still had four ahead of us—two days at each island. Despite the deck of the boat still being draped in longline, by the next morning we had rallied. We had all travelled unbelievable distances to dive at Darwin and Wolf. One sobering glimpse of human waste and cruelty wasn't going to stop us from diving. The crew, who had done most of the hands-on work of bringing in the line, seemed largely unaffected. When I asked them how that could be, they told me it was nothing every one of them hadn't seen and dealt with many times before. Their attitude caught me off guard. I wasn't naive enough to think that all of them were diehard nature lovers, but I had at least expected them to resent the damage longlining was doing to an ecosystem they depended on for their livelihoods. It didn't make sense to begrudge the crew their desensitization, though. They had, after all, been the ones cutting sharks from the line. The outrage was that they had been exposed to longlining at all, let alone exposed to so much of it they were numbed to the practice.

We were scheduled for four dives a day, each lasting between an hour and an hour and a half. This was hard diving: ripping currents, rock bottom and knife-sharp barnacles everywhere. When I'd scoped out articles on the Galapagos in my dive magazines as a kid, there had always been an accompanying editor's note saying something like "Experienced divers only." In the water here, I understood pretty quickly why it said that, and it felt pretty good to dive it. Not quite a rite of passage but definitely an accomplishment.

It seemed like the sharks were everywhere as soon as I jumped in, but I began recognizing patterns pretty quickly. If I resurfaced close to the reef, I'd maybe be able to hang out with a passing whale shark. If I came up out in the blue, I'd definitely see some silky sharks—the aggressive teenagers of the ocean. Hammerheads turned out to be incredibly shy and hesitant animals. If I got close to them it seemed like even my excited heartbeat was enough to startle them well clear of me and my lens. And I needed to get close because the water was so full of plankton and other organic debris you had to be near to get an image that didn't come out feeling cloudy or gritty.

Hammerheads have beautiful faces that you can't really see without getting close. The undersides of their hammers are covered in intricate patterns made up of ampullae of Lorenzini—tiny, oil-filled pits that detect electromagnetic fields. Like a fingerprint, the pattern of the holes swirls across their faces in a way that's completely unique to each individual. The positioning of their eyes

You can't see how beautiful the head of a hammerhead shark really is unless you get close.

allows them to see 360 degrees around them, and the eyes themselves have huge, round pupils. They have really sharp-looking teeth and small oval mouths and their distinctive head shape allows them to move through the water with incredible agility.

The first step in getting near hammerheads was to get the hell away from everyone else. I always dove alone. I'd either be the first in and catch the current early or I'd wait for everyone else to dive in and swim off, then go. Diving alone is a big no-no for recreational divers, but for me it's useless to dive with a group of people. They make so much noise just kicking and breathing, you don't have a hope in hell of getting close to anything. Even if an exceptionally brave creature comes toward you, half the time a fellow diver will swim in and block the shot. I needed to venture off by myself to get good shark photos. Keeping my heart rate as slow and even as possible also helped. If I had to cover some distance to intercept the school, I had to time everything so that I could stop, calm myself down and slow my heart rate and breathing, otherwise the hammerheads really wouldn't come anywhere near me.

I also had to be careful to limit my breathing even though it's not the greatest idea to hold your breath on a dive. Holding air in your lungs makes you more buoyant. If you've got air trapped inside you and you rise too much in the water, the pressure change can pop your lungs, causing an embolism, which can travel to your heart, giving you a heart attack, or to your brain, giving you an aneurysm. Exhaling, however, caused a stream of bubbles to escape my regulator, which was often enough of a disturbance to scare away any nearby hammerheads. I opted to take the risks, assuring myself that I'd be especially careful not to let myself float too far.

On one dive I photographed a Galapagos shark with a length of fishing line fluttering from a hook in its mouth. It could've been one of the few living animals we'd cut loose; it was trailing the right amount of filament. While we'd been dealing with all of the dead and dying animals the day before, I kept thinking, *Well, there are tons of sharks here in the Galapagos. Even if the line has killed this many, there are still tons out there.* To then go under water and come face-to-face with one of the sharks we'd just cut free shattered that rationalization. There aren't that many sharks. Even in an ecosystem as abundant as the Galapagos, a single longline had a noticeable impact. I tried to get close enough to the animal to work the hook free but it wouldn't let me. I had to settle for a picture from 5 metres away.

I could've photographed those same sharks on those same two islands every day for the rest of my life and never gotten bored. I'd estimate that I saw hammerheads on 75 percent of the dives at Darwin and Wolf. You'd think that would've given me ample opportunity to get the shots I wanted, but I was only able to get close to them on, at most, 5 percent of those dives. Sharks, especially hammerheads, are living, moving pieces of art. But they're pieces of art that you get just a rare and fleeting glimpse of. If you're lucky you have four seconds to get a shot. Even then, you haven't chosen the angle, the shark has. In their reluctance to get near you and their willingness to change their minds and bolt, hammerheads severely limit your options as a photographer. There are hundreds of things you want to do to photograph them, but they give you the choice of a handful. There was always going to be another angle, more sharks in the frame, a slightly better thing I could do or see. If the boat hadn't taken me back to Santa Cruz and my flight home, there's no way I would have left.

Chapter Eleven

Dancing Lemurs

I returned from the Galapagos a month before I was supposed to move back to London, Ontario, for my third year at university. As much as my run-in with longlining had affected me, I was going back to school in the fall. That was the plan, that's what was expected of me and it was what I was going to do. When I swore to myself that I was going to do whatever it took to stop sharks from being killed, I meant it. I just didn't know what to do next. I had discovered some of what was happening out in the oceans and I knew I wanted to be part of making change, but I was still far from an activist. I was twenty. I was going to do everything I could to stop long-liners and save sharks. I had a mission. But first, I thought, I better finish school.

The momentum I'd built up on the trip survived the return flight to Canada. In my first few days back, I got my piece for *Canadian Wildlife* together, editing the thousands of photos I'd taken down to the real keepers. The story was mostly a straightforward travel piece on the Galapagos, but I tacked on two pages at the end that dealt with illegal fishing and shark conservation and included some of the photos I'd taken of the crew of the *Aggressor* pulling in the longlines. In addition to running it in *Canadian Wildlife*, I sold versions of the article to the *Globe and Mail* and *Asian Diver* before handing it over to The Cover Story, a syndication company that continued to sell it all over the world. It was the first time I'd had something published anywhere other than *Canadian Wildlife*.

Returning to the day in, day out routine of school was a shock. I had sort of breezed my way through the last couple of years of high school, bored but doing the work and getting the grades. I don't know if anyone actually ever said it in concrete terms, but there was always this promise that university would be different. The unfailing enthusiasm of my high school teachers and the starry-eyed reminiscences of my parents had me believing that I'd get to university and suddenly I'd be challenged and find myself surrounded by a group of intelligent and like-minded peers, all interested in the things that I found so exciting. My interest in wildlife and the natural world had always been my own thing. My high school friends showed passing interest now and then, but it definitely wasn't something they were passionate about too. I'd never gone diving with any of them and only rarely persuaded friends of mine to visit a pet store with me. It was the obligation of university—the fact that I enrolled, and that my parents and everyone expected me to finish—that kept me from skipping classes that bored me to tears and kept me handing in assignments I could've done in my sleep. I thought you put up with high school to prove that you deserved university.

I hope that post-secondary education makes good on its promise to other people at least. I went to university for the wrong reasons. I actually got accepted by a bunch of schools that catered to my interests, such as Dalhousie, the University of British Columbia, and the University of Hawaii. But in the last year of high school, I discovered partying. And when it came time to pick a school, I went to the school David Letterman rated as the best party—the University of Western Ontario. I did meet some undergrads there who felt fulfilled by their studies, but that wasn't the case for me. It was worse than high school: boring work, a bunch of kids more interested in getting drunk and high than in learning. The partying also got boring very fast.

Instead of allowing me to plunge deeper into my studies, my lifelong interest in animals meant that I already knew most of what they taught to zoology majors like me. The science was new, but I wasn't interested in interacting with the science. I found animal behaviour fascinating, and it didn't seem like my seminars and textbooks were teaching me anything I hadn't already seen first hand.

For the first two years of university I'd overcome my apathy with extracurricular work. I'd carried a normal course load, taken that correspondence degree from the New York Institute of Photography, become certified as a scuba instructor trainer, taught scuba diving and taken on whatever photo assignments I could dream up for *Wild* and *Canadian Wildlife*. Even doing all that I'd found a fair amount of time to get wasted and piss away my time. Still, I hadn't really felt like I had any other options. I thought you needed a degree to do anything of value, and since I was already earning credits towards a degree in a field that I was interested in, I thought that it didn't make much sense to drop out or look for something better. The Galapagos trip hinted that I might be able to make a living taking pictures (if only because it showed me that someone other than my parents' magazines would publish my work). More importantly, it showed me how much happier I could be when I had something bigger than myself and my own pleasure to dedicate my time to.

Just because I finally knew how unhappy I was, though, doesn't mean I did anything about it. Considering how much I felt university had let me down, the effort I made to try and stick it out at Western is mind-boggling. I stumbled through an entire semester, half-asleep through lectures, drank three to five nights a week and filled out the occasional multiple-choice Scantron test.

I even joined a frat, thinking that things might improve if I met some new people. I did meet a bunch of new people but, predictably, I just ended up doing the same unfulfilling things with them.

I wanted more, much more, and then I came across a poster for a study abroad program in Kenya. Canadian Field Studies in Africa was a full semester program available to zoology, biology and anthropology students from all across Canada, run as a collaboration between McGill, Dalhousie, the University of Victoria, the University of British Columbia and a few other schools. I applied, got accepted, coasted through my exams and headed home to my parents' for Christmas.

Getting forty-two students to Kenya was complicated. Flying in from all over Canada, we congregated in a terminal at Heathrow in London to wait for a connecting flight to Abu Dhabi's ridiculous Fabergé egg of an airport. From Abu Dhabi we were to catch yet another flight to Nairobi. It was the first time all of us students were together in one place, and there was a predictable amount of sizing up going on. I don't know what makes you gravitate to one total stranger over another, but kids seem to have a preternatural sense for deciding who might make a good friend before you've ever exchanged words. I found myself pulled towards a hulking blond Viking of a guy.

Doug was well over 6 feet tall with biceps the size of my thighs. I initially approached him expecting to find a rival, someone I'd have to be in constant competition with for the next three or four months. But thirty seconds into our conversation it was clear to me he was a total puppy dog. He also shared my love of animals. A biology student from Simon Fraser University in B.C., he was as excited as I was to get out into the Kenyan bush and start catching some critters.

After picking up our bags at the airport in Nairobi, we were trucked off to our first campsite — a cleared field bordered by a lake on one side and thick forest on the other. When everyone had arrived and unloaded their gear, we were told to pick tentmates for the semester. My pelican cases of photographic equipment and I tented with Doug and an older student named Ian. Ian was a fun-loving, always smiling, always joking kind of guy and he kept our guts pretty much continually busted. We camped 100 metres from the lake, which none of us were allowed to even touch let alone swim in because of the risk of picking up schistosomiasis—tiny, bladder-dwelling parasites. We arrived to find a welcoming party of black-and-white colobus monkeys that hung out at the edge of the forest and watched us unpack our gear and set up camp.

The Canadian Field Studies program offered a wide variety of courses, but its students were divisible into two rough groups that had surprisingly little overlap: people there to study animals and people there to study other people. We all camped together at the same sites and had the opportunity to mingle a bit at meals, all of which were served buffet-style, outdoors, under a collapsible canopy. But during the day we split off to attend classes. I barely interacted with anyone besides Doug, Ian and a couple of girls in our program named Tasha and Lisa.

Each class spanned a certain portion of the trip, during which the professor assigned to teach it would arrive, jump on our caravan and live in tents alongside us for a week or two. I loved two classes above all: herpetology, the study of reptiles and amphibians, and entomology, the study of insects. We hit that part of the program about a month into our trip, while we were camping near Kakamega Forest, which was as far west in Kenya as we went. Entomology class basically consisted of running around spraying the coolest bugs we could find with Raid and bringing them back to dissect and study. It gave me an excuse to catch and keep Richter, a scorpion I carried around in my breast pocket for a couple of weeks near the end of the trip. I found Richter when our caravan, travelling between campsites, made a rest stop. While other students used the facilities, I ran out into the sandy shrub grass that surrounded us and flipped rocks over until I came across a giant, forest-green scorpion. Instead of spraying him dead, I caught him and tucked him into a neoprene camera case that fit in my pocket. Richter easily could have jabbed me through the neoprene, but he never did—he had an easygoing personality. I fed him bugs and when we gathered for dinner, I would let him run free on the table—to the chagrin of the African staff, who knew him to belong to a fairly deadly species of scorpion.

Herpetology class was tailor-made for me. Near the end of each day's classes, our professor would canvas for volunteers to head out at night into a nearby swamp to catch tree frogs and snakes. Doug and I were about the only people who ever volunteered, and we spent every night hip-deep in swamp water scanning the dark with miner's headlamps. Why we could wade into the swamp without having to worry about the schistosomiasis that had been such a concern at the first campsite was never explained to me.

On one of our excursions, I spotted a menacing-looking, ash-coloured snake frozen in the beam of my headlamp. It was hanging from a tree, hovering over a clump of reeds and, like Doug and me, likely searching for tree frogs. I didn't know what kind of snake it was, but it seemed so hypnotized by the light I figured I had a pretty good shot at catching it. I knew that something like 97 percent of the snake species native to the swamp were poisonous, and to catch it safely I'd have to grab it behind the head as quickly as I could. I psyched myself out so badly thinking about how poisonous it might be, that I began to shake uncontrollably. Still, I shone my light directly into its face and lunged, catching it correctly. Then I pulled it from the tree. I ran over to Doug and our driver, with the snake clutched in my hand and consulted with them about what to do next. Neither of them knew what kind it was, either, but agreed it was likely poisonous and the only safe place for it was in a Rubbermaid container kept in the back of the Land Rover to hold some tools. Our driver dumped out the tools and Doug held the container open, using the lid as a shield. I dropped the snake in and he brought the lid down fast. Unbitten, we waited for the rush of adrenaline to subside.

By the next morning, word had gotten around camp that I'd managed to catch something truly dangerous and everyone wanted to see it. I'd kept the Rubbermaid container in my tent overnight and before breakfast I hauled it out into the centre of the camp. My herpetology professor stood on one side and I stood on the other, with most of the students circled around us, and the African staff keeping a safe distance in a second ring. I pulled off the lid and immediately there was an outburst of frantic Swahili and all of the staff scattered.

My instructor quickly and calmly took the lid from me and secured the container, the snake still safely inside. He said, "That is most likely a black mamba and you need to take it far away from here and let it go." I had caught a snake that is not only one of the ten most venomous land snakes in the world but also the fastest bar none, and with a reputation for extreme aggression. I carried that container through the woods for about fifteen minutes before letting it go. It darted away without incident.

Even when I wasn't introducing highly poisonous snakes into camp, I was a very different kind of student from my peers. I rolled around covered in cameras that I never took off, one of which would be equipped with a two-foot lens. I'd brought three hundred rolls of film with me and made it clear from the start of the trip that I was there primarily to take pictures. I attended classes like everyone else, but if there were a bunch of monkeys pounding back mangoes while the instructor was speaking I was guaranteed to be with the monkeys.

By the time we'd made it to Kakamega Forest, I'd bargained my way into a bunch of special exemptions and privileges, one of which was the almost exclusive use of one of the program's Land Rovers and its driver. Between campsites I still rode with everyone else—under weather-proof tarpaulin on crippling wooden benches in the back of a couple of World War II-era lorries for up to twelve hours at a time—but once we arrived, Doug and I would grab our driver and head out into the bush.

I shot every place we set up camp as though I was covering it for a story. A lot of the places we visited were really cool national parks and I shot them all in a way that would allow me to assemble photo stories on them when I made it back to Canada. In exchange for the preferential treatment I received, I offered the program's organizers the use of any of the photos I took to promote the course in years to come.

It was near Kakamega Forest that I first got to know Jane. I had been aware of her since she'd arrived—late and separate from everyone else—at our first campsite, but I hadn't had a chance to get to know her because she was there to study people not animals, and I was shy. We'd gotten a break on a night when we didn't have any school work to deal with, and Doug, Tasha and I had settled down to hang out and drink a few beers. Jane joined us and for the first time I got a chance to have a conversation with her.

She wasn't into animals as much as I was, but she loved to take pictures and had a gorgeous Contax camera, a high-end, Carl Zeiss–lensed thing of beauty. She also had a boyfriend who ran a bungee-jumping operation for tourists in Zambia. She was tall and had giant lips and long, wavy dark hair and a cute ski-jumpy nose—she looked like a cross between Cameron Diaz and Angelina Jolie. I liked her. A lot. When she told me about her boyfriend I immediately starting devising my plan to oust him. By the end of the night, we were alone, drinking and flirting, and I was laying it on as thick as I have ever laid it on in my life. I had found the first person who held my focus as much as catching reptiles and taking pictures.

The last three weeks of the trip were on the coast, south of Watamu in a place called Tiwi. The main semester of study had ended by this point and Tiwi was an optional add-on course in marine biology that many of the forty-two Canadian Field Studies students chose not to take. Doug, Ian, Jane and I all signed up.

We lived in small huts on a 15-metre cliff that fell away into the ocean. When the tide was out, it exposed 100 metres or so of tidal flats. You could follow a path that ran down the side of the cliff and walk around amongst coral and algae, and tidal pools that would occasionally have some cool stuff in them. When the tide was in, the area was still really shallow. If you wanted to go snorkelling, you slipped in and snaked your way out into the deeper water. Doug, Ian and I lived together in a hut about 20 feet by 20 feet with a little bathroom off of it. We had our three cots, covered in mosquito netting, and our gear and that was it.

By the time we were in Tiwi, the program no longer felt like school; it was basically a vacation. Unlike the main body of the trip, in which you always seemed to be studying or packing up camp in preparation for the next move, on the coast we had every night free. There was a bar, and every night Jane and I would pair off and talk, drink Smirnoff Ice, and flirt. We'd head down to the tidal flats and walk around or we'd sit on the steps right above the water and look out over it, leaning into each other just a little bit.

I spent my days taking pictures under water or taking my friends diving in the Indian Ocean. The marine biology course had a boat of its own, available 24/7. I was a higher-level scuba instructor than the diving teachers in the program, so I was allowed to take the boat out by myself. Technically, the boat was for trips to observe animal behaviour and ecosystems relevant to whatever was being taught that day, but I was the only one who wanted to spend all day, every day under water. Whenever the boat wasn't being used for a class trip, I could take it out.

I was surprised at how good the diving was. I expected the coast of Africa to be ravaged and instead I got warm water, beautiful soft corals and an incredible number of species. Most of the diving I'd done to that point had been in the Caribbean, where people have found between three hundred and five hundred different species. In the Indian Ocean that number jumps to between one thousand and two thousand species.

The whole time I was there I didn't see big animals or sharks, but there were a couple of cool wrecks and I would take Jane out diving, just the two of us. She wasn't that experienced and whenever we went out, I felt like I was letting her see something secret that belonged to me. It was like showing her around my childhood bedroom, holding up teddies and trophies and telling their stories. I taught her to be patient and let the coral come to life. With hand signals I'd motion to her to sit still and wait, and a moment later, corals would open up and moray eels would appear and things would start mating all around us.

Anytime I went out to shoot pictures, Doug came with me. He made my life easier, helping to lug gear, doubling the number of eyes we had looking out for animals and keeping me company. He had a blast doing it because he got to see and do things that he wouldn't have otherwise. We soon decided to go on another trip together when the course finished.

A few times during our travels with the program, a guy named Andrew had joined our student caravan. He was the son of Deiter, Canadian Field Studies' South African fixer. Deiter, never without a giant hunting knife strapped to his hip, was the badass who made sure things went smoothly. If at any point we found ourselves in a sketchy situation, Deiter was the guy who got off the truck and did all the talking. Deiter also owned a fleet of Land Rovers that he rented out to bush tours and to our program. Andrew had grown up in South Africa and been shipped away to England for school. Since returning he hadn't been doing much and his dad was eager to set him up with a gig. I made a deal with the two of them to get the use of one of Deiter's Land Rovers with Andrew as our driver, to whip Doug and me around Africa after we were done with the course.

Jane planned to head off to another part of Kenya to photograph tribal communities, so we had to say goodbye in Tiwi. I had been in intermittent e-mail contact with Michael Buckley, the travel writer, who was trying to set up a trip down the Mekong River from Saigon. Before I took off from Tiwi, I made a plan to meet Jane in Vietnam to do this photo story with Michael Buckley. I hadn't been too interested in Buckley's assignment, because it didn't have too much to do with animals, but with Jane on board— excited at the possibility of photographing people all through Southeast Asia—I got on Buckley's case in a big way. We had the trip confirmed within a few weeks and I sent Jane an e-mail letting her know when we'd be meeting in Saigon.

Andrew, Doug and I spent the next month and a half criss-crossing Kenya and Tanzania. We did the Masai Mara National Reserve and then met Doug's dad in Nairobi and took him with us to see the first rainfall of the year in the Ngorongoro Crater in Tanzania. After it rained the whole crater exploded in purple and yellow wildflowers and beautiful tall grasses. I shot elephants and rhinos standing up to their knees in them. We spent almost two weeks there, sleeping in tents on the rim of the crater. We had two tents. Andrew slept in one and Doug, his dad and I slept in the other. We set up camp in a well-maintained campsite near an outhouse. The outhouse had no roof and was really just a bunch of cement-walled stalls over top of holes in the ground. One night, Doug was in the outhouse when he heard an animal panting. Alone in the dark and caught literally and metaphorically with his pants down, Doug's mind started racing. Leopards, lions and hyenas are all common enough in the area and, in the dark, all Doug could tell about the animal was that it was big. Making its way farther into the outhouse, whatever it was stopped for a moment in front of the door to his stall, still panting, and Doug was sure he was about to be mauled or killed. After a bit of snuffling, the animal moved deeper into the washroom. As soon as he was sure it was clear of his stall, Doug kicked the door open and bolted. I was standing by our truck, about 30 metres from the outhouse, when Doug came flying out of the dark with a terrified look on his face, ran right by me without saying a word and locked himself in the Land Rover.

Doug is about 6 feet 4 inches tall and easily weighs 230 pounds; seeing a guy that size in full retreat with no explanation of what he was running from was pretty unsettling. I followed his lead and got him to let me into the truck and explain what the fuss was about.

We decided we needed Andrew's set of antique night-vision goggles. They could've dated to World War I. You put them on and looked out through tiny green pinholes. We found the goggles in the truck and I put them on, and we carefully headed back outside. From the outhouse we could hear snorts and panting, but all the information the goggles provided was the occasional flashing set of eyes—something with a strong white strip down its back and black sides.

Finally we realized the outhouse had been invaded by giant bush pigs, 350 pounds a piece, with long trunk-like snouts and tusks; they were rooting around looking for food. Apparently bush pigs can be quite dangerous, especially when cornered. They're powerful animals and can gore you with their tusks if they feel threatened. For the most part, though, they're nothing to be afraid of, and when we decided to chase them away they spooked easily and took off without much trouble.

The bush pigs often came back in the middle of the night, and would snuffle around and sniff at the sides of the tent. You'd hear and sometimes feel their breath inches away from your head, and sometimes they'd push a snout or a foot into the tent. They got Doug's dad pretty freaked out, because you could never be 100 percent sure it was a pig and not a leopard or lion. To mess with him, Doug and I would wait until he was almost asleep and then whack the sides of the tent. He'd bolt up screaming in his sleeping bag, and Doug and I would burst into gails of laughter. Then Doug would tease him, pretending to be ashamed that his dad wasn't tougher, and then we'd all settle down. Just as he was about to fall asleep, we'd do it again and he'd start screaming again, every time. It was pretty funny. But it was a wonder he didn't kill us.

After Tanzania, Andrew drove us back to Nairobi, where Doug and I caught a flight to Madagascar, and Doug's dad flew back to Canada. We spent a week photographing giant lemurs, called indri, in a national park near Antananarivo and then headed south to a private wildlife reserve in a place called Berenty. My parents flew over to hang out with us in Madagascar for two weeks. The ring-tailed lemurs there were so accustomed to people that I remember at one point my mom was holding a banana and a ring-tailed lemur jumped out of a tree and onto her shoulder to steal it.

Most days I wandered around trying to get pictures of sifakas dancing. Sifakas are a genus of lemur particularly famous for the way they move across the ground. Up in trees, they're powerful climbers and leapers, and if given the choice that's where they'll stay. But occasionally, getting from one tree to the next requires them to cover a patch of ground, which they do on their hind legs, hopping sideways with their arms raised above their heads for balance. It's quite a sight. The only real challenge of photographing in Berenty was trying to get the sifakas dancing without catching a house, a sign, a person or a painted rock in the background.

By that time, I'd been on the anti-malarial drug Lariam for six months straight, and in Berenty that caught up with me. One of the listed side effects of the drug is "hallucinations." People have gone to the loony bin on account of the stuff, which seems to be able to cause some kind of elemental shift in brain chemistry. I'd had some weird dreams in Kenya, but in Berenty they intensified. Early on in our stay, I woke up in the middle of the night and saw that the corners of my room where the walls met the ceiling were full of lemurs. I called for Doug to come check them out and when he came in and turned the lights on they disappeared.

In Madagascar, a dancing sikafa lemur.

The next night, I woke up and saw lemurs again. This time I touched my eyeballs to make sure they were open, and still there were lemurs everywhere. I screamed for Doug and as soon as the lights went on they disappeared. Ten years later, I still have dreams that continue after I've woken up. I've woken up in bed with people I shouldn't be in bed with; leapt out of bed because there's was a ghoul in it; I've tried to put out non-existent fires. In Berenty, I had to get used to falling asleep under the smiling eyes of dozens of imaginary lemurs. These lingered effects have taught me, for better or worse, to question the reality of anything exceptional or different. When confronted with such things, I have to ask, "Is this real? Could this be real?"

I left Madagascar in June 2001 and had a week or two back in Toronto to collect myself before flying to Saigon. Buckley had conceived of the trip as the first riverboat journey down the Mekong from Saigon in Vietnam to Angkor in Cambodia. He had successfully pitched the idea to an in-flight magazine and assured me that the bulk of our travel and accommodations would be comped because of the magazine's commitment and his reputation. Buckley would write the story, I'd take the pictures and Jane was along as a photographic subject. We would explore Saigon and Vietnam and then follow the river through Cambodia and into Angkor. In Angkor we'd stop and explore again and then travel overland by bus to Thailand, where we'd spend a week or two in Bangkok planning our next move.

It wasn't a wildlife trip; it was a travel story. I was to photograph popular tourist sites, spas, hotels, floating markets, temples, that kind of thing. I'd never shot anything like that before, but it turned out to be a lot easier than wildlife photography. Vietnam went smoothly; it was beautiful and I ate a lot of fruits I'd never heard of. But making it to the river revealed a fundamental flaw in Buckley's plan: there was no riverboat that would take you from Vietnam all the way to Angkor. Buckley and I each put up $500 to rent a boat and driver for two days to take us into Cambodia. The boat was a war machine, massive and almost fully enclosed in metal. It looked like something the coast guard would use in giant ocean swells.

In Cambodia, we hired a guide so we wouldn't step on any land mines and rode rented dirt bikes out into the countryside. Jane was terrified of being on a motorcycle. To get her on the back I had to promise that I'd drive carefully and we wouldn't crash. I was so nervous about scaring her or having her slip off the back of the bike that I became the least decisive motorcyclist in the world. The roads were muddy and deeply rutted. At one point, my back tire slipped into a pothole and we fell over. After that she was too freaked out to ride with me and she spent the rest of the trip on the back of our guide's bike instead (which was a bit emasculating). Still, we saw

On the Southeast Asia trip.

tons of gorgeous ruins that tourists normally didn't go to and both Jane and I got some great pictures.

As we explored Bangkok from our base off Khao San Road, I got in touch with *Asian Diver* magazine to arrange the next leg of our journey. I was desperate to get back under water and wanted to do a dive story on a group of four small islands around Borneo. They liked my pitch and agreed to run the story, but Jane was a tougher sell. She was stubborn and independent and had gotten fed up with what she perceived as tagging along on my trip. She agreed to come along to the first two islands, Sipadan, Malaysia, and Sangalaki, Indonesia. Instead of doing the others, she flew back to Cambodia and travelled around talking to and photographing land mine victims, which was where her real passion lay.

Buckley also bailed on me after Sangalaki. He had written the Bradt travel guides for Tibet, Bhutan and Nepal, and left to travel in that region and write his latest update. I shot the other islands and then got on a plane for Toronto. It was almost September and I intended to head back to university and finish my degree.

Chapter Twelve

How I Became a Filmmaker Instead

Coming back to Ontario and the prospect of a last year at university after spending nearly eight months abroad was a serious bummer. I felt like my career as a photographer was just taking off and instead of allowing that to happen, I was putting it on the backburner. Not only that, I was in love with a beautiful girl who lived almost nine hours away in Montreal. I made an appointment with a guidance counsellor at Western to find out my options and get some advice, who helped me decide that I should not be going back to school; I should settle for the three-year degree I'd already earned and call it a day. If the whole point of university was setting yourself up for the job you wanted, then I had already succeeded.

I decided the best place for me was with Jane in Montreal. She was still locked into her degree, and I could be a photographer anywhere. All I wanted was to be with her. She came to London to help me pack. We loaded my stuff into the back of a rented truck and drove straight through to Montreal. We'd found a loft on Boulevard Saint-Laurent, near Parc Jeanne-Mance. It was one giant room on the fifth floor of a former warehouse or factory and had 16-foot ceilings and a little bathroom enclosure with walls that gave up three-quarters of the way to the roof. All we had in the way of furniture was a bed, a couch, my light table, and Jane's desk, but the place came with an old metal bathtub and had a wall of windows that rose from about hip height to the ceiling. The sill was big enough that I could sit on it with one leg in the apartment and the other dangling out over the street. I'd sit there in the morning

I spent a long time sitting on this window ledge in Montreal, figuring out what to do with my life.

when the light was best, looking at slides in the sun, and thinking.

Jane had decided to start school again in January. She spent the fall semester modelling and working on her own projects, while I started culling the shots I'd taken on our trip with Buckley. I edited them down to the cream of the crop and got my final selections to Buckley's in-flight magazine.

Then I had to figure out what to do with myself. Through Buckley I had managed to make some amazing contacts in Southeast Asia. Those contacts helped me arrange a series of one-off trips to Thailand and a trip to Borneo, again with Buckley, which kept me busy clear through to January.

Buckley and I had been talking about the Kinabatangan River in Borneo off and on since we'd met. The area was great for photographing Asian elephants and also allowed for the possibility of shooting proboscis monkeys. Proboscis monkeys are decked out in orange-golden fur, tinged red around their heads and across their shoulders; they have a great, round gut for digesting leaves, an orange face, and a giant nose bulging out like a fleshy gourd. As far as I could find out, no one had done a good photo story on proboscis monkeys. So if I came away with good shots, they were guaranteed to be in high demand.

In preparation for the trip, I studied every picture that had ever been published of proboscis monkeys. The decent ones were all taken by a guy named Frans Lanting. He was likely the best wildlife photographer in the world at the time, but his pictures of proboscis monkeys were not groundbreaking, and I figured I could get a better photo story than he had. After all, I'd watched Lanting's Nikon Wildlife Photography instructional tapes over and over again in university.

And I did; I blew the story out of the water. My masterpiece was a shot of a proboscis monkey jumping right over top of me at sunset. The sky is completely purple and he's fully extended in mid-air with an erection. At the time, I thought I'd created the best photo story on any non-human primate I'd ever seen. It was published in major wildlife magazines all over the world: *BBC Wildlife*, *Asian Geographic* and *GEO*, a German magazine that's the European equivalent of *National Geographic*. More than anything else I'd done, that story put me on the map.

In January, Jane went back to school. It didn't take long for her classes to pick up and pretty soon she was spending most days on campus. I kept myself busy sifting through and editing the thousands of images I'd shot on my trips to Southeast Asia, searching for the real keepers, categorizing them and figuring out which articles they would work best with. This was before digital photography really took off—the interesting thing about shooting with film is that you never really knew what you'd actually managed to captured until you got the film developed. Also, once I'd figured out which pictures were worth trying to sell, I had to take them in to a lab to get them duplicated so I wouldn't be sending out my originals.

Unlike digital photos, the quality of the image in physical slides tends to deteriorate when you have it copied. Film is basically just a plastic sheet covered in silver halide crystals. When exposed to light, the crystals react and that's what creates the image. No line

This shot of a proboscis monkey put me on the map as a wildlife photographer.

in a picture is actually straight; every one is composed of a bunch of little crystals. When a developer duplicates your film, it's hard for them to recreate small lines and details without picking up a few extra silver halide crystals. The resulting effect is similar to blowing up a low resolution digital image to the point that it starts to pixelate; lines, especially smaller ones, blur and fuzz out and in some cases you can almost make out the shape of the crystals.

It was rare to get a really good dupe but for the most part they'd be passable. I usually needed between five and ten copies of each image. When I got my dupes back, I'd go through them and weed out the bad ones. The good ones would get slipped into slide sleeves and FedExed to anyone I thought might buy them. If a publication wanted to use a few of my images, I'd send them the original slides or they'd just use the dupes. Most magazines were fine with the dupes.

It took me a couple of weeks to get all of my Southeast Asia pictures out the door. I sent them along with accompanying articles, written either by Michael Buckley or myself. I could usually sit around for a while after a push like that without feeling like a total waste of life. I found out pretty quickly, though, that my ability to enjoy a few days of downtime depended on knowing what I was going to do when I was done taking it easy. And I didn't.

In the year and a half since my last trip to the Galapagos, I'd reworked the article I'd written on longlining at Darwin and Wolf dozens of times for publications across the globe. I'd always offer pretty shots of the Galapagos to help entice readers but, I bolstered the conservation angle of the story with shots I'd taken travelling through Asia—photos of local fishermen catching and finning sharks and of markets with tables of dried shark fin waiting to be purchased. I ended every article with a call to readers to help fund a second patrol boat for the Galapagos through the Charles Darwin Research Station, and I was now giving the pieces free to any publication that would run them. In all that time, only $1,300 in donations has rolled in. I'd spent way more than that getting the material for those stories. Clearly, I'd educated a bunch of people about the plight of sharks, but why weren't they doing something about it? I needed a better way to show people that sharks are not the menacing predators they've been portrayed—to show them sharks through my eyes.

As I sat around trying to plan my next destination and the story it would inspire, my failure as a shark conservationist started to get on my nerves. I looked over the photos I'd taken at Darwin and Wolf again and remembered how strongly I'd felt in that moment and how sure I'd been that my images would put a stop to the practice. Africa and Asia had been a blast but apart from falling in love with Jane, I hadn't felt anything close to the intensity of my resolve to save sharks. I decided that I had only failed because I hadn't tried hard enough. I was still going to try to end shark finning, and I just had to put all my energy into accomplishing that goal.

It didn't seem like I could do it with a photo story. No matter how compelling I made it, no one wanted to pay me to do shark conservation stories. Dive and travel magazines had never cared for the conservation angle. Their raison d'être was to attract readers interested in beautiful faraway places and undersea pictures in the hopes of enticing resorts, airlines, travel insurance companies, dive and tour boat operators and scuba equipment manufacturers into advertising in their pages. The last thing they wanted was to publish something a reader might find discomforting. They were about escaping realities, not facing ones you didn't even know existed.

Nature magazines like *Canadian Wildlife* were supportive of my mission, but the wildlife photo industry was so competitive they had no reason to commission a shoot. The only ones that might bother were *National Geographic* and *GEO*, and their slates were fully booked for years. I needed a way to get more and better shark photos without relying solely on funding from the magazines I'd been working with. My solo efforts hadn't amounted to much and it seemed like my chances of getting any trips to shoot sharks had dried up. To continue, I needed to find a group of people already actively working to save sharks.

Disappointed with my failure to raise enough money to get the Charles Darwin Research Station a patrol boat, I had asked for their help in brainstorming new and different ways to inform and mobilize people on the issue of longlining in the Galapagos. They told me that an organization called the Sea Shepherd Conservation Society, based in Washington State, had just accomplished the exact goal I'd failed so miserably at: they'd donated a patrol boat to the Galapagos. I'd been killing myself to raise this money for them and beating myself up about it. Finding out that they had gotten the boat gave me some comfort that maybe I wasn't doing this alone—that there were people out there in the world who were as concerned about sharks as I was.

I knew of Sea Shepherd and its president, Paul Watson, who was one of the original activists at Greenpeace. I knew Sea Shepherd had been battling whaling for years, but I hadn't realized that they were doing anything to save sharks. I spent a few days reading everything about Sea Shepherd that I could lay my hands on. Then I sat down to write them an e-mail. In it I described my efforts to help sharks, the magazine articles and the fundraising efforts on behalf of the Charles Darwin Research Station and expressed my admiration for the work they had done.

While I was waiting for a response, my dad told me about a new camera he'd heard about from a friend who worked at Lucasfilm. It was a high-definition camera that shot video but also allowed you to pull still images; George Lucas was using it to shoot the next *Star Wars* movie. I had never shot digital before, and hardly anyone had used HD cameras at that point, but I decided that I was going to get my hands on one of them. To get people to finally take action to save sharks I figured I had to do something much, much bigger than I'd been doing. A movie was bigger.

It helped my cause that HD cameras were brand new. Since few really knew how to use them, the fact that I was trained as a photographer and not a filmmaker or cameraman made a lot less difference than it might have. I signed myself up for a two-day HD-camera training course over a weekend in Toronto and came out the other end with an unframed paper certificate saying I'd passed. Certificate in hand, I headed back to Montreal and set about trying to find someone willing to rent me a brand-new camera worth several hundred thousand dollars.

Sea Shepherd got back to me with an invitation to come aboard and document their next trip. They told me where they planned to go—to Cocos, Costa Rica, another shark sanctuary, and the Galapagos—and roughly when. In my response, I let them know that instead of just taking pictures, I was going to see if I could turn the trip into a movie. Sea Shepherd was insistent that we draw up a contract to make things official. They had an office in Malibu and I asked David Dizenfeld, a Los Angeles–based lawyer and family friend, to represent me in the contract negotiations. He'd known me since I was a child and had kept tabs on what I was up to, showing particular interest when I started travelling as a wildlife photographer. He was happy I'd found a career doing something I loved and seemed genuinely excited to help me move forward with it. I sent him the contract Sea Shepherd had come up with and he met with them and worked it out. It was as easy as that.

With the contract finalized and the trip a sure thing, I began pitching it as a photo story to every magazine editor I'd worked with. All most people knew about Sea Shepherd at that point was that it was a radical group that occasionally made the news for ramming whaling ships. I thought that one of them would be interested in a piece that explained who the people with Sea Shepherd actually were, what they were fighting for and how they were going about it. The response was dismal. A lot of editors expressed interest in looking at my photos once I got back, but only a couple were willing to give me any money up front.

I was a little more successful pitching the trip as a movie. My parents' connections got me meetings with representatives from Kellogg's, Ingersoll Rand, Cinema Guzzo, Warner Bros. and Universal Studios. I'd written a treatment and had it printed up to hand around at the meetings. The film was going to be about the depletion of shark populations around the world and the human actions that were causing it. I had no story structure at that point; the treatment just gave some statistics and explained that I'd be travelling on the Sea Shepherd Conservation Society's boat to some of the most shark-rich waters in the world, including the Galapagos and Cocos Island, off the coast of Costa Rica. The working title for the movie was *Saving Sharks*.

My only real selling point was the HD angle. I promised that this was going to be some of the first underwater footage shot in HD (provided I could get my hands on a camera). I also played up the savings the project would enjoy since I'd be travelling with Sea Shepherd—something in the neighbourhood of $400,000 that I wouldn't have to spend on flights and dive boats. In short, I argued, I didn't really need that much money. Somehow I managed to get all of these different companies to give me (relatively) small amounts of money. When I put it all together, I had enough that I could conceivably get started. All I needed was that camera.

The most readily available HD camera at the time was a Sony that shot at twenty-four frames per second. Since I was planning to film sharks and since sharks move quite quickly, I was dead set on using a much harder to come by Panasonic HD camera that shot at sixty frames per second—the VariCam. I'd been combing high-end rental places in Los Angeles and Toronto for weeks looking for someone willing to rent out a $100,000 camera to a twenty-two-year-old with no luck. I'd located a couple of places with Panasonic HD cameras for rent but in order to get my hands on one for the month and a half I intended to travel with Sea Shepherd, I'd have to put down $100,000 I didn't have. Then I stumbled across a company called LYCA, which was based in Montreal.

Despite the fact that I lived there, I hadn't really thought of Montreal as a movie-making city and so I'd been looking everywhere but. I swung by LYCA and introduced myself to Jacques Lamontagne, who ran the place. He seemed to like my vibe and admire what I was trying to accomplish, and he offered to rent me one Panasonic VariCam sixty-frames-per-second piece of gorgeous HD camera with lens for the low, low price of $35,000 a month. I accepted.

Knowing I had a camera lined up meant the movie was actually going to happen, which in turn meant that I needed a crew. Doug was the most obvious choice. I knew we worked well together and he was just wrapping up the school year at Simon Fraser. He said yes immediately, but told me that he'd have to miss the first leg of the trip in order to finish his exams. We were scheduled to board Sea Shepherd's boat in Los Angeles in the middle of April. From Los Angeles, we'd sail down the Pacific Coast of the Americas and dock in Costa Rica at the beginning of May. Doug would fly down and meet the boat in Costa Rica.

My other crewmember was supposed to be my childhood best friend, Tyler. We'd lost touch near the end of high school, but had grown close again when we realized we were both ducking out of university after three years. Six days before we were supposed to leave, Tyler got offered a job hosting a cable-TV show on the Outdoor Life Network. It was an incredible opportunity and he had to take it.

I frantically started trying to find someone to replace Tyler. I called everybody I knew but it was such short notice I kept striking out. My last-ditch attempt was a guy named Geordie who had been a student of mine in an Advanced Diver course I'd taught in Kingston, Ontario, two years earlier. I called him on April Fools' Day and said, "I'm going to Cocos Island in Costa Rica and to the Galapagos in Ecuador to film a shark documentary. I can't pay you but do you want to come and help out?" He told me he needed to think it over. Three hours later he called me back and told me he was in. I had a crew and a camera.

Packing up my gear in preparation for my trip with the Sea Shepherd crew.

PART TWO

SHARKWATER

Chapter Thirteen

Sea Shepherd

Geordie and I landed at LAX a little after 10 p.m. local time. I'd hired a limo bus, the kind of van that moves celebrities and their entourages around, to get us from point A to point B for the three days we were scheduled to spend in Los Angeles. The bus was waiting for us at the airport. Geordie and I loaded our gear into the back and then I hopped in a cab to head to our hotel to check in and make some final arrangements, leaving Geordie with the job of getting our gear over to Sea Shepherd's boat. We had thirty-five pelican cases—large waterproof plastic suitcases—of diving and camera equipment with us and no way in hell was it all going to fit in our hotel room. Geordie and the gear made the trip to the *Ocean Warrior*, the Sea Shepherd's ship docked at Port of Los Angeles, arriving close to midnight. The first impression we made on the crew was to wake them up in the middle of the night and make them lug cases of gear off the docks and onto the boat. Geordie came back to the hotel that night fairly grumpy, but the prospect of watching me try to win everyone over the next day appeased him somewhat.

Mid-morning we went over to the *Ocean Warrior* to meet Paul Watson and check out their diving setup. I had had no contact with Watson up to that point and also had no idea what to expect with regard to the equipment I'd find on board. I'd been told that they had an air compressor and a handful of tanks, but no one had been able to give me a sense of the shape the equipment would be in. Geordie and I only had the three days to turn the boat into a functional diving and filming platform.

The *Ocean Warrior* was a 165-foot steel ship at least 50 years old, maybe more, with a loud diesel engine. It was grey, with its name painted freehand in orange on the bow, along with kill flags representing the flag of every boat it had rammed or sunk. Almost every surface had the texture of something that had been painted over and over again. It had cabins below deck, a two-storey-high galley and bridge about halfway back, just in front of the helicopter pad, and a structure rising from the bow to elevate the davits, cranes for lifting smaller boats in and out of the ship. Those davits looked a lot like cannons, which made *Ocean Warrior* look even more bad-ass. Rumor was that it used to tend oil rigs in the North Atlantic before Sea Shepherd bought it and turned it into a ship deserving of its name. The boat was equipped with a can opener—a steel blade on hydraulics that came out of the bow—and water cannons. It was an old, but formidable ship, and one that was going to take Geordie and me to sea further and for longer than either of us had ever been.

I was anxious to meet Paul Watson, but it was a nervousness born out of excitement rather than fear. As a kid, I'd dreamed of being a James Bond-type environmental activist, parachuting onto fishing boats and dispatching entire undersea headquarters worth of faceless bad guys in order to foil devious international plots to hurt species I loved. Paul was the closest thing to such a person in real life. I had an image of him as a man of constant action, travelling the world doing battle with evil and greedy whaling and finning ships. I hoped to meet a kindred spirit and maybe a mentor, someone who understood the mission I was on, saw its value and couldn't wait to help me make it happen.

Reality turned out to be a lot more . . . realistic. The man I encountered was a seasoned, slightly jaded environmental activist. Surely he had seen kids like me come and go and felt no need to express interest or confidence in the movie or the good it could do. During the half hour or so I spent explaining myself and the project, I got mostly one or two word responses from him. I was so eager for us to hit it off that I talked almost non-stop. He didn't say anything that was outright discouraging but his silence and aloofness were slightly crushing. I had had so much faith that what I was doing was going to change the world—that we were going to save sharks and publicize him and his work —that I'd assumed his enthusiasm in advance.

After telling Paul our plans, we had to deal with the logistics of getting all the equipment we'd need in working order—most

Paul Watson.

notably the scuba tanks and air compressor we would use to dive at Cocos and Galapagos. I was led by the first mate, Frasier, to a supply room in the bow where all our sponsored gear and donated goodies were stored—Vector cereal and cereal bars, cases and cases of Cott beverages, Kryptonite bike locks and Cinemas Guzzo jackets and shirts, the distribution of which I hoped would bring the crew on side. He also showed us the enclosed space on the bow that was to be our scuba centre. At the top of the portside stairs that led below decks sat the air compressor, about 2 metres distant from outside air. Ideally you want an air compressor somewhere it can easily pull in fresh air for your tanks, but this would have to do.

The inside of that scuba centre was a far cry from what I was used to. Along with not being in the ideal place, the compressor was both ancient (not great news but not really a problem) and broken (really a problem). Its air filters probably hadn't been changed in ages and the buildup of filth on them had taxed the rest of the machine. At the very least, we'd have to find new filters and whatever backup parts we could lay our hands on in the next two days and hope that Geordie and the boat's engineers could figure out how to get the thing going. As promised, the *Ocean Warrior* did have a handful of oddly sized and painted scuba tanks, but they were ancient. Tanks are made from aluminum or steel and after every safety inspection and pressure test, the inspector takes a mallet and hammers the date of the test right into the tank; *Ocean Warrior*'s scuba tanks hadn't been pressure tested in years. They might be fine but if we tried to fill one and it turned out to be cracked or otherwise damaged, it could explode and injure or kill someone. I wasn't too fond of that idea, so we added scuba tanks to our shopping list, hopped off the boat and set about locating, visiting and buying out every dive shop in Los Angeles.

Over the course of that day and the next, Geordie had the air filters and other parts for the compressor shipped to us via overnight delivery. We bought scuba tanks and the other bits and pieces still missing from our inventory and loaded everything onto the boat. Three days later, we officially boarded *Ocean Warrior* for the two-week journey to Costa Rica. We were given two small rooms directly above the propeller for ourselves and thirty-five cases of equipment. The amount of engine noise and vibration inside the hindmost room ruled it out as a sleeping cabin, so we used it to store the equipment, nailing and screwing chargers and monitors into desks, walls and ceilings, mounting hard plastic waterproof cases for the soon to be precious tapes, and creating hiding places for expensive stuff we didn't want sitting out in plain view.

The other room had a graduated bunk bed that Geordie and I would have slept on had the temperature not been about a thousand degrees. Instead, we stored our clothes and personal items there, and slept on the bow of the ship, with the majority of the crew, on Therm-a-rest inflatable mattresses, in one giant outdoor slumber party. We figured it was going to be a filthy, noisy, fun and incredibly hot trip to Costa Rica.

My excitement about finally being en route was somewhat tempered by my having to make a speech to the crew as soon as we left the dock, explaining that Geordie and I were making a movie that was going to save sharks and increase Sea Shepherd's profile. The entire forty-person crew (minus Paul who'd heard my speech already and had sequestered himself in his cabin) gathered in the galley and I tried to get them excited about the project and urged them to sign release forms in order to make this film a million times easier. The awkwardness continued after the speech as Geordie and I rolled around the ship taking Polaroid pictures of everyone and writing their names on them so we'd remember who was who and have a visual record to associate with the releases we were asking them to sign.

I was twenty-two, but if you've seen *Sharkwater* you know that I looked about twelve. The disbelief coming off most of the people on board was palpable: how had anyone been willing to give me a camera or the money to make a movie? The only way to get by on that boat was to be confident. Confident that I was working for good; confident because I was the only trained scuba instructor on the boat, and the only one who'd ever been diving with sharks; confident that I was the only published photographer and the only one with the ability to take Sea Shepherd and their cause to the next level; and confident that I *could* actually make a movie. I didn't think about anything else, I just tapped into that confidence and pretended I knew what I was doing.

As soon as we left port in Los Angeles, the entire crew went to work disguising the very famous *Ocean Warrior*, turning it into the *Farley Mowat* in blue, grey and black ocean camo with sharp lines that would make it tough to see on the horizon. As the crew chipped paint, sanded and soldered, I went to work learning how to make a movie. First I needed to figure out how to use the VariCam. The manual was 400 pages long, and included terms like white levels, black levels, chroma and gamma, but it didn't explain any of them. I read it over and over again, but could only understand about half of it.

Then I read the two books Jane had gotten me on how to make movies: *The 5 C's of Cinematography* and a blue paperback on documentary filmmaking. I watched *Snatch* and *Amélie* on my laptop and practised shooting scenes with Geordie. We visually demonstrated the "5-second rule" with vegan pancakes, shot the ship and its crew working to transform the *Ocean Warrior*, shot ourselves bored a dozen ways. Talk about self-taught.

Chapter Fourteen

My First Naval Battle

The boat first appeared as a blip on our radar off the Pacific coast of Guatemala, on or around our twelfth day at sea. Paul's personal policy (and, by extension, Sea Shepherd policy) was to investigate any vessel we came near that might turn out to be an illegal fishing boat. So, when the blip appeared, he angled us toward it. News from the wheelhouse always had to work its way down the ranks through Frasier, the veteran Sea Shepherd campaigner who functioned as Paul's first mate. Word that maybe there was something about to happen came around six in the morning, as I was asleep on deck, tucked underneath the Zodiac on the port side of the ship. Soon a black spot smudged the horizon.

Our trip to that point had been a mundane grind for the crew. The sight of a boat after days of manual labor had people milling around on the deck. Soon enough the smudge grew into a small, wooden fishing boat trailing a longline—the *Varadero I*. Crew took down the license number painted on the side and relayed the information to Paul. Before contacting the ship directly, Paul wanted to find out as much about them as possible, so he radioed the Guatemalan port authority to find out if the ship was legal and whether we had any power to do anything about it if it wasn't. Paul found out that according to the Guatemalan authorities, the *Varadero I* did not have any permits to fish in Guatemalan waters, and welcomed Paul's request to be allowed to escort the ship and its crew into port for arrest.

I didn't hear Paul's initial conversation with the Guatemalan authorities. But I watched the crew of the *Varadero I* through the HD camera lens as we drew closer, and they definitely looked like they were operating illegally. People at sea often project an air of ease. Not usually in relationships on their own boats (which tend to be stir-crazy pressure cookers of human drama), but in the way they encounter other vessels. There's a relaxed, full-arm wave that you've probably seen and returned on a cottage lake or from the deck of a cruise ship. It's like a mutual acknowledgement that you're out of your element and at the mercy of a force much greater than yourself, so you may as well just relax and make the most of it until you're back on dry land. The crew of the *Varadero I* weren't doing any waving.

The crew of the *Varadero I* were pulling in their lines, the same sort of lines marked with black flags that I encountered in the Galapagos. They worked at a pace that became frantic as we neared. They butchered the sharks in open view, quickly removing the fins and throwing bits of shark back into the ocean. They even threw a shark head in the direction of the camera. The line lay in tangled heaps on the deck.

On board the *Galapagos Aggressor I*, we had treated the animals we cut free with care, and the experience had still traumatized me. What was taking place on the deck of the *Varadero I* was very different: I was witnessing firsthand what I'd been fighting for the last two years to stop. Mixed in with my anger and disgust I also felt excited. I was excited to film this; I was excited we were going to bring these bad guys to justice; and I could tell that others on board the *Farley Mowat* shared that feeling.

Word reached us that the Guatemalan authorities had given the okay for us to bring the *Varadero I* into port, but it wasn't clear exactly how we would do that. The mood on the deck was confused and feverish and it didn't feel like anyone was prepared (or preparing) to tell us what to do.

I made my way up to the wheelhouse. When I got there, Carlos, the only person on board who spoke fluent Spanish, was on the radio to the crew of the *Varadero I*. He seemed to be acting as a translator for Paul who was bellowing demands that they stop pulling in the longline and follow us into the nearest port. Unsurprisingly, the crew of the *Varadero I* refused to stop their work in order to be arrested and instead focused on putting some distance between the two ships. Then all hell broke loose.

As the crew of the fishing boat continued working their catch, a handful of Sea Shepherd volunteers began trying to pull in the section of line nearest to us. They managed to hook it and haul some of it on board but none of them had gloves or knives with which to handle it or to cut the animals loose. Without gloves they couldn't even safely take a firm hold of the line itself (let alone deal with the hooks), so I sent Geordie down to our cabin to grab a few pairs of dive gloves and a knife. Around then, Paul gave the order to man *Farley Mowat*'s three water cannons and a few crewmembers leaped into position and waited for them to kick on.

One of the sounder strategies for apprehending the *Varadero I* was to render it immobile by flooding its engines. In a perfect world, we'd get close enough that the water cannons were in range, give the *Varadero I* a good soaking and then tow it into port. But when the water cannons started up, we were too far from the *Varadero* to have any hope of hitting it. Complicating things further, many of the cannons had rusted in place since they'd last been used. They shot straight up into the air, off at odd angles or, worst of all, back into the boat. Everything and everyone was getting absolutely soaked. When the water cannons first fired up, Geordie got hit by some nasty rusty water. Thinking that this must be some kind of acid or toxic goo that Sea Shepherd was using to battle the *Varadero I*, Geordie hid in an closet for much of the battle trying to save himself from the toxic ooze. The misfiring cannons upped the sense of urgency. It felt like we'd been cooking and accidentally set off every smoke detector in the house.

With things on the deck getting more and more chaotic, I stopped filming and retreated to the wheelhouse to try and get a bead on the situation. I wanted to figure out if there were going to be radio calls I should tape; I needed to know where it made the most sense for me to be in order to capture the story. No one knew.

We followed the boat around for hours, long after their line was out of the water (some of it on board *Farley Mowat*; most of it on the *Varadero I*). Despite the persistent sense of urgency on the ship, it was all actually kind of boring. Mostly we stared at the "bad guys" boat bobbing up and down off the side of the ship.

I was awaiting new developments when Geordie burst into the wheelhouse with a shotgun and treated us all to a vigorous *chk-chick*, as he cocked the gun. I had no idea what to do about it, so I just pointed the camera at him and started asking questions.

"Geordie, why do you have a shotgun?"

"It's loaded with flares."

"You're planning on shooting flares out of a shotgun?"

"Yeah, exactly. I'm going to strafe a couple of flares over their bow."

"Why?"

"As warning shots."

Doug and Geordie.

Geordie had overheard a group of Sea Shepherd volunteers discussing the shoot-flares-at-the-other-boat plan. Joining in, Geordie found out that he was the only one on board other than Paul who had ever fired a gun. Deciding that he was therefore the least likely to accidentally hit someone on board the *Varadero I*, he nominated himself as the gunman. He was given the shotgun and then ran off to find me.

"So," he asked, "are you going to come film me shooting flares at these dudes or what?"

I followed Geordie out onto the deck and watched him shooting off three or four flares (successfully and without any injuries) as the rest of the crew worked the water cannons. Everyone on our deck was drenched and wild-eyed, and the boats were writhing closer and closer together.

I was back in the wheelhouse when I heard someone yell, "We're going to hit!" I ran out onto the deck with my camera and pushed record just as the two boats collided. All the energy that had been building in intensity for hours disappeared with

The *Farley Mowat* trying to stop the *Varadero I*. The volunteers got soaked.

one great shuddering jolt. On both decks, people just stood there stunned.

After the collision, the *Varadero I*'s crew radioed their submission and agreed to let us tow them into port. Two Sea Shepherd volunteers zipped a towline over to the *Varadero I* in a Zodiac. Then we took off for Guatemala. The speed, waves and jerking of the towline made the *Varadero I* lurch violently. Eventually, Paul decided we had to cut it loose so it wouldn't flip. By radio, Carlos and Paul got the crew to agree that if we released the towline they would voluntarily trail us into the nearest port.

As we neared the coast, Paul again radioed the Guatemalan authorities to let them know that we were almost there. The authorities said that they were sending out a gunboat to escort the *Varadero I*, but that we would also be taken into custody. At that point, it wasn't clear why we were being arrested but we assumed that the crew of the *Varadero I* had pulled some strings.

Wanting to avoid a major Central American court drama, Paul decided that we'd set the *Varadero I* free and sail on. With the little fishing boat shrinking once again into a black smudge on the horizon, we set our sights on Costa Rica.

Chapter Fifteen

Too Close a Call with the Costa Rican Legal System

The citizens of the city of Puntarenas had just managed to get a new national marine park—an area of protected seas—created near the coast, just south of the port. The *Farley Mowat* came into harbour in the middle of a giant festival celebrating the achievement. Sea Shepherd had been invited to Costa Rica by the president at the time, Miguel Ángel Rodríguez Echeverría, to help raise awareness about the epidemic of illegal shark finning in the country. The plan was to touch down in Puntarenas for a few days and await word from the office of the president. We'd then meet him for a press conference or photo op before ripping out to Cocos Island, a marine reserve, to patrol, dive, film and save sharks.

It felt as though all of Costa Rica had turned out to welcome us. Everyone we encountered in the city seemed to know who we were and why we'd come. The people Geordie and I passed making our way into the centre of town were full of love and seemed optimistic about the good we were there to do. It was completely intoxicating and we all felt like heroes coming to save the day.

The festival's epicentre was a square in the heart of the city, three blocks from the water. The first time we visited the square, a crowd of about three hundred had gathered around a small stage on which a group of face-painted dancers stomped and spun in sparkling turquoise outfits. The music was loud and the beat that infectious one-two-three, one-two-three Latin shuffle. The crowd clapped along and danced, calling out slogans I didn't understand and proudly waving banners and flags. Geordie and I just stood there grinning at each other and everything around us. When the song ended, the dancers poured off the stage and a bunch of politicians filed up to replace them. At some point we figured out that one of the politicians was Costa Rica's environment minister. I filmed them all giving impassioned speeches, figuring that if anything cool or interesting was said we'd get it translated and sort it out later (though I confess we never did). When the speeches were over, the crowd dispersed and we made our way back to the boat.

For the next few days we rode the high of our arrival, getting more and more excited for the trip to Cocos. Doug was done his exams and made it to Puntarenas on his own. He called me and Geordie on board and I took a Zodiac to shore and picked him up. With Doug safely arrived and our first chance to get under water only days away, it felt like things were finally coming together.

Then we found out we were being charged with attempted murder.

It turned out that the *Varadero I* had headed home to Costa Rica instead of Guatemala. Though it docked miles up the coast, word of our arrival in Puntarenas had reached the crew. Arriving three or four days behind us, they'd made their way to the local courthouse and brought charges against us. They claimed we had intentionally rammed their boat in an attempt to sink them and had fired guns at their ship. The first time I knew anything was happening was when two coast guard ships full of Costa Rican police jetted out to the *Farley Mowat* and Carlos, by way of explanation, told me, "They're coming to search the boat."

That initial encounter, as well as much of the bureaucratic nonsense that would follow, was complete mayhem. The deck of *Farley Mowat*, already crammed with gear, garbage and young activists, was swarming with cops who didn't seem to have any idea what they were looking for. I knew Paul was likely to be the centre of attention, so I grabbed my camera and stuck as near to him as I could. Relying on Carlos to translate when their broken English proved insufficient, the prosecutors or lead investigators (who everyone was, exactly, was never clear) explained that we had been charged with the attempted murder of the innocent souls that crewed the *Varadero I* and that they had a warrant to search the ship for weapons and anything else that might incriminate us and help their investigation. Paul, as captain of the ship, would take the most heat.

Paul appeared only slightly provoked by the situation, and, despite occasional bouts of sarcasm, showed the requisite politeness and satisfied the dozens of demands that cropped up. He led the officers on a tour of the ship and handed over the shotgun that was used to fire the flares. My presence didn't go unnoticed and I was asked to surrender all of my footage. I explained that even if I gave them the tapes, short of purchasing a $100,000 HD tape deck, they'd have no way to view them. After a practical demonstration in which I showed them the impossibility of loading one of my tapes into a regular VCR, they tried to commandeer my camera (never, ever, ever, ever going to happen) before giving in and demanding that I surrender a set of duplicate tapes to the courthouse the next day. I ended up making the duplicates they wanted. I quickly couriered the originals to Canada.

We spent the next ten days under house arrest on the ship, lost in legal limbo. At first, we all expected that the case would quickly be exposed as total nonsense and we'd be back on track. But the longer we sat in port with most of the crew confined to the boat, the more dejected we became. I jumped at every opportunity to leave the ship and head into town. Paul, Carlos, Frasier and I were run through an endless series of meetings with lawyers, judges and port authority representatives, and I tried to make sure I was present at all of them, filming, since someone needed to document what was happening to us. The few times they forgot to let me know about an upcoming meeting or, worse, went to one without me, I made sure to remind them that my presence wasn't just useful, it was necessary.

Mostly the meetings were conducted in Spanish, which made it difficult to know when and what to film. We were represented by a local lawyer named Milton. Paul, Geordie, Doug, sometimes Frasier and I would sit there watching a bunch of people debate our fates. At any natural pause in the conversation, we'd all turn to Carlos who would then distill everything to the salient points. Carlos's way of explaining things wasn't too subtle. Often he'd leave you even more confused and stressed out than when you had absolutely no idea what was going on. After a long, heated exchange, for example, he'd turn to us and say something like "You're probably going to jail." Then he'd turn back to the conversation, leaving us staring at one another in wide-eyed consternation—and terror.

Our main concern was figuring out what we would have to do to get the charges dropped. The story changed a lot, but it was always presented in a way that made it seem like we only had one more hoop to jump through before we would be free to go. The hoops we were supposed to jump through were almost exclusively monetary. If we just paid the next round of court fees, we'd be free to go. Oh wait, there was also just one last permit we had to pay for and then get stamped at the port authority office. Oh, and a docking fee. On and on it went.

The fact that we were in trouble at all also seemed perpetually up for debate. Someone would arrive to tell us that the charges had been thrown out of court and we'd spend an afternoon celebrating on the boat. Then evening would come around and we'd find out that, nope, the charges were being reinstated. There also seemed to be some confusion about what we were actually being charged with.

Paul seemed to have a limitless energy store for dealing with the crisis, but for most of us the lack of a clear solution was demotivating in the extreme. We'd spend two days in talks with someone or other trying to negotiate a permit to leave only to find out that there was something else we'd be required to do instead and maybe those two days had been a total waste. It's hard for me to imagine a method of controlling people and breaking down their spirits that's more effective than endless, mystifying bureaucracy.

We had been stuck in Puntarenas, confined to the *Farley Mowat* for ten to fourteen days when I heard that we were going to be allowed to spend a week at Cocos Island, patrolling, diving, filming and finally saving some sharks. The charges hadn't been dropped and the politics and legal niceties remain a little beyond me, but basically the authorities decided that because we had been invited to Costa Rica by the president to help stop illegal fishing practices plaguing the country, it would be okay for us to spend a week patrolling the waters around Cocos despite the charges against us. We didn't ask too many questions, we just started getting our act together for the trip.

Chapter Sixteen

Finally, Finally *Some Sharks Get Filmed*

As well as being a protected national park, Cocos Island is also a UNESCO world heritage site and one of the seven underwater wonders of the world. The island is 25 square kilometres of rainforest on top of a 5,000-metre extinct volcano rising from the floor of the Pacific Ocean. It sits all alone about 550 kilometres from the coast of Costa Rica, a thirty-six-hour boat ride from Puntarenas. Like the Galapagos, deep undersea currents converge here, running into the side of the volcano, and bring waters full of nutrients from dead and decaying plant and animal matter from the deep ocean to the surface; there tiny marine plants (phytoplankton) use those nutrients to create oxygen and life. This proliferation means that every big animal in the region is either at Cocos, on its way to Cocos or leaving Cocos. The island is known to have the greatest concentration of sharks in the world, as well as dolphins, whales and manta rays. Except for a single park ranger station, Cocos is uninhabited, but because of all the big animals, it's a go-to destination for live-aboard dive trips.

We paid a port fee and got the necessary permits and other assorted paperwork as together as possible then left Puntarenas.

We'd made it all of a few miles when a 25-foot Zodiac pulled up alongside us, loaded with three uniformed men carrying automatic rifles (presumably also loaded). They were pointing their rifles at us and moving them up and down in that slow-down-and-stop, we're-the-police kind of way. Paul got on the radio with them and we found out that, apparently unaware that we'd been given permission to sail to Cocos, the Costa Rican coast guard thought we were making a break for international waters. Their entire side of the radio conversation consisted of yelling orders at us in Spanish. (Carlos translated them for me later: "You've got to stop, you've got to stop. We're going to shoot you if you don't stop.")

Paul immediately gave the orders to cover the easily boardable areas of the ship with barbed wire, and for everyone to stay below deck and out of sight. The *Ocean Warrior* by any name would take a serious commitment from the authorities to board at speed from a 25-foot Zodiac. But with barbed wire hung like Christmas lights, there's no way they were ever going to be able to board us. At the same time, none of us felt like getting shot.

I was out on the deck and unable to take cover because I needed a clear line of sight to the Zodiac in order to film everything. I'd duck away and take breaks when the situation really freaked me out. But eventually we reached the conclusion that they weren't likely to shoot the cameraman, and for the rest of the chase I stayed out in the open.

In the bridge, Paul was screaming over the radio, trying to explain that we'd been given a permit to go to Cocos and that shooting us would be ridiculous. Eventually he got the patrol to agree to leave us alone if we showed them our permit. Paul photocopied it, rolled it up, stuck it in an empty wine bottle and corked it. Without ordering the ship to stop or even slow down, he walked to the side and threw the wine bottle overboard. The Zodiac circled back to pick up the bottle, and at that point we knew we were in the clear. I don't know how they intended to get that piece of paper out of the wine bottle, but they didn't try to renew the chase. If they managed to fish out the permit on board their little soft-sided Zodiac boat, they were geniuses. Maybe they smashed it with a rifle butt.

The only trouble on the rest of the trip was that the weather was absolutely sweltering. Playing around to get more familiar with the camera, I shot a series of scenes with Doug and Geordie in which we'd head to our cabin and wait to see how long it took us to start pouring sweat. We averaged about five seconds.

Now everyone aboard the *Farley Mowat*, except Paul and Charlie—who was the engineer and the only paid crew member—slept on the deck of the boat. Early on the second morning, as people around me began to stir, I woke up and there was Cocos shooting out of the ocean right in front of us, this beautiful, tiny rainforest pinnacle, surrounded by clouds and riddled with undiscovered pirate treasure—most famously that of Captain Bennett Graham, who is said to have buried 350 tons of gold bullion on the island sometime around 1820.

Knowing what was under the water around me—so many sharks—made me want to slip on my dive gear and throw myself overboard, but we hadn't come just so I could go diving. Our first priority was to pick up some park rangers from the island and brainstorm with them about what exactly Sea Shepherd could do to best patrol and protect the area.

The *Farley Mowat* had two Zodiac boats on board: a 16-footer and a 25-footer. Before we'd even arrived at Cocos, I'd managed to talk Scott, one of the crew, into driving Doug, Geordie and me out to some dive spots in whichever of the Zodiacs was free. Hindsight being 20/20, I can now say with confidence that we should never have set up our dive trips the way we did. The currents at Cocos are so severe that a few people get swept away and lost every year on well-organized, professional diving expeditions. Finding people in the open ocean is incredibly difficult. With no captain, no dive guide and no one but a Sea Shepherd volunteer manning the boat, it's surprising that we didn't get lost at Cocos—we didn't even use a down line to get from the surface to the dive site. I had never been in that poor a diving arrangement before but at the time it didn't matter—we were diving at Cocos!

There were three live-aboard dive boats in the area at the time— *Sea Hunter*, *Undersea Hunter* and the *Oceanos Aggressor*. Knowing how valuable they could be to our success with filming sharks, I made one of my first priorities whipping over in our Zodiac to introduce myself. Not only did they provide me with the oxygen necessary to fill my rebreather but, after I explained the *Sharkwater* project and handed out some *Sharkwater* t-shirts, they told me where the best dive sites were and when I should go there. Over the course of the week, we managed two or three dives a day, at varying locations, as well as a regular night dive, always at a spot called Manuelita off the northeast corner of the island.

At night I had to provide myself with light as well as air. Night divers usually go down with two flashlights and a Glow Stick that attaches to their buoyancy compensation device and allows other divers to mark their position in the water. I had the standard Glow Stick but instead of a flashlight I had two 400-watt halogen lamps attached to either side of my camera on six-foot arms. When I got the hundred-pound camera rig overboard and under water, with another 40 pounds of light batteries strapped to my chest, then flipped the switch, I became a small sun. It felt like those halogens lit up the entire ocean.

Manuelita at night was full of whitetip reef sharks. My ability to create a swath of daylight through the dark allowed me to team up with them to hunt smaller fish, concentrating huge amounts of sharks in my field of view and allowing me to get killer footage.

Whitetip reef sharks get their very literal name from their dorsal and caudal (tail) fins, which look like tiny snow-capped mountains. Their backs and sides are grey-brown, sometimes dotted with a pattern of scattered black leopard-spots unique to each individual. They have big, milky white eyes with beautiful, dark vertical pupils. Their mouths are small, or maybe just seem that way beneath their broad noses, and lend the whitetips a serene and serious air that is

Under water with a lighting rig.

only undermined by a pair of distinct, tubular nasal flaps, which make it look like they have short straws stuck up their noses. They only grow to be 6 or 7 feet long and have very sweet dispositions, which is pretty great if you're going to be surrounded by a hundred or more of them. The sharks at Manuelita were so plentiful you could reach out and grab one in almost any direction. As far as I'm concerned, to be able to touch a shark, hold it with one hand even, instantly alleviates a good chunk of the fear and stress you might feel about swimming with so many of them. At Manuelita, you could hold one gently by the tail and stop it from swimming for a second before letting it go.

When fish are woken up in the middle of the night by two 400-watt halogens, they act a lot like we would. They stay put, stunned and wondering what could possibly be going on and when it will stop so they can get back to bed. In that moment of disorientation, while the fish are stammering, "Oh, oh, what? Oh," the sharks arrive and just *hammer* them. The pickings were so easy it took no time for the sharks to learn to hunt in my light. Whitetips are pack hunters, and so whenever I turned the camera on a fresh patch of water, dozens of them would show up and go for any fish that moved. All I would have to do is turn my lights towards some fish and the sharks would go for them.

Once in awhile, when I was moving around to find a new shot, I'd accidentally bump the back of the camera into the battery packs strapped to my chest, making a deep clunking noise. The sharks at Manuelita grew to associate the noise with the easy hunting available in my light. After a while, I realized that any time I made that noise the sharks came right to me. So I started doing it on purpose. I'd go *gunk gunk*, double-tapping the camera against the packs on my chest. Instantly, any shark in the area would swerve right toward me no matter what. I got killer shark footage on every night dive. I'd never seen anything like it in my life—fifty to a hundred whitetip reef sharks smashing into the coral right in front of me.

A few days into our trip we started diving at Bajo Alcyone. Named after Jacques Cousteau's wife, Alcyone is an undersea pinnacle that peaks 95 feet below the surface of the water. Despite being an absolute nightmare to get to, it quickly became our favourite dive site on Cocos.

Farley Mowat's position, relative to the island, changed pretty drastically from day to day, but it always ended up being at least an hour away from Alcyone by Zodiac, and depending on conditions, sometimes as much as two and a half hours. In the smaller of the Zodiac boats, with a nine horsepower engine, the trip could be challenging. The swells were big enough that waves would crash over and into the boat, and we'd have to bail it out by hand. Near the end of the trip, I managed to talk Paul into letting us take out the 25-footer, but only by offering to pay for all the gas.

Surviving the ride out to Alcyone was less than half of the battle, though, because once we got to what we hoped was the right spot, we still had to find the peak 30 metres below the surface, about 2 kilometres from the island itself. At first, we'd just huck ourselves in roughly where we thought it should be and swim down. If we missed, we'd try again, as many times as it took to hit the pinnacle. Eventually, experience triangulating our position in reference to the island increased our chances of starting off in the right spot. I eventually asked my parents to courier us a GPS so we could find the site more easily than with visual triangulation.

I was always the first one dropped in because it took two people to lift the hundred-pound camera out of the boat and get it safely in the water. Once I had the camera secured, and Doug and Geordie were in, I'd go under and kick as hard as possible straight down, pushing the giant camera in front of me. Diving straight into blue water is a pretty unnerving experience. Your bubbles are flying off behind you, so you don't always know which way is down, and there are no landmarks to help orient you. At Alcyone, the currents often shifted perceptibly on the way down; you crossed through one and into another, making it nearly impossible to predict whether you were being carried off course, or in which direction.

Sometimes I'd get 120 feet down and not see anything but unbroken blue in all directions. At that point it's a serious decision whether to stay down and try to find the peak or just kick back up to the surface and try again. Chances are you're not going to find it, and you're going to have to go up and try again. Staying down is appealing because going up and down and up and down is really hard on your body. Having Doug and Geordie with me changed things a bit. If I spent a whole day hauling them up and down and one of them got "bent," I was going to feel pretty guilty about it, so I dove a lot more carefully than I would have if I'd been alone.

For the most part, diving is a safe sport. But you're only a visitor underwater, surviving on the small pressurized cylinder of gas you brought down from the surface with you. That cylinder contains a mixture of gasses that are toxic at certain pressures, and in different ways. When too much oxygen (hyperoxia) is forced into your blood by the pressures of depth, you convulse in a seizure that usually results in your drowning. Not enough oxygen (hypoxia), and you slowly pass out, often with similar results. But most of the time you only run into oxygen problems when diving really deep or when you're using a rebreather.

It's nitrogen that you really have to worry about; it makes up almost 79 percent of the air in your tank, with oxygen being the other 21 percent of the mix. If you've been diving deep for a long time, you're going to go into decompression. As you breathe air at pressure, the gasses in the air dissolve into the liquids of your body. With too much nitrogen in your blood, you can get the bends. It's like opening a can of soda: You remove the pressure from the liquid in the can by popping the top, and bubbles form and come out of the solution. When you surface with a lot of nitrogen in your blood, bubbles of nitrogen congregate in your joints and other susceptible areas and can kill you. You can't safely surface without time to off-gas at predetermined safe "ceilings" on the way up: 30 feet, 15 feet and so on. Often it can take quite a while to surface, which is problematic if you're diving in strong currents in the middle of nowhere.

If you do a bang-up job of controlling your breathing, you can stay under a couple hours at 30 feet and about 40 minutes at 100 feet. If you do an average job breathing—because you're kicking hard to avoid being swept away by the currents, or battling those currents with an enormous camera—then you've probably got more like fifteen minutes, maybe less. The hammerheads you're after are most likely hanging out at 150 feet. There, you've got five minutes before you go into decompression.

Using a rebreather, depending on the depth, you have a lot more time: up to six hours. Rebreathers constantly re-circulate the air that you breathe, injecting oxygen, and scrubbing out the carbon dioxide. They can give you more oxygen in the mix, which reduces the amount of nitrogen you absorb, but sometimes if you're not careful or there's a glitch they can give you too much oxygen.

When you surface from a dive, you're supposed to do it slowly, at least as slow as your bubbles. If the currents are strong on your way up and you also have to spend several minutes at 30- and at 15-feet ceilings, the chance of getting swept far away from the boat that's supposed to pick you up is huge. To combat this problem at Alcyone, most diving expeditions have one giant 125-foot dive boat planted on top, with a rope down to the pinnacle and two 25-foot Zodiacs that rip around and pick people up. We were out there in a little 16-foot dinghy and our main boat was often on the other side of the island, out of radio range. But to me none of this mattered, really. What mattered was getting the best hammerhead shark footage ever.

Hundreds of hammerhead sharks congregate at Alcyone, in greater numbers than possibly anywhere else on earth. The eastern equatorial region of the Pacific is hugely rich and hugely diverse. Currents from every corner of the world—from the north, from Antarctica, the Humboldt Current from the west—collide and intermingle and bring with them all sorts of different animals. If you're a shark and you're navigating somewhere in the area, you stop in to hang out, find a mate and grab a bite to eat before heading into the relative desolation of the open ocean. During La Niña, an irregular cooling pattern that when it hits usually stretches from late spring until early fall, Cocos attracts massive numbers of hammerhead sharks, and Alcyone is the best spot for filming and interacting with them.

Even though I was still figuring out how to use the camera, I needed the footage I got at Cocos to be perfect. I had to nail it because I didn't have the time or resources not to. Before I boarded the *Ocean Warrior* I had watched a couple of IMAX films (figuring they represented the apex of wildlife movies) to get some sense of what I was aiming for, and I noticed that the camera never moved. It was planted on a tripod and didn't pan, didn't tilt, nothing. I was relieved as I thought the major difference between still and video shots was the camera movement. Not so—the movement could come from the subject. So I decided all I needed to do was start filming and just keep the camera steady, almost the same as shooting stills, except I was shooting sixty of them every second.

On any given dive, whichever side of the peak was bearing the brunt of the currents was the place to find sharks. So once we got down to Alcyone, we had to work our way up current. I would leave Geordie and Doug up to 300 feet away from me and downstream on the pinnacle, so they didn't frighten the hammerheads with their excitement, bubbles or movement.

With hammerheads so sensitive, I had to keep my heart rate down despite having to fight the current, and make most of my movements while they weren't looking. This required finding a good vantage point on the face of the pinnacle, wedging myself in and staying put until they arrived. I often had to hold the camera between my legs and drag myself hand-over-hand across the barnacle-encrusted rocks to get to a spot where I couldn't be dislodged by the current.

Hammerheads group together in schools that are almost entirely composed of females, called shivers. Their position in the school depends on their size and dominance, which is established with a variety of awesome, aggressive displays. Using their pectoral fins they'll arch up like a pissed-off snake and undulate their entire bodies. They'll also combine the undulation with a spastic head shaking that brings their hammers around in a figure eight or, stepping it up a notch, they'll do corkscrews—sometimes three or four in a row.

The schools tended to swim in circles with Alcyone (and me perched on its face) serving as a point on the circle's perimeter. Hammerheads swam in and past me, planted on the side of the pinnacle, for a second and then disappeared into the blue. Occasionally, they widened their circle and passed over top of me, closer to the rocks, but very rarely. The hammerheads were visiting cleaning stations on the pinnacle where dozens of butterfly fish swim out and start picking dead skin and parasites off them. There could be as many as twenty bright yellow butterfly and angel fish swimming alongside a 9-foot hammerhead, pecking and plucking all over its mouth and body. The hammerheads seemed to genuinely enjoy this cleaning, swimming slowly with their mouths agape to signal their intent to be cleaned.

But most of the time the sharks stuck to the usual pattern and with my rock-steady camera technique all I got on the majority of the dives was side-on shots, albeit many with cute entourages of cleaners. I started watching the footage at night back on board the boat and all I had was shots of sharks entering and leaving the frame.

I knew I had to get something better. So, as the hammerheads circled in, I started trying to predict their path. Just before they arrived, I'd hold my breath, gather myself and launch out from the face, hoping to intercept their circuit so they would swim right at me, over me, around me and into the camera. Holding my breath was dangerous because it created the possibility of rising up in the water and bursting my lungs. But since the hammerheads angled away from me if I let any bubbles escape my regulator, the only choice was to hold my breath and do my damnedest to swim out and level or out and down.

Ideally, I would have been using a rebreather at all times. With a rebreather, not only can you stay down a lot longer, there are no shark-upsetting bubbles when you exhale. The *Farley Mowat* only had the air provided by its ancient compressor. The only access I had to the pure oxygen necessary to refill a rebreather was when I could arrange a meeting with one of the live-aboard dive boats kind enough to let me mooch theirs. I maybe managed that four or five times.

Air's not a bad second choice because there are only two ways it can fail you. Either you run out of it, which is only possible if you completely ignore the gauge on your wrist that tells you how full your tank is, or your regulator fails. Even if your regulator fails, it fails in the open position and starts free-flowing air. This can bring a longer dive to a pretty quick end, but you can still breathe from the free-flowing stream of air.

Rebreathers can fail in dozens of ways. The nastiest of these is when it decides to give you the wrong concentration of oxygen. The concentration of oxygen in regular air, 21 percent, is toxic 250 feet under water. At 150 feet, 50 percent oxygen is toxic. You control the mix of oxygen in your rebreather's airflow and usually you try and stay just above toxicity so your body accumulates the least amount of nitrogen and you can stay down longer. If your rebreather decides to act strangely and give you an extra big hit of pure oxygen, you're going to go into convulsions, spit out your mouthpiece and die.

At one point on Alcyone, I was at 150 feet and I noticed the computer on my forearm that monitored the mix of oxygen from my rebreather was beeping and reading 50 percent oxygen. I couldn't figure out why I wasn't already in full convulsions. I had no idea how long it had been giving me 50 percent; I'd been filming sharks and not really paying attention to anything else. I immediately shut my rebreather mouthpiece, grabbed the bailout regulator hooked up to a small scuba cylinder called a pony bottle and headed for the surface, figuring that if I was going to go into convulsions it was best to have it happen as close to the surface as possible. I made it without convulsing or getting the bends, but the experience was enough to keep me out of the water for a few hours. I never did find out what the problem was, but afterward I triple checked the rebreather, cleaned it, and then went to see if one of the dive boats could fill my oxygen cylinder.

Near the end of our week at Cocos, on our second dive of the day, when Geordie and Doug's cylinders were empty I kicked alone with my rebreather and camera, straight down into blue water and hit the peak of Alcyone on the first try. There was nothing but empty blue as I approached but right as I settled on the rock the hammerheads came, hundreds of them, gliding from just below me up the face and right over me. All around me were these 2- to 3-foot heads, swaying as they slowly swam by. For some reason, they were completely unafraid.

I pointed the camera, hit record and everything was white. I had forgotten to flip a switch on the inside of the camera that alternated the iris between auto and manual, so it was wide open and everything was overexposed. I couldn't do anything to adjust the camera to let in less light. I knew the film wouldn't be useable, but I shot the scene for five seconds anyways. I just wanted a little bit of a record so that I would remember what it was like. The footage shows hundreds of surreal albino hammerheads swimming around in a white turquoise wash of awesomeness, their giant heads being cleaned by butterfly fish right in front of me.

I've never had an experience quite like that. You spend so much time trying to see these sharks. And once you've spent days just trying to see them, then you try and get close to them. And once you get close to them, then you try to get underneath them. And then finally you get underneath them and you're like, "Okay. Now what?" Underneath them *and* in front of them so they've got to swim right over the camera—that's the best. That's what you're looking for. And that's what they did, heaps of them. I've only ever had a few of them swim over me any of the other times I've had the chance. To get a hammerhead shark close to the camera, so you can see detail in its face, and have a bunch of them in the background, so you can see there are 150 of these suckers and three of them are a foot away from you. Of any footage that I could shoot in the world, I want to shoot that. Hammerhead sharks. Close to the camera. Hundreds of them.

With such a profusion of life in the waters around Cocos, it is home to predatory displays of epic proportions. Sharks and dolphins routinely collaborate to bring schools of fish to the surface. With no avenue of escape, the school forms a bait ball at the surface, and the sharks, dolphins and seabirds feast on fish. The way to find one of these spectacles is to track the seabirds. Lots of seabirds means a good bait ball.

Footage of bait balls and their predators was high on my list of things to film, so our crew was on constant watch for seabirds dive-bombing the ocean. At least once or twice a day, we'd spot a likely congregation and jet out in one of the Zodiacs as fast as we could. I'd jump in with just snorkel, mask, fins and camera. Most of the time I'd get there just as the last fish was eaten, or find a school of fish that didn't have enough predators around it to ball up. But

Free diving.

every time presented an exhilarating adventure, as I never knew what kind of animals and action I was jumping in on.

When you free dive, you usually look for a spot on the bottom and aim for it. It's calming and grounding to know where you're going. Free diving in blue water is a totally different experience. You can't see the bottom, and often descend past the point where you can still see the surface, so you have no idea how deep you are. Free diving and filming in the blue, I'd often end up following or being followed by sharks, and I'd be spinning around upside down and sideways. When I had to get to the surface, with no bubbles or sharks to orient me, I wouldn't know which way to go. This little period of not knowing was really disorienting. But sharks really don't like bubbles and free diving is often the best way to film them.

To help the park rangers on Cocos, when our week's grace was up we agreed to transport thousands of pounds of garbage back to mainland Costa Rica. The rangers composted everything they possibly could, so the waste that built up was all batteries, scrap metal and hunks of plastic. It seemed like every spare inch of deck space on *Farley Mowat* had been given over to landfill. Garbage was piled up around the Zodiacs and on the helicopter pad, in all of the places on deck we usually slept. There wasn't much in the way of organic waste, so it didn't stink that bad. But still, piles of garbage weren't the most pleasant companions to have on a ship that already felt a bit claustrophobic. Adding to the unpleasantness was the fact that we were still unsure of our legal status in Costa Rica, no matter how ridiculous the whole situation seemed to us. Our garbage barge might be taking us back to prison terms.

But Cocos had been good to us, and we did our best to stay optimistic. Geordie, Doug and I organized mini-screenings of our underwater footage for the crew. We'd invite a few people at a time to brave the sweltering heat of the cramped camera room. Stuffed in and dripping with sweat we'd show them masses of hammerheads, swarming whitetips, underwater volcanoes and vast expanses of blue on a 7-inch monitor. For an hour or so at a time, we could transport people away from the garbage barge to jail and into this beautiful alien world. It was a way to finally get people really excited about what we were doing. Seeing the response my footage got was great for my spirits. Beyond the visuals themselves, everyone seemed taken aback by the quality of the footage; even I was pretty blown away by how professional looking it came out. The screenings didn't necessarily win over everyone on board, but they did create the illusion that Geordie, Doug and I knew what we were doing.

Much the same way we'd crossed paths with the *Varadero I*, about halfway back to mainland Costa Rica Paul noticed a blip on the radar and swung us toward it. When we reached its source we found a Taiwanese longliner. It wasn't as brazen as the *Varadero I* and chose to peel away rather than haul in its illegal catch in front of us. We opted to deal with the line this time rather than chasing the boat. As Paul and the crew tried to sort out just what "dealing with the line" entailed, Doug and I grabbed our camera, suited up with fins and snorkels and hit the water.

The camera creates a sense of both purpose and detachment that can be incredibly useful when dealing with something as grim as a longline. It allows you to focus all of your attention on the question of how to turn what you're experiencing into a visual that will hit its audience with the maximum emotional force. Doug and I swam along the line for several kilometres. Whenever we found something, I'd pass the camera to Doug and he'd film me using my dive knife to cut it loose. In the hour or so that we swam the line we only came across one living thing, a dorado, swimming in circles as big as the hook through its cheek would allow. Doing my best not to frighten it, I crept along the main line to the point at which the hook branched off. Taking hold of the section of line it was caught on, I pulled the dorado as close as I could and cut the line. It swam off trailing a couple feet of filament.

Because of all the garbage we had on board, there was no place to pile the line if we pulled it in. By the time we got back to the boat, Paul had decided that the best way to deal with the line was to sink it. The logic behind sinking the line was that there would be less life at the bottom of the ocean to take the bait. There are animals at the bottom of the ocean that could bite a baited hook, but less than at the surface, and when the bait wore off the hooks, the line would pose no threat. It was the lesser of two evils—given the options it was probably better to have the line on the bottom than floating at the surface. We cruised along the line, tying hunks of metal to it. After awhile it sank and we continued back to Puntarenas.

Chapter Seventeen

A Short Trip to the Ugly Edge of Town

The port at Puntarenas only had permanent docks for cruise ships and fishing boats. Since we were neither, we had to drop anchor a few hundred metres out in the harbour and use the Zodiacs to cover the last stretch. This was inconvenient if you wanted to take a quick stroll into town, but it did have the benefit of preventing people from dropping by unannounced—particularly handy in giving us a little time to brace ourselves before visits from the authorities. Technically, the whole crew was supposed to be confined to the boat anyway, at least until we had been cleared in court. Since Geordie, Doug and I weren't part of the Sea Shepherd organization and hadn't had anything to do with the decision to pursue the *Varadero I* (let alone the actions that caused us to hit the boat), I decided we were exempt from house arrest and free to come and go as we pleased. Besides, my camera equipment was costing $7,500 a week and we had a movie to make.

The three of us became easily recognizable fixtures in town; I always had a giant camera and everybody soon knew us as the white guys from Sea Shepherd. There were a handful of local environmental activists who were interested in sharing their struggles and successes. When any of them wanted a chance to speak with Sea Shepherd, they usually chose to approach Geordie, Doug and me in town. Before our trip out to Cocos, our main contact in the Costa Rican environmentalist movement had been a guy named Eduardo, a joker who enjoyed being on camera. He let me interview him and gave us a cursory backgrounder on the shark fin trade in Costa Rica. Eduardo was a pontificator who loved to hear himself talk. He was entertaining, but not the most useful of guys.

Shortly after our return from Cocos, we were approached in the street by an activist named William. William was soft and childlike on the surface, but you didn't have to dig very deep to find a passionate environmentalist. He had barely finished introducing himself when he began to tell us, in broken English, about a warehouse he knew of in an industrial area on the outskirts of Puntarenas that trafficked in illegal shark fin, said to be run by the Taiwanese mafia. I invited him to a sit down meeting aboard the *Farley Mowat* that evening and we parted ways.

William showed up that night with a folder of newspaper and magazine articles about his battles with the tuna industry. For years he had been active in exposing the slaughter of dolphins by tuna fisherman. Now, he was interested in helping us end the illegal finning of sharks. He agreed to take us to the shark fin warehouse the following morning.

The next day, William, Carlos, Doug, Geordie and I all piled into a little red cab with the camera. William gave the driver directions and we set out towards the edge of Puntarenas. The road was in terrible shape and our driver had to swerve constantly to avoid car-swallowing potholes and slower, less-ballsy motorists. It was a hot, dry day and the road spat up a thin rooster tail of dust in our wake.

We drove for fifteen minutes before pulling to a stop on a blasted-out gravel patch surrounded by high cement walls. We asked the cab driver to wait and got out. Each of the walls had a heavy metal door set into it with crudely spray-painted logos containing images of sharks and fins. There was a transport truck parked off to the side of the gravel patch, against one of the walls.

I banged on all the doors. None of them were unlocked and no one answered. At the end of one of the walls was a stretch of chain-link fence that bordered the water. Through it you could see the back corner of a large warehouse, five wooden longlining boats just like the *Varadero I* moored on a muddy brown estuary, and about a thousand shark fins lying on the ground.

William believed there would be more shark fins drying on the roofs of the warehouses. He explained that once the fins were offloaded onto the dock, they had to be dried in the sun before they could be stored or transported anywhere. Since the roof provided the largest open space and plenty of sun, and was out of the view of authorities, it was likely that that's where the fins would be drying. The transport truck parked near the wall offered our best chance of peeking over the top. I climbed up on it and Doug passed up the camera.

From the top of the truck you could see far more than a small sliver of the facility. Lining the banks of the muddy river as far as I could see were dozens of docks with longlining vessels, each with a corresponding cement warehouse and fins drying on the corrugated metal roof. On the roof closest to me, thousands of shark fins lay drying in the sun. I trained the camera on the fins. I had taken all of thirty seconds of footage before three or four guys came tearing out and started kicking and pushing the fins off the roof and out of sight of my lens. As soon as I saw how frantic they were, I knew we had to get out of there. But I continued filming until they seemed to realize the futility of pushing all those fins off the roof, and instead decided to come after us. Maybe they realized, as I did, that shots of them pushing the fins off the roof was far more dramatic and revealing than just fins on the roof.

I handed the camera down to Geordie, jumped off the truck and made a dash for the cab. We were intercepted by a man from the

Shark fins drying on the factory roof in Puntarenas, Costa Rica.

warehouse, a Latin American, dressed well in a tieless suit, who demanded to know what we were doing and tried to stop us from getting into the cab. Avoiding his questions, I was the last to pile in and then we took off. We spent the entire ride back through town looking out the rear windshield for pursuers.

Showing that footage to the crew of *Farley Mowat* was a pretty triumphant moment. Thanks to William, we had filmed a massive illegal shark-finning outfit operating in Costa Rica in broad daylight. Paul finally started to warm up to us. We'd gotten footage everyone could use and we'd shown him that our project could actually do something to help sharks. He started to say hi when we ran into each other instead of walking right past me; I even heard him bragging once about the footage and the good we could do with it.

On a trip to town the day after we'd visited the warehouse, Carlos spoke to someone who gave us a fairly ominous warning: people were looking for us and maybe even wanted to hurt us. Carlos was told not to show his face in town anymore and to tell us to do the same. I didn't really see what these ominous and powerful invisible people could do to me. Were they going to grab me off the street in broad daylight? Still, I made sure that on my subsequent trips to town I had a buddy to walk around with, and I always tried to move with the confidence of someone who wasn't going to get kidnapped.

Worrying about whether or not I'd be attacked didn't have to occupy me for long. The day after we filmed the warehouses we got word that the Costa Rican authorities intended to arrest Paul and hold him in prison indefinitely. This came at the same time as we were learning about Taiwan's huge investments in Costa Rica, donating major highways, bridges and buildings to the country. One source cited $95 million dollars a year in donations flowing from Taiwan to Costa Rica. With shark fins a billion-dollar global business, we were getting ourselves into serious trouble.

The decision to flee Costa Rica was made within hours, and like any other decision on board it was made by Paul alone, passed on to Frasier and only then spread amongst the rest of us. Once word got around that we were going to make a run for Panama, the closest friendly port, five crew members instantly decamped. Life on the *Farley Mowat* hadn't turned out to be the nature-saving high adventure they'd hoped for. For most of them it had involved months of confinement on the boat with very little to keep them occupied. One of the Zodiacs ferried the five to land while the rest of us prepared for the trip. When the boat was in order, we gunned it towards Panama as fast as we could, barbed wire and water cannons ready. But no coast guard boats chased us this time.

Chapter Eighteen

Crisis in Panama

Finding and filming the shark fin warehouses had felt like a minor victory: we had managed to collect hard evidence of illegal shark fin trafficking. But instead of putting the footage to use, we were fleeing a country to which we had been invited by the president himself having done nothing much to save sharks. We hadn't even managed to unload the garbage from Cocos. In two weeks, Costa Rica had transformed us from a band of righteous environmental heroes to a floating trash heap of attempted murderers.

Fearing the exorbitant dumping costs we'd face in port, the crew decided to burn every combustible piece of garbage. For days they burned plastic, treated wood and other odds and ends in barrels on the back deck of the ship. As our environmental crusade soldiered on to Panama it farted out a wake of noxious smoke.

Panama was a good place for us to regroup. Almost anyone is free to stop there. It was also nicely situated between Costa Rica and our next scheduled stop, the Galapagos Islands. Despite what I was assured were Sea Shepherd's best efforts, upon our arrival in Panama we still hadn't managed to arrange permits to visit the

Galapagos, let alone film there. Stopping in Panama allowed us to explore the option of going to Malpelo Island, a Colombian territory and famed shark diving site similar in nature to Cocos, if the Galapagos fell through. We also needed to refuel and restock the boat, and fix the fiberglass hull of the larger Zodiac, which the crew had managed to snap clean in half on the return trip from Cocos when the crane operator tried to bring the Zodiac onboard in two-metre swells. When the *Farley Mowat* listed to one side, the Zodiac was yanked out of the water with such force the bow snapped.

Upon our arrival at the mouth of the Panama Canal, Paul decided that we would drop anchor a few hundred metres from shore and use the single intact Zodiac to ferry people to land. We were anchored around one of the busiest shipping lanes on the planet, and we would have to jump waist deep into the water every time we needed to get the Zodiac boat safely ashore and unloaded.

I have to admit it was fun hopping in and out of the little Zodiac, and Doug, Geordie and I leaped at any excuse to go into town. We all tagged along for most of the restocking grocery trips and we helped get the supplies necessary to mend the big Zodiac. Betting on the crew's ability to fix the hull, I bought a $3,500 dollars' worth of gas for Doug, Geordie and me to use on dive trips in the Galapagos or wherever it was we ended up. Considering the state of our budget at that point in the trip, it was a pretty significant bet.

We had only been in Panama for a few days when I started experiencing pains in the lymph nodes of my left leg. The only time I'd ever felt anything similar was recovering from surgery to repair my anterior cruciate ligament and cartilage in my knee after I wrecked myself snowboarding in high school. Since my only frame of reference for what I was feeling was something so extreme, I took the pain seriously. My feet had been cut to shreds diving at Cocos and jumping in and out of the little Zodiac. I'd been wearing flimsy little sandals our entire stay in Panama and had been pretty loosey-goosey about keeping the cuts clean and covered. Figuring there was a pretty good chance I'd managed to do something nasty to myself, I persuaded Carlos to come with me to the Hospital Nacional in Panama City to act as a translator.

I wasn't naive enough to expect dirt floors and meat hooks, but the Hospital Nacional was definitely better than what I'd been preparing myself for. Both the facility and the process of getting to see a doctor were exactly as they would have been in Canada, except everyone spoke Spanish, of course. Carlos guided me through the admittance process, and then we spent a good chunk of time sitting in the emergency room waiting for an available doctor. When I was called, Carlos came with me and translated my description of the pains I was feeling. As Carlos spoke, the doctor stared at my leg and I dutifully pointed out the areas in which I'd felt pain. The doctor ran through a quick examination of my leg, turned to Carlos and gave a diagnosis that Carlos managed to distill into something along the lines of: "He says you are fine. Come back if it gets worse."

By the next morning the pain had intensified. I roped Carlos into taking me to the hospital again. Just like the first time, he helped me through admission and sat next to me in the emergency room. Carlos was a seasoned activist from Spain, about forty years old. He was the kind of guy who didn't give a shit what he looked like as long as he was doing his job, saving something. He had been on campaigns with Paul before and was a regular aboard Greenpeace and Oceana ships sailing the Mediterranean; we always got along really well, though we rarely talked about environmental issues. Instead we chatted about life, girls, and what was coming next. All told I sat in that waiting room with him on four separate occasions. On our second visit I was given some anti-inflammatory drugs and sent on my way, and the third only yielded more anti-inflammatories and a bottle of painkillers.

On our fourth visit I finally had Carlos impart a Spanish version of, "Look, what you've been giving me isn't working. There's something seriously wrong here and I need you to do something about it." A nurse drew some blood, which was taken away to be tested. Carlos and I ended up back in the emergency room waiting for the results.

Soon, I got my own room. A series of doctors and nurses showed up, some of whom spoke briefly to Carlos. Eventually, they (Carlos included) set about trying to explain to me what was going on. It was all deeply surreal. They managed to communicate that they had found staphylococcus—a bacteria that causes flesh-eating disease—in my left leg. As if the news weren't nasty enough, the way a translator, even a well-meaning one like Carlos, conveys that kind of information is in itself pretty unpleasant. The nurses and doctors would speak for a little while and then one of them would make a sawing motion and point at my leg. As I tried to get Carlos to give me a better sense of the actual chance of full amputation, the best he could offer was, "Your leg might come off." I was told that a doctor who spoke better English, a department head, would visit me later in the day and fully explain my situation. Until then, I just had to wait and let them take care of me.

I told Carlos that it didn't make much sense for him to stick around and he should head back to the boat. He promised to tell Geordie and Doug what was going on and told me that he would come back the next day to check in on me, and left.

The HD camera went everywhere I went, so I had it with me in the hospital. Alone with my flesh-eating bacteria for the first time, facing the prospect of a total failure, I set up the camera at the foot of the hospital bed and pointed it at myself. There's a self-consciousness that comes with having a lens trained on you, which for some people can be intensely uncomfortable. But everything that had been said to me in the hospital room, about my leg and whether or not it might come off, had felt as though it was being said to someone else. The language barrier had also added an element of (very) dark comedy to the proceedings. Through the whole thing I hadn't had any chance to absorb the dangers and consequences being described. Filming myself made it possible to think clearly as I explained the situation to the camera. (I included

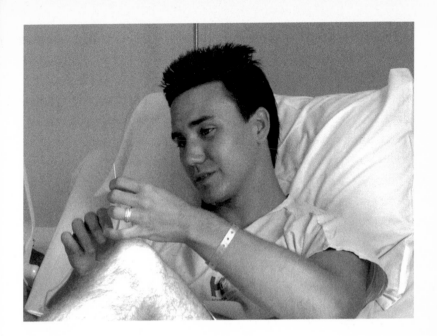

In the hospital in Panama with flesh-eating disease.

some of that footage in the final cut of *Sharkwater*. I'm in the hospital room by myself. I'm still in street clothes because the nurses haven't given me a gown yet. I'm breathing deeply and look pretty shaken up.)

The English-speaking head doctor arrived before Doug and Geordie got there. He was middle aged with silver hair and a peppery beard. He was relaxed and pleasant and I asked if he would take over my case. He told me he couldn't because he specialized in a different kind of medicine, but he assured me that he would keep tabs on what was happening and would be available once in a while to answer any of the more complicated questions that might arise. He explained to me that, yes, I had contracted a flesh-eating bacteria in my leg. He showed me a rashy, red line under the skin on my inner thigh. The line marked the progression of the bacteria up my leg. If it reached my groin the prognosis wasn't very good: to prevent the bacteria from spreading to the rest of my body, they would have to cut my leg off. If they didn't, I would die.

He told me that they were going to put me on a course of intravenous antibiotics that they hoped would kill the infection. The red line on my thigh would serve as an indicator of the effectiveness of the antibiotics. Once I started treatment, the line shouldn't climb any higher. I asked him to write down the name of the drug they were putting me on, so I could find out a bit more about it. He obliged, wished me well and left. I sat in silence trying to cling to the fact that losing my leg wasn't yet a sure thing.

When Doug and Geordie showed up, they immediately started putting pressure on me to return to Canada. Geordie, being a paramedic-in-training, told me that as soon as Carlos had brought them up to speed, he had jumped on the satellite phone and begun arranging a repatriation program for me through contacts he had at his school. A specially chartered plane with its own medical staff would pick me up at the airport in Panama City, still hooked up to an IV, and fly me back to Toronto for treatment. All I had to do was give the go-ahead.

Doug backed Geordie's plan, though I could tell that he understood that my decision wasn't so cut-and-dried. Going back to Canada was the safest thing to do, but first we should figure out whether the treatment I was getting in Panama was the same as what I'd be receiving back home. Doug offered to call an American doctor who was a family friend of his and would be willing to give us some advice. If the treatment wasn't up to North American standards or if at any point my condition deteriorated, we would hop on Geordie's plane and head home.

Armed with a piece of paper listing the names of my antibiotics and a phone, we got the number for Doug's family friend and gave him a call. I described my symptoms and the diagnosis the Panamanian doctors had given me, and then listed the drugs they had me on. He told me that the diagnosis fit the information I'd provided and that to treat staphylococcus I'd be on the same drugs in Canada as Panama. Feeling the first small taste of peace of mind I'd enjoyed since being admitted, I thanked him and hung up.

The nurses came in a little while later and hooked me up to an antibiotic IV drip. Doug and Geordie stayed with me for the rest of the day, even napping for awhile in the waiting room, but around six in the evening, they were asked to leave to let me get some rest.

I hadn't yet called my parents, but alone again with the camera and a phone on the desk beside my bed I knew I couldn't put it off any longer. As much as I knew they deserved to know what was happening to me, I was terrified that they would make me come home. It's crazy how much parents care, unfathomable, actually, for someone who doesn't have any kids. My parents cared so much about me, I knew this news would devastate them. I was still young enough that they also had considerable sway over my decisions. They had put up with the way I travelled and lived my life up to that point because, barring an ear infection or two, I had always been okay. In a few of my earlier phone calls home I had told them little bits and pieces about the attempted murder charges in Costa Rica, so they were already worried about me. Here I was in Panama with a hugely expensive rented camera. I knew that if my parents freaked out and put pressure on me to come home, I'd have to give the camera back to the rental house. I was already massively over budget and in debt, with no movie to show for it. All I had a little bit of shark footage from Cocos, the shark fins on the warehouse roof and our run in with the *Varadero I* and the Costa Rican court system and legal authorities. If I went home now, I'd never be able to get my hands on that camera again, I'd lose my chance to make a movie, and maybe my one chance to save sharks. I had to stay.

Needing to stay in Panama and persuading my parents that I should stay were two different things, however. I wanted to go into my conversation with them armed with as much information as possible. Doug's family friend had helped. Prepared for an emotional rollercoaster, I made the call.

And my dad answered.

Of my parents, my father is by far the more emotional. He's not touchy-feely or a crybaby, he's just from the heart. He doesn't guard himself. He dives into emotion quickly and he dives deep. He later told me that that phone call marked the worst day of his life.

As I explained my situation, Dad became more and more distraught. I tried to construct my explanation in a way that lead naturally and rationally to the conclusion that I should stay in Panama, but he begged me to come home, offering to pay whatever it would cost to get me back to Canada. When I turned him down, using the fact that the treatment in Panama was the same as I'd get at home, he was crushed. I asked him to put my mom on the phone but she was out, so I had to call her on her cellphone. Mom too was shocked, but she seemed to understand my reasons for staying and trusted in my ability to decide what was best. I promised her I would succumb to Geordie's repatriation program if my condition showed any signs of worsening. When the nurses came in and asked me to get off the phone and take a small blue pill, she let me go with the same quiet reluctance as my dad. I told them I'd call again first thing the next morning. I later learned that they checked every possible flight option to get down to Panama, including asking to borrow their friends' planes.

Geordie and Doug showed up early with unexpected news. Paul had left Panama and the *Farley Mowat* to attend a speaking engagement. His instructions for the crew were to continue on to the Galapagos where he would meet them. Deciding they couldn't afford to wait for me to recover, they were shipping out that day.

My ominous red thigh-line hadn't progressed in the night, but it hadn't receded either. I figured that if the doctors could estimate a discharge date for me, I might have a shot at talking Sea Shepherd into sticking around for awhile. But when Carlos arrived in the early afternoon to lend me his linguistic skills, he told me that the doctors couldn't even say for sure that I would recover until they got some confirmation that the antibiotics were working—the line would have to give up some ground—and that would take at least a week.

I decided to send Doug on to the Galapagos with the camera.

Nothing of relevance to the movie was likely to happen on my end of things. If the worst came to pass and I had to take Geordie's emergency flight, maybe leaving the camera in the Galapagos with Doug would give us a second crack at getting some footage. I couldn't return a camera I didn't have. When I was released from the hospital, Geordie and I would fly to the Galapagos and meet Doug and the *Farley Mowat*, and go diving at Darwin and Wolf. Doug and I said our goodbyes and Geordie went with him back to *Farley Mowat* to pick up our few personal bags.

In addition to the antibiotics, the doctors had me juiced to my eyeballs on painkillers and sleeping pills, so I didn't feel any real pain in my leg after I began treatment. Discomfort came in the form of unbearable restlessness. Geordie showed up religiously, but there were still large chunks of day for me to fill. I wrote a lot—ideas in my journal, plans and calculations for finishing the film in the Galapagos when I was discharged. I had a book or two, but I'd sent the camera manual on with Doug in case they ran into a story worth filming. I spent a lot of time meditating, listening to music and monitoring the red line's retreat. I also started to make calls to try to arrange a filming permit for the Galapagos.

I also spent a lot of time on the phone with Jane—maybe too much. I'd been gone two and a half months and our relationship had been showing signs of strain the entire time. On the boat, I had run up a satellite phone bill into the thousands of dollars ($14,000 actually), our conversations losing more and more ground to awkward silence. The less we had to say, the more I felt the bad kind of butterflies in my stomach, and the more those calls became a chore, something to be got through. I could tell she felt the same, but neither of us knew what to do about it. In that one regard, I saw the bacteria eating my leg and threatening to kill me in a positive light—it gave us something to talk about, and maybe would elicit some compassion from her for my situation.

Despite my best efforts to keep myself distracted, I was in a bad place. The movie wasn't coming together, I didn't know if I'd get a chance to finish it and if I got the chance I didn't know how I was going to take advantage of it. I was somewhere around $150,000 in debt, and had nowhere near enough good shark footage to show for it. Then there was the mental effort it took to not think about losing my leg, and the low moments when it was all I could think about. I had to stay positive. I called Jane again and again, looking for sympathy and distraction, hoping to feel some of the love that had been so present in Montreal and doing my best to convince her to fly to Panama. I got none of that. Our conversations were almost comically laden with miscommunications. I'd call and catch her in class or out with friends, unable to talk to me for more than a minute or two. She'd respond to my pleas for her to come visit with, "No way, I'm just getting over you."

I had the best shot at an actual conversation if I called Jane around dinnertime, after she'd gotten home from class and before she'd headed out with friends. The problem was that dinnertime often coincided with the day's last round of medication, which featured a distressingly fast-acting little blue sleeping pill. The pills gave me twenty minutes of leniency before reducing my conversation skills to those of a just-dumped drunk dialer. I'd slur incomprehensibly, fall asleep midsentence and forget entire conversations, causing me to repeatedly bring up the same things—none of which helped me lure her to my bedside. I hung up feeling more alone and more hopeless than ever. I kept calling anyway, a few times a day for my entire hospital stay.

After three days and nights on the antibiotics, the line on my thigh started to fade. That same day I got a call from Doug, who'd taken my satellite phone with him in order to keep Geordie and me posted. The *Farley Mowat* had broken down. They were two days from land in any direction—literally the middle of nowhere—and had no engines at all. To make matters worse, the generator had given up on them and the only batteries they had on board were the ones in the satellite phone. Needless to say, Doug couldn't talk for very long. We wished him luck and hung up.

After seven days, I was released from the hospital with my leg intact and my body free of flesh-eating bacteria. I had already booked a flight for the day I was supposed to get out, so Geordie and I went straight from the hospital to the airport and boarded a plane for Ecuador. In Quito, we had dinner and went to bed early. The next morning we flew to Guayaquil, and from there caught a TAME flight to the Galapagos Islands. Both my legs got there before Doug and *Farley Mowat*.

Chapter Nineteen

The Shepherd Loses Part of Its Flock

Geordie and I had made it to Puerto Ayora on Santa Cruz Island, but we were completely in the dark as to the whereabouts of Doug and the *Farley Mowat*. After the call to the hospital to let us know the boat had broken down, we hadn't had any contact with him. I was sorely tempted to call the satellite phone just to check on him (and the camera), but Doug had stressed the importance of the sat phone's battery and I wasn't going to waste any of its potentially life-saving juice finding out they were still generator- and engine-less and gently floating closer and closer toward the Pacific gyre. If there was anything we needed to know and he had the means, Doug would get hold of us. I kept my cellphone close to hand at all times.

I hadn't managed to make much headway on getting film permits in the hospital. Knowing how valuable a local who was familiar with the hoops we were meant to jump through could be to the process, I put in a call to Valerio—the guide I befriended on my solo trip to the Islands as a photographer—and asked him to meet us for some bodysurfing and planning.

Valerio picked us up in his truck and we drove out into the highlands to check out some tortoises. There is a different species of Galapagos giant tortoise on each island. Some have shells with huge saddle-like openings allowing them to reach their long necks high into bushes and shrubs to eat, while others have shells that only permit their necks to extend straight out and down. They are thought to live more than 150 years, and can weigh more than 500 pounds. They have been almost wiped out of many of their original island ranges, as they made great food for ocean travellers, since they could last alive for months on ships without food or water.

Afterwards we headed for the beach. We went bodysurfing and then sat out on the end of the dock, watching a bunch of marine iguanas and laying the rough framework of a plan of action if Sea Shepherd crew didn't show up or they couldn't get permits to take us around the islands. Valerio offered to spend the following day digging up some options for alternative boats. He seemed pretty sure that if he asked around among the local fisherman he'd be able to find us a decent boat for a good price. Back at the hotel bar, I bought Valerio a couple of whiskeys and then he disappeared. The permit office, it turned out, was within walking distance of our hotel. Valerio claimed that I could just show up and ask for a clerk named Fabian Oviedo. Fabian would hold my hand through everything.

The next morning I met with Fabian at the permit office. We were barely into our conversation when he claimed he would be able to set me up with a film permit that same day if I could put up a $5,000 deposit. Ecuador's travel and tourism commission, he explained, would hold the money, until I sent in proof that the footage I shot was actually being used in something credible and didn't cast Ecuador or the Galapagos Islands in an unfavourable light. When I sent in the proof, they would repay the deposit.

The film had next to no budget to begin with and I had long since resorted to dumping our operating costs onto my own credit cards. I asked Fabian if he would be willing to accept a personal cheque, figuring he'd never be able to find a bank in Ecuador willing to honour it. He agreed and I wrote him the cheque.

I now had my permits, but did Sea Shepherd crew have theirs?

Fabian, a little giddy with my five grand on his desk, began checking through files on his computer. The *Farley Mowat*, he told me, had yet to be granted a permit to dock in the Galapagos. The news was discouraging, but I knew better than to write them off on the strength of Fabian's word alone. Our experience in Costa Rica had hammered home how often bureaucratic barriers were just thinly veiled under-the-table propositions. On top of that, you never knew whether the next person you spoke to would tell you the exact opposite or give you a whole new set of requirements. Until Paul and the boat showed up and he applied for permits in person, nothing was set in stone.

Valerio called as I was walking back to the hotel to tell me that he had cobbled together a selection of boats we could rent if Sea Shepherd crapped out on us. I told him I'd managed to get the permits.

Doug called later that afternoon. After four days of tinkering, Sea Shepherd's mechanic had managed to get the engine operational again. They had just anchored, Zodiac-distance from the docks, but couldn't come any closer because they hadn't yet managed to sort out their docking permits—they were in port on a "fixing boat in an emergency" kind of entry. Doug himself *was* allowed off the boat and would head over as soon as he got his gear and the camera together.

Doug arrived at our hotel a few hours later with a couple of *Farley Mowat* crewmembers—Nathalie and Lisa—in tow. Understandably sick of being on the boat, they had come to spend a few days hanging out at the hotel with us. Though this was the girls' first time on the boat, from talking to lifers on the crew they had figured out that the prospects for a permit to patrol the Galapagos weren't looking good. What I didn't know was that, a few years prior to our trip, Sea Shepherd had exposed some corruption among Ecuadorian military officials and Galapagos National Park employees who had been allowing illegal shark finning to take place in protected waters. The controversy had resulted in the loss of a lot of jobs, including the second in command, and significant embarrassment for the all-powerful navy, on what was still a very small group of islands. The sense that Sea Shepherd's main purpose was to stir up controversy had fostered a general distrust that almost guaranteed they'd be shunned this time around. They had left Panama fully aware that they didn't have permits to be in the Galapagos, and were officially denied entry into the park. They would have to fix their ship, and leave. Sea Shepherd and the *Farley Mowat* was officially out of the picture. It was time to call Valerio.

Our budget was already in the negative, but it was just debt. The key was to keep the debt reasonable by opting for the minimum outlay necessary to get the job done. From the beginning, the only boat for us was the *Rumba*. There were bigger, better-equipped boats available but they were considerably more expensive. I didn't even check them out. I did look at a few of the cheaper options, but none of them had beds. If I went for one of them, we'd spend the seven-day trip sleeping on benches. Having just been released from hospital, that was not the most appealing arrangement.

The *Rumba* was a 40-foot wooden fishing boat crewed by a middle-aged captain and a fifteen-year-old boy we all took to be the captain's son. It had three tiny cabins—one for the captain and the boy and two for us—equipped with wooden bunk beds and little else. In the bow, there was a room the size of a walk-in closet full of electrical outlets where I could store the camera equipment, charge batteries and so forth. It was a heap, but it would be mine. I'd already spent much time, effort and money in camera rentals, flights and waiting around on Sea Shepherd, and I had barely any aesthetic footage to show for it. Just knowing I'd have my own boat for a week, willing and able to take me wherever I wanted to go, gave me shivers.

It took a couple days for us to get the *Rumba* ready to set off. In addition to organizing and loading our gear, I had asked Valerio to find me a dive guide. Valerio was great on land, but I needed someone to put me at dive locations that would be teeming with wildlife. He recommended a friend of his named Macaron, who, like Valerio, had been a fisherman and nearly everything else under the sun. With Macaron, the captain and Valerio, I sat down and plotted a route for our trip that would take us to the two islands in the Galapagos I most wanted to see, Fernandina and Española.

When everything was in place, we set off from Santa Cruz. I had yet to set eyes on the *Farley Mowat* but through Nathalie and Lisa I had arranged to pick up the rest of our gear and one of the three tanks of fuel I had purchased for the Zodiac before we left port.

I had heaps of fuel, my own boat, Doug, Geordie and two Galapagean friends with me. Finally I was in charge, and was ready to shoot some film.

Chapter Twenty

Eyefuls of Wildlife and Some Very Bendy Poachers

There were tons of fascinating animal behaviours that I'd witnessed or heard about on my earlier trips to the Galapagos but had never managed to catch on film. Marine iguanas fascinated me, and now that I had my own boat I was determined to head to Fernandina Island, with the largest and most abundant marine iguana populations in the archipelago.

Marine iguanas are the only lizards known to have adapted to a life entirely dependent on the ocean. Fernandina is an active volcano and its coastline is made up of thrusting, pitch-black lava rock, broken up by a very occasional soft sand beach. The iguanas sit cooking themselves on the rocks, every now and then diving into the (usually) bitterly cold ocean to feed off green algae blooms and the thick seaweed that carpets the sea floor. On my first trip to the Galapagos, I'd snapped a ton of photos of marine iguanas preparing for the plunge. On this trip, I was going to get footage of them feeding under water.

All of the islands in the Galapagos are volcanoes of varying levels of activity sitting on a continental plate that is sliding east, underneath another plate. The volcanoes gradually climb higher and higher in the west, building on themselves with each eruption. Once they age and begin to drift east, they lose their power as volcanoes, and sink back beneath the water. The newest islands are all found in the west, and the land mass grows older as you move east. Fernandina is the most westerly island in the Galapagos. Being farthest west is also what makes it such a wellspring of plant and animal life. The Humboldt Current that hits Galapagos comes in from the west, bringing travellers from way out in the ocean. Not only is Fernandina the best island for interacting with marine iguanas, it also has the most whale sharks and boasts massive numbers of rays, Mola mola, sea lions, seals, flightless cormorants and even Galapagos penguins.

Filming the iguanas was a pretty rough-and-tumble endeavour. It was too dangerous to bring the *Rumba* close to shore, for fear of smashing it to pieces on the rocks, so for the last little bit we'd hop into this tiny dinghy that was towed behind the boat (there being no room for it on the deck). The sheer quantity of iguanas was overwhelming. They carpeted sections of the beach, forcing you to step slowly over and around them. The footage I got was amazing. Every new place I pointed the camera seemed to top whatever had preceded it; it made me bolder, pushed me farther out into the pounding surf. The swells came in a couple of feet high. They would pick you up and slam you back into the water and against the rocks that lay just below it. All the rocks were covered in barnacles, which are sharp and tend to be covered in bacteria. My wetsuit got pretty scuffed and scratched, and even though I had better footwear than in Panama, so did my feet.

We found a surf break that the Galapagos sea lions were particularly fond of, and I jumped in with them, excited at the prospect of filming surfing sea lions. One particularly nasty wave caught me with my guard down and crushed me against a rock. My right leg took the full force of the impact and a barnacle cut clean through my wetsuit and left a 2-inch puncture in my leg.

Back on the *Rumba* when we'd wrapped shooting, Geordie cleaned the cut and sutured it together, but the next day I noticed that a fresh rashy red line was ripping its way up my leg from the cut. It wasn't accompanied by the same pain I'd felt in Panama, but it shook me pretty badly.

We had a pretty serious medical kit on board, so for the next couple of days I took the most powerful antibiotic we had. After a course of Zithromax, the line disappeared. Unlike my time in hospital, on Fernandina I had real distractions from my bacteria-filled appendage. As the Zithromax coursed through my blood-stream, kicking ass, I got some of the best footage of feeding marine iguanas and surfing sea lions I'd ever seen. It's in *Sharkwater*.

Our second day at Fernandina, Doug, Geordie, Macaron and I left Valerio with the kid and the captain and hit the water. Having three extra people under water with me made filming a lot more difficult. They got in the way as I was trying to shoot and the added noise of three more bodies thrashing around scared the animals off. Since we were under in some fairly challenging conditions, it was hard not to get distracted checking to see if they were all okay. The best reason to bring them along was for life support. Doug, Geordie and Macaron all carried pony bottles on them in case of emergencies. If I ran out of air (which never happens if you pay attention), having one of them near me could mean I had just enough air to get a spectacular shot or avoid getting myself bent. This wasn't regular diving. I felt that everything was riding on me getting great shots—the film, my career, the future of sharks.

The spot Macaron had picked for us was on a steep slope off the west coast of Fernandina. The current rushed in from the open ocean and crashed into the island, causing the usual feeding frenzy all up and down the face. Rays and Mola mola—giant sunfish that weighed over 1,000 kilograms—were a common sight as were Galapagos sharks. We made our way down to

90 feet and cruised around near the wall, hoping to film some large predators hunting.

Near the end of the dive, I spotted a whale shark out in the blue, roughly 60 feet away from me, 30 feet from the slope. Checking the computer displays on my wrist, I saw that I was running low on air and already had eleven minutes of decompression—to avoid getting the bends I'd have to spend 11 minutes at 15 feet underwater letting my body eliminate nitrogen from my blood before I could surface. I decided that the risk wasn't worth it just to film a whale shark and started heading toward the surface, but as I was setting off I noticed a half dozen Galapagos sharks rocketing at the whale shark. When they reached it, they began swarming, swooping all around it, below and above. It was too far away to film or see exactly what was going on, but it looked as though the Galapagos sharks were attacking the whale shark. To my knowledge no one had ever even seen this before, let alone filmed it, so I immediately kicked as hard as I could against the current to get close enough to film them. It was a stupid, dangerous decision, but it was also the opportunity of a lifetime and all I could think was, *Okay, my movie's in the shit right now. But if I film this, I'll win awards.*

When I got close enough, I took the camera off my shoulder, turned it on and took what I hoped would be a steadying breath. Nothing came through my regulator—nothing. I had completely exhaled and had nothing at all in my lungs. Frantically, I turned looking for any of the three people who I hoped would be waiting behind me with a pony bottle ready, and found out I was alone. Not only were Doug, Geordie and Macaron not near enough to hand me an air canister, not one of them was even in sight.

The only choice was to bail hard. I put the camera on my shoulder and started kicking toward the surface as hard as I could. I was more than 90 feet underwater covered in mere millimetres of wetsuit. I had my air tank, the camera and all my other equipment strapped to me, making my escape to the surface almost impossible. I have ten seconds of footage of a group of Galapagos sharks going after a whale shark shot from far away. Then the camera spins abruptly, points straight up and turns off.

When you bail underwater, which I'd only taught people about and never actually had to do myself, you have decisions to make, but you have to make them fast. Do you ditch your camera, the 3-foot-long, 100-pound behemoth? Should you ditch your scuba tank and BCD to eliminate drag? Should you just ditch your weights so, no matter what, you end up floating at the surface, dead or alive. I didn't seem to be able to make any of these decisions.

As a kid I used to hold my breath until I fainted, so that I would know if I was about to faint while free diving. I have a lot of experience fainting. I have low blood pressure and often ride the line between being here, and fainting. I also fainted pretty frequently when I was hung over in university. Before I faint I get a warm, flushed sensation in my forehead and face, and tunnel vision. As I kicked for the surface I noticed my vision narrowing and thought, *Oh, oh no, I'm screwed*. If I passed out with no one around under water, I was going to die. At such a point, the only thing you can try to do to not faint is to focus on expanding your awareness. As you fight to keep your world vivid, this comfortable, dark, lazy weight tries to overwhelm you.

Thirty feet from the surface, I saw bubbles in the direction of the rock face and spotted Macaron rummaging around after frog fish or something. The current must have pushed me back toward him while I was trying for the surface. Racing over to him as fast as I could, I snatched his spare regulator before he'd even seen me and took my first breath in what felt like forever. Macaron was pretty surprised but he clued in quickly.

Air has weight under pressure, which helps to keep you under water. As your tank empties, it gets lighter and you become considerably more buoyant. With two empty (or one completely empty and one nearly empty) tanks, Macaron and I gradually became so buoyant it was difficult to stay down, and very awkward, too, bound by three feet of hose attached to the same tank. Not to mention the giant camera. Showing each other our wrist computers, it was clear neither of us had logged anywhere near enough time decompressing, so we started grabbing rocks off the slope and stuffing them into our pockets. We hadn't quite managed five full minutes of decompression and, even with several pockets full of rocks, I was floating toward the surface against my will. In a last-ditch attempt to stay under, I found a large boulder and held it between my knees. But with a boulder between my legs, one arm for the camera, and my mouth gripping the regulator attached to Macaron, the current started flinging us around wildly, bashing us into the rocks. I was trying to protect the camera, which required me to put my entire body between it and incoming rocks. We took the beating for a couple of minutes before retreating to the surface, still in need of another five or six minutes of decompression. Offering little explanation, we grabbed fresh tanks as fast as possible from Geordie and Doug, who were sitting bewildered on the dinghy, and went back down. For the full life of the new tanks, we hung out at 15 feet, shivering in the cool water, and letting our bodies adjust. Then we headed for the surface again.

Doug and Geordie, it turned out, had also run low on air (right around the time I'd taken off to film the shark fight). Macaron and I were both lucky enough to avoid the bends, one of many minor miracles under the circumstances.

On our final day at Fernandina we were scheduled to go out diving again. As close as Macaron and I may have come to getting bent the day before, not to mention me drowning, in the end just as I always told my parents, I was okay. I had leaped at a chance to get some unbelievable footage and hadn't (really) put anyone but myself at risk. I had done what I was supposed to, and come out alive.

When we reached the spot Macaron had chosen for us we found

it already occupied by a crew of sea cucumber fishermen. We had the captain hail them over the radio and waited for a response. Initially, they were reluctant to communicate or get too close to us. Though there were still twelve days left in the Galapagos' sea cucumber fishing season, they were fishing in a restricted area. They would catch as many cucumbers as they could in the next twelve days and then return to port pretending never to have strayed from the legal boundaries.

Macaron, himself a former cucumber fisherman, took our dinghy over to talk with them. He convinced them that we could film them ripping around under water, harvesting the cucumbers and they would remain anonymous so long as they kept their masks on. They agreed. We all suited up and I filmed them for awhile, the whole time keeping my eye out for a more engaging subject. It was a pretty dull dive. Someone saw a Mola mola, but I missed it.

I still wasn't sure what was going to happen with the footage I was getting. Figuring that one worst-case possibility was that it could be turned into a travel show, I got Doug to shoot a bunch of segues and introductory segments. Most of them featured me, sitting with Valerio and Macaron, describing the dives we had just done or were about to do—what animals we were hoping to see, where we were and any interesting facts that I could spout off the top of my head. They were pretty unnatural-feeling moments to film, and we soon stopped doing them.

Later that day, after the dive, a couple of the cucumber fishermen came over and, through Macaron, told us that two of their crewmembers were bent. One of them had bent himself diving that day and had managed to get back under water in time to let his body readjust—a technique they told me they had seen in a movie. The other wasn't so lucky. He was severely bent and had been for at least four days. He sat shivering in a corner and was complaining of unbearable pain in his shoulder. He too had tried going back under water, but it hadn't done him much good.

I dive with tanks, and a computer to tell me when I go into decompression and to guide me safely out. Cucumber divers dive with a hose that runs all the way to a compressor running constantly at the surface, and they don't dive with computers, or pay attention to dive tables. The captain of the fishing boat asked me what I could do to help the sick man and I immediately made it clear that the only way to help someone in his condition was to get him back to Santa Cruz and into a recompression chamber. The round trip to Santa Cruz would cost them four days of fishing, the captain responded. Taking him back would cost them too much money. He would have to hold out until the season ended.

I assumed I had failed to make the severity of the sick man's condition clear to him.

"If someone is paying them to go diving for cucumbers, someone should be able to pay to take them back to Santa Cruz to get to a chamber," I told him. "Because he's really sick. He could die if he doesn't get to a chamber."

Macaron's translation set the captain fidgeting. From the tone of their brief exchange I could tell that the captain was seeking sympathy for his situation; he was asking Macaron to explain things in a way that I could understand.

Without waiting for the captain's response I gave him an ultimatum: "Lose four days of fishing or lose your man."

The captain's fidgeting intensified. He aimed an awkward smile at me and began shrugging and shuffling his feet as though I was asking the impossible of him, as though my suggestion was indecent. In a plaintive tone he again asked Macaron what I could do to help.

We all knew that the only thing I could do to help was to take the sick man back to port. Clearly, though, they could do that too, and in my eyes it was their responsibility. He had fallen ill aboard their ship and in their employ, and the only reason they didn't want to take him was they were making money fishing illegally. If I took him back to Santa Cruz on the *Rumba*, I wouldn't get the footage

I needed for the movie. I couldn't afford to take him into port and then head back out to finish filming. It was a strange moral dilemma.

Picking up on my hesitation the captain again began speaking to Macaron. When he finished, Macaron turned to look at me and asked, "Could *you* take him into port?"

I felt in that moment that it was Macaron who was asking me. It was weird and uncomfortable. Here were a group of men who could risk a man's life—a friend's even—in the name of profit and not even think twice about it, while simultaneously trying to manipulate me into taking on that exact same moral burden. They were trying to make me choose between my movie and the life of a man I didn't know. Why was that my decision to make? They were the ones choosing to let him suffer.

I knew I had the potential to save the sick man's life, but despite my confusion I hung onto the belief that the responsibility was theirs. I told the captain I couldn't take the sick man and again insisted that they should, but I couldn't shake the guilt. I gave the captain a bottle of Tylenol (the strongest painkillers we had), told him one last time to take the sick man back to Santa Cruz and then we left them.

I hope they took my advice, but with twelve days of fishing in front of them I doubt they did.

We began our crossing from Fernandina to its closest neighbour, Isabela, after the sun had fallen on our fourth day. All of us were out on the deck, talking and watching the sky.

The storm arrived quickly. There was a gathering silence, a change in pressure like the one just before a kettle comes to a boil. Then the wind picked up, whipping in and blowing out the stars, the moon, leaving us in near-total darkness.

The first of the larger waves hit before we had any chance to prepare ourselves. As the swells grew from 6 to 10 feet, the boat was picked up and dropped again and again. From the deck, I caught sight of the equipment room. It was filling with water. I struggled down to try to protect the delicate electronics, camera and batteries, but when I got there I couldn't figure out how the water was getting in—it was already to my ankles. Then we dropped over the lip of another wave. As the *Rumba*'s bow slammed into the bottom of the trough, I was flung directly at the forward bow wall, as water shot through each plank, soaking myself and the equipment. The *Rumba* was entirely wooden, the seal between its planks was betrayed by the immense pressure of the whole ship slamming down bow first. As we crashed down into the trough every slat in front of me burst into liquid, shooting salt water at me like a 3D movie. Everything I could see in front of me was rushing, cold water. I thought the boat was going under.

As we climbed the next wave and the rush of water abated, I started to throw the gear into waterproof pelican cases as quickly as possible. Whatever I could lay my hands on went into the closest case, along with any dry fabric in the area. Then I chucked each case up the stairs and out onto the deck, so we'd all have something buoyant to hold onto if the boat did sink, along with the cameras to film it.

Back on the deck, I started to feel violently ill. The nausea rolled through me in rhythm with the waves, and I came close to throwing up all over myself. I sat down where I was, somewhere in the galley, and spent a moment regaining my composure. I tried to get to work again, but I was too sick. We all were. For at least an hour in the worst part of the storm, everyone on board except the captain was completely incapacitated. I was so sick I climbed into my bunk and wedged myself between the mattress and the wall with pillows so I couldn't be rolled around and valiantly fought the urge to puke. Inside I was a dark nauseous void of waves, my breath and my heartbeat interacting with each other, with my mind trying not to let one overtake the other.

When the weather let up, I stumbled out onto the deck to take stock of our situation and realized that the kid was missing. When the weather got bad, I hadn't been the only one frantically packing and throwing gear around—stuff had started flying everywhere. In the chaos, no one had a clear idea when the kid had disappeared, but we figured out he hadn't been seen for at least three hours. We were sure he had been lost overboard. A strange mutual guilt overwhelmed all of us, as we realized we had no idea where he was or how to find him. We wandered the ship aimlessly looking for him in the last spasms of the storm.

Then he climbed down from the top of the *Rumba*'s wheelhouse. Seasickness had hit him early in the storm. Looking for a flat place to lie down and collect himself, he'd climbed onto the roof and then the weather got so bad he couldn't get back down. He'd spent the duration clinging to the top of the boat for his life. We were stunned from the physical toll of the storm and seasickness and the shock of seeing him alive. No one said much. The celebration of his return was decidedly restrained.

I spent my last day on the *Rumba* at Española Island, the furthest southeast island in the Galapagos. Española is the only island in the Galapagos that can guarantee you regular access to waved albatrosses. They gather on the island's seaside cliffs in unbelievable numbers to mate. That's what I was hoping to get on film.

Valerio, Doug, Geordie and I tried to get to shore in the little dinghy, but the surf was too heavy and we couldn't get the boat close enough to land without running the risk of flipping it over. Leaving the captain to take the dinghy back to the *Rumba* and await our call, we hucked three pelican cases into the water, dived in and kicked them through the surf to shore. We spent the day filming waved albatrosses and Galapagos hawks hanging out on the rocks and soaring around above us and out to sea. At the end of the day, we radioed Valerio to come pick us up and dove into the surf to get thrown around on top of our pelican cases. It was fun, adventurey shit. Exactly what I wanted to be doing with Geordie and Doug on my last day as boss of the *Rumba*.

Chapter Twenty-One

At Least Robinson Crusoe Had an Island to Be Lost On

By the time we got back to Santa Cruz, I had managed to organize spots for Doug and me on a live-aboard dive boat called the *Lammer Law*. It was an eight-day trip with five of the days at Darwin and Wolf. The odds were pretty good we'd see silky sharks, hammerheads and green turtles and we'd have a shot at whale sharks as well. Live-aboard trips are usually fully booked at least a year in advance. We got on board out of blind luck. A couple of people had dropped out and I'd pulled strings with dive operators who respected the mission we were on. After our eight days on the *Lammer Law* were up, I'd found a single spot on a ten-day dive with the *Galapagos Aggressor*. I'd have to say goodbye to Doug, though, as I didn't have enough money for both of us. I also couldn't afford to bring Geordie on either trip. He decided to hang out in Puerto Ayora for a couple of weeks before heading back to Canada. (When I saw him two weeks later, he was scruffy and tanned and looked healthy and relaxed—as the result of the amazing power of sitting around on a beach all day.)

The plan for the *Lammer Law* trip was to do three days of diving at Darwin Island, the northernmost of the two, then move on to

Wolf. The first two days at Darwin were unexceptional. We saw some silky sharks and got some half-decent footage but nothing great. So I was itching pretty bad to hit the water on the third day, our last before moving on to Wolf. The first dive of the day began sometime around seven in the morning. We were dropped close to one corner of the island and were told by the dive crew that the plan was to hop in and drift with the current to the right.

What they weren't aware of on the boat was that a strong current was hitting the corner of the island and splitting. As soon as we were under water, I realized that in order to go in the same direction as the group, I was going to have to swim into the current for a few hundred metres before I could get around the corner. I tried for a minute, but the drag of the camera was like swimming with an open parachute strapped to my back. If I continued trying to follow, I'd use up all my air in the struggle and the dive would be totally lost. I motioned to Doug that the plan was changing and we gave in to the current and headed the exact opposite direction from the one the *Lammer Law* operators were expecting.

We stuck close to the island filming for a bit, but nothing much was going on so we ventured out into the blue to hang out with some silkies—some of the ballsiest sharks you can dive with. As hunters, silky sharks are really curious and persistent, and when you're diving with them these qualities transform them into the shark equivalent of overly aggressive teenagers. They come at you in your blind spots, never dead on, and sometimes bump into you before retreating in fear. They're brave and brazen until you look at them, and then they're scaredy cats. At 5 to 8 feet or so, they seem to fulfill every negative stereotype about sharks. They love to circle you and circle you and circle you. Really, they just want to know what you are and whether you're food. They're beautiful, with long pectoral fins and a sleek dark khaki-coloured body, which makes them great subjects to film.

We spent about 20 minutes at the end of the dive filming silky sharks and surfaced without incident, though most of the footage was shaky, as they only approached close enough when I wasn't looking and I had to spin around a lot. But as soon as we came up, in 6-foot swells, we knew we were in serious trouble. I'd never surfaced so far away from the island before. At first I was struck by the strangeness of seeing it from such a distance and perspective, but that experience was serene compared to the realization that we couldn't see the boat. The *Lammer Law* was a 130-foot trimaran with a huge mast. Even in six-foot swells, it should have been visible. If we couldn't see it we were really far away.

I'd been lost briefly on my first trip to Darwin and Wolf. That time I'd surfaced where I was supposed to and it still took forty minutes for the dive boat to find me. Doug and I had surfaced in the wrong spot, on the other side of the island with the boat nowhere in sight. The initial rush of panic was intense as everything I knew about getting lost at sea, and how we were going to die, collapsed into my psyche.

What are the chances of them finding us? How are they going to find us? How fast is this current going? How long do we have out here? How tired am I? How tired is Doug? What's going to get us first: dehydration or hypothermia? What can we do to stay close to the island?

As the string of questions ripped through my head, I gradually managed to slow my breathing and focus on the answers. The thing that hit me strongest was that if we drifted more than a kilometre from the island we'd never be found.

Ocean rescue operations circle where they last saw the person, making larger and larger orbits until they find the diver—or not. If we drifted farther than a kilometre, the amount of time it would take any rescue boat to do a circle that massive would be enormous, and we'd have almost no chance of being found. The fact that the island was still visible gave me some hope because I knew that, worst-case scenario, if we ditched all of our equipment, including the camera, we'd have about a 50 percent chance of being able to swim to the island, and pull ourselves out on a rock. The island, however, was not your typical island. Its sheer rock faces erupt

straight from the ocean, rising 50 metres. Only those with heli-
copters had ever set foot on Darwin. We could see some rocky
outcroppings at the edge of the island that I figured we could
scramble onto, and even spend the night on if necessary. We
had a ways to go until then though, about nine hours until sunset,
and a kilometre to the island.

In the first few minutes after I realized we were lost, time slowed
down. I inflated my 2-metre orange safety sausage, the one visible
marker for where we were, and made sure either Doug or I held
it erect at all times. We used our mechanical and manual whistles
at regular intervals, and started kicking towards the island. The
first hour passed. To that point we'd been able to see the bottom,
but we were still ripping in the currents that had got us into this
mess, and they'd finally pushed us far enough that the bottom was
no longer visible. And now there were silky sharks circling below
us, investigating. Ironically, now they weren't scared, and didn't
mind coming at us head on. Had we not been fighting for our lives
and the most afraid we'd ever been, I could have gotten amazing
silky shark footage.

I actually shot our situations for a few seconds here and there
because I couldn't help myself, but then I'd turn the camera off and
return to freaking out. Despite our best efforts, we were drifting
farther from the island.

I don't feel like I have any fears except of being really unhappy
and being lost at sea (which combines both and adds a bunch of
other nasty stuff). I spent long stretches of the time lost in a battle
between optimism and realism: calculating how long it would take
us to expire from hypothermia, dehydration or exhaustion, and
where, based on our current trajectory, we'd end up. I believed the
next land mass in our path was the small island nation of Kiribati,
thousands of miles away. Every once in a while, Doug or I would
shake off the fear, however briefly, and tell each other, "It'll be
fine, they'll find us." Pushing the camera and all that gear was
exhausting and I kept falling behind, so Doug took the camera

when I couldn't kick any longer, allowing me to turn on my side or back and find some more comfortable way to kick.

Occasionally I turned the camera on and panned down to those silky sharks whipping around below us. I wanted to keep filming but I was too scared. You hear about a few people every year who go diving at Cocos or the Galapagos and disappear. I couldn't believe that I might end up as one of those people. I was going to be the idiot who got lost in the Galapagos. Not only that, Doug was going to go down with me.

Blended with the exhaustion and fear was a nice hit of anger and frustration. We'd been kicking for at least two hours. I couldn't believe that the *Lammer Law* hadn't managed to find us. I couldn't believe I had gotten myself and one of my best friends into this mess, that I didn't have some sort of GPS device that could locate us, and that I skipped breakfast to get into the water faster.

As we got more and more tired and drifted farther away from land, we had to start ditching gear. Our dive weights went right after the initial adrenaline rush had subsided and we could think clearly again, but ditching our BCDs and tanks was a pretty major decision because of how expensive that equipment was. If we ditched it and the boat showed up fifteen minutes later, I was going to feel like an idiot. I used a similar line of reasoning for keeping the camera. There was no way I was going to dump it unless I knew I could no longer swim with it. Like my leg in Panama, I was only prepared to part with the camera if my life was placed on the other end of the scale. We weren't quite there yet.

As the hours passed, the sun moved in the sky, we bobbed in the swell, kicked like our life depended on it, on our stomachs, sides and backs as muscles cramped, spasmed or were exhausted. Once in a while when we were spent, or had swallowed too much salt water, we stopped to whistle, wave our safety sausage and encourage one another. Many times, Doug seemed far more together than me. As much as I felt terrible for having gotten him into this mess, I was so glad he was there. Doing this alone would have been way worse.

Meanwhile, the *Lammer Law* had put the word out to every boat in the area to look for us. We were found by the tender of another dive boat just before sunset, after eight or so hours in the water. The relief of hearing a boat approaching, not to mention actually laying eyes on it, is completely inexpressible. I'm not even going to try.

When we made it back on board the *Lammer Law,* I was embarrassed at having had everyone out looking for us all day, and didn't want to explain what happened, and so I just slunk to my cabin. As soon as I closed the door, the physical and mental exhaustion hit me. I'm not even sure I made it to the bed before falling asleep.

I always travel with a couple of redundancies for every piece of equipment I use, so Doug and I were able to get back in the water the next day. I feel like I was normal on the remaining dives, but I probably was more cautious. I definitely surfaced closer to where I expected the boat to be, closer to when they'd expect us to surface, and went in the same direction as the rest of the group.

If I'm honest, I'm still a little traumatized from that experience. A lot of things coalesced for me after we were found. How easy it is to get lost. How diving in a place like the Galapagos you're relying on a couple of people you don't understand and who don't speak the same language to know where you're going to be when you surface—people who have very little experience diving with you and who don't know your style. I realized, concretely, how amazing it is that people aren't lost all the time. I still have trouble staying near any group, or going with a plan, but if I do a dive where I know I could be swept away, I bring locator devices so that satellites will know where I am.

But I was found, and I had one hell of an experience.

In hindsight, it's not entirely surprising what happened to us. The camera is a huge distraction. It's also an enabler of really unsafe behaviour. You would never do what I did if you didn't have your entire career, hundreds of thousands of dollars of debt, every personal relationship you've ever had and all your dreams riding on getting good footage. If you're just going for a dive, you stay with the group. If things look sketchy, you go to the surface right away.

There was always more at stake than that for me. I didn't think twice about the danger when it came to getting footage for the movie. It was just, "Yes, of course I'm going to do that." That may seem brave but it's not. When you're going for it, there just isn't another option.

Chapter Twenty-Two

Things Fall Apart

We had nailed the shoot in the Galapagos, but still had very little footage of Cocos, and the sharks there. I had one Visa card that wasn't maxed out, and so Doug and I started making our way from the Galapagos to Ecuador, back to Costa Rica. We knew going into Costa Rica was a risk, but I figured the authorities were far more interested in Paul Watson than me, and thought it unlikely that my name would be on any wanted list at the border. We flew from Baltra and, after a couple stops, arrived in San Jose, Costa Rica. I went through customs, disguising my fear and apprehension with a childish giddiness that distracted the customs officials, and got Doug and me and our thirty-five cases of equipment into the country without issue. We boarded a bus to the coast, and a couple of hours later we were back in Puntarenas, looking over our shoulders for any mafia men still pissed about the fin thing.

I had booked two dive trips to Cocos on the *Undersea Hunter* and *Sea Hunter*, but I didn't have enough money for Doug to join me on either of them. Fortunately, his father met him in Puntarenas and they hung out together and kept each other entertained while I was gone.

On those trips, I was in my element, had all the dive assistance I ever needed, a rebreather, and lots of time underwater. I got better footage of hammerheads than I had in the Galapagos and better stuff on the dive boats than I had with the Sea Shepherd crew. Alcyone was still my favourite spot and my fellow divers were still a nuisance to be navigated, though they all realized if they hung out next to and behind me they would see a lot.

I did the two ten-day dive trips back to back and then met Doug in Puntarenas and got the hell out of dodge. His dad had flown back to Canada a few days before my return. The night before we left, Doug and I had dinner with a William Munoz who ran the environmental group, Friends of Cocos, and then went out drinking in San Jose. I was so exhausted and preoccupied I didn't really care about any of it. I was in debt to a level I couldn't imagine, I was worried about my relationship with Jane and I still had no idea how I was ever going to get a movie made. I needed some time to get my act together and it definitely couldn't happen in Costa Rica. Doug and I said our goodbyes at the San Jose airport—he was headed back to B.C. Then, with all thirty-five cases of equipment, I boarded a plane and finally, almost four months after I'd left, flew back to Montreal.

Jane picked me up from the airport in a rented cargo van. I'd been hoping that the tension, awkwardness and miscommunications that had dominated our phone calls were just products of missing each other—something that could be blamed on distance and little blue pills—and that we'd shed them as soon as we were back together. But when I saw her, I could tell that things had definitely changed. Instead of a tearful loving reunion, she was kind of cold and indifferent. Despite the way our phone calls had been going, the lack of affection shocked me and I didn't know how to handle it. We loaded up the van in silence and she drove me back to our loft.

I had come back to Canada with 137 HD tapes. On them was footage from more than 150 dives, a mafia-run shark fin warehouse, near-death experiences, a courtroom drama, a naval battle and every-thing else that added up to the craziest thing I'd ever lived through. It was enough raw material, I felt, to make a movie people would want to see. But not only did I have no experience editing film, having returned the camera to LYCA my first day back, I couldn't even watch the tapes (at the time, the deck it took to play them cost $100,000).

Before I could think about making a movie, I needed to figure out what I thought was the most important thing in my life—my relationship with Jane. In my absence, she had made a new life for herself. She was preoccupied, gone all day and with plans that didn't include me at night. I spent a lot of time while she was out sitting in my window, dangling a leg out over the street and thinking. When she was home, things were so miserable between us that I usually ended up leaving the apartment. I'd walk to the bookstore and buy books on relationships and I'd sit in the park on Mount Royal reading them, looking for answers.

Jane didn't love me anymore. It didn't take any great insight to figure out that part; she came right out and told me. When I had first left, she said, she'd missed me so much she could barely function. She felt like her world was crumbling and just sort of dragged herself through the days. It had pissed her off that another person could have such an effect on her. The longer I stayed away, the more her sadness and loneliness turned into resentment. She resented the fact that we'd become so interdependent and she resented me for leaving. While I was away she'd had found a way to be happy without me: she'd basically had to get over me. At the same time, she did remember how good things had been between us. She no longer felt love or affection for me, but she was sure that if we gave it time and worked through our problems those feelings would come back.

From the start, the idea that if we just logged enough time together feeling like shit eventually we'd fall back in love had seemed crazy. I had just been through one of the most gruelling yet awesome experiences of my life. I'd almost died. I'd almost lost my leg. I was spent. One of the relationship books said that if you're unhappy in your relationship and you're not married, don't have kids and aren't bound to it, move on. That advice provided the last little push I needed to leave. Less than a month after returning to Montreal, I loaded my tapes and a couple of suitcases of clothes into my truck and hit the road. On my way out of the city, I pulled over dozens of times, crying and beating myself up. Deep down I wanted to be with Jane and I was leaving because I was too proud to fight for her. I thought I was enough of a catch that I shouldn't have to work to win my girlfriend back.

My last stop on my way out of Montreal was at a post-production house. To make a movie I had to be able to watch what I'd filmed. I negotiated a pay-you-later price of $14,000 to convert the tapes to DVDs. With that in the works, I headed for Toronto. At twenty-two, broken-hearted and hundreds of thousands of dollars in debt, I'd survived flesh-eating disease, but it turned out I was infected with dengue fever, West Nile virus and tuberculosis. I was also moving back in with my parents for the first time in four years.

When the DVDs arrived, I could finally watch my footage, but there was still the problem of finding a place to edit it. At the time, there weren't many post-production companies in Toronto that could handle HD footage. The equipment you needed to be able to watch it, cut it, even just digitally store it, was incredibly expensive. On top of that, there were so few people working in HD, companies had a hard time justifying the cost. Eventually, I found a post-production house called Stonehenge that could handle Panasonic HD. They agreed to give me an amazing deal on cutting together a trailer for the film that I could use to try and drum up financing. The understanding was that when I was further along in the process and putting the movie itself together, I would go back to them with more work. Unfortunately, *Sharkwater* ended up taking four years to get off the ground and by the time I was in post-production, Stonehenge no longer existed.

I didn't have the technical knowledge to differentiate one editor from another, so when Stonehenge gave me a bunch of reels to choose from, I just picked the one I thought was the coolest. I wrote the trailer and my editor of choice spliced it together. It was really straightforward. It flashed titles like "The Beauty" and "The Cause" that walked you through the story, with the most arresting visuals I had connecting them, and a track from Moby for emotional oomph. When it was done, I launched myself on the film festival circuit. I had a movie to sell.

On one of the live-aboard trips I'd done to Cocos, I'd had a dive guide who had past experience working with Howard Hall, a filmmaker who's done a bunch of underwater movies. The guide told me about a circuit of three wildlife film festivals that were my best bet for getting the movie picked up by someone with the money and expertise to see it through to completion. I'd started looking into them when I got back from Costa Rica, and it just so happened that the Wildscreen Festival—dubbed the "most influential and prestigious event of its kind in the world"—was taking place in Bristol, England, a couple months after I moved back to Toronto.

The experience I had at Wildscreen would become a familiar one. In addition to a festival pass, which allowed me to go to screenings, lectures and schmooze parties, I arranged to screen my trailer and give a short talk. My presentation was effectively a sales pitch, but it was also a declaration of all of the ways I intended to separate myself from every other wildlife filmmaker. I would explain, in brief, the horror of what was happening to sharks and the urgency of informing the general public about it. Then I would try and sell the audience on my vision of what a wildlife movie should be. Most nature films, I argued, were unwatchable. They had no story, no human element, and were infinitely boring. What we needed to be doing was making wildlife films that had the narrative structure of Hollywood blockbusters. Particularly because of the urgency of the messages we were all trying to get out to our audiences, we needed to be making films that would draw people in and then hold them, engrossed, until they actually cared about the issues we were bringing to light. At Wildscreen, two old British guys stood up at the end of my talk and applauded me, shouting, "Hear, hear!" The rest of the audience stayed in their seats and their expressions ranged from pissed to uninterested. That was basically the response I got at festivals for the next two years.

The presentations were stressful, but they weren't the worst part of the festival circuit. My time as a scuba instructor had acclimatized me to speaking in front of a group. Not a group of three or four hundred people, but still. The worst part was the networking. The networking and schmoozing and waiting in line to meet famous people or fabulously wealthy people or anyone at all who might be able to help make *Sharkwater* a reality. When I began, I was still only twenty-two. It was tough for me to walk up to a stranger—usually twenty or thirty years older than me—and just start talking, trying to make the necessary connections. I'd never had to do that before. I wanted to be able to hang back and have someone else sell me. There was no one else who could do it though: I was alone. Eventually I figured out that the best tactic when I felt fear or anxiety creeping up was to stop thinking and just start walking toward whoever or whatever it was I was afraid of. To force myself into the situation I was afraid of before my mind could rationalize a way out of it, and have faith that I'd figure it out. That somehow made everything way easier.

Despite the lack of enthusiasm at my talks, the response I got was by and large very positive. Though none of them panned out, at various times I was in discussions with Discovery, National Geographic and PBS. I met a lot of amazing people. I had shot some of the first underwater HD footage on earth, it was good, and I'd come out of nowhere at twenty-two with a crazy story. To them, I was something totally new.

I was flattered that people were taking me seriously as a film-maker and for two years I was able to ride that high from festival to festival, optimistic that things were going to work out. When I got right down to it, though, I wasn't getting anywhere. The effort and expense had taken it out of me. I no longer had absolute confidence that *Sharkwater* would ever be made, and I knew that doubt would affect my ability to make it happen. In 2004, on my way to the Jackson Hole Wildlife Film Festival in Wyoming, I finally gave myself an ultimatum. I decided that it would be my last festival. If I couldn't get the movie going by the last day of Jackson Hole, then I was going to shelve it and move to Australia. My parents had generously assumed the debt I'd racked up filming *Sharkwater*, I wasn't with Jane anymore and it didn't look like my dream of making a movie was going to come true. Unless something changed at Jackson Hole, there was nothing keeping me in Canada.

Jackson Hole proved as much of a success as every other festival I'd attended. Everyone liked me and said they respected what I was trying to do, they just didn't want to give me any of their money unless I took on a more experienced partner (thereby ceding creative control of my movie). They also said that they had no obligation to air conservation content; they wanted entertainment that put bums in seats and got ratings, and my conservation story would turn people off.

I may not have gotten any funding at Jackson Hole, but I did meet Dave Hannan. He was an underwater cameraman, director and cinematographer who ran a production company based in Australia. He couldn't front me any money for *Sharkwater*, but he did make me the most appealing offer I'd had to that point. He invited me down to Australia to help him finish filming a documentary he was putting together on crown-of-thorns starfish, the venom-spiked sea stars that are eating the Great Barrier Reef. He had his own boat and HD camera equipment and intended to cruise up and down the reef diving and filming. Sweetening the pot even more, he told me that I could keep any of the footage I shot for use in *Sharkwater* or any other project I dreamed up. I'd gone into Jackson Hole waiting for it to tell me whether or not I should head for Australia. The answer couldn't have been clearer. *Sharkwater* was dead, at least for now. I was moving to Australia.

Chapter Twenty-Three

How to Give Up In Order to Get Going Again

I stayed in Australia for a year, initially as a house guest of Dave Hannan and his girlfriend, Lucy, on North Stradbroke Island, near Brisbane. At first, since I'd given up on *Sharkwater*, I occupied myself working on Hannan's projects, shooting my own footage and developing scripts and plans for a couple of other movie ideas I had—one on the dragon fish, the Asian arowana, found in the rivers of Indonesia, Malaysia and Singapore and believed to be reincarnated dragons, and another on tuna. As I worked on the other scripts, trying to find a story to piggyback the message of conservation I wanted to build into the films, I couldn't shake the thought that nothing I was working on was as compelling as the story I already had with *Sharkwater*. Dave's business partner, Ian Bates, an ex-lawyer turned camera guru, owned a camera rental and post production house called ProCam. He took me under his wing, showed me the tape-to-tape HD processes of post production, and was willing to let me use the house editing suites at night or whenever else they were free in an "I'll pay you when I get some money" kind of way. For the first time in my life, I had millions of

Dave Hannan and me.

dollars of HD cameras and editing equipment to play with. I got my 137 tapes shipped over from Canada, and started editing my footage, finding the good stuff and compiling it onto massive HD tapes. I was starting to believe that maybe I had all the support I needed to finish the film, that maybe we could do this ourselves, and that I didn't need to sell *Sharkwater* in order to get it done.

Around the same time, I heard from a friend named Michael Clarke, who I'd met at Wildscreen. Michael was an award-winning film director, producer, tech expert, and he was also an editor. He told me that he was between jobs for awhile, and I started talking to him about working on *Sharkwater*. I asked what was the smallest amount of money I could get away with paying him for his services. We agreed that we'd go to work editing *Sharkwater* for eight weeks and see what we had. After a last round of filming with Hannan, I packed up my stuff and left the Stradbroke Island beach house I'd rented for the beauty that is Toronto in October.

Michael and his wife, Patricia, also a filmmaker, lived in the west end of Toronto in a three-storey building. We took over the basement, and began editing *Sharkwater* from the 137 DVDs I had created. After six months of work, Michael and I had a really beautiful, cool and artsy underwater movie with an amazing soundtrack and little story. Michael was basically my mentor, the most experienced and knowledgeable filmmaker I knew. He taught me everything I know about the process of editing and telling a story with film and moving images. Michael believed you had to find the story of a documentary within the footage, and couldn't impose one; if you did, it would all feel fake. The problem was I hadn't shot a particular story, I'd just filmed everything that went on and figured we'd work it out later. Michael and I continued to re-work that beautiful art film a number of ways, until we realized we needed a change.

After our seventy-seventh rough cut, we showed the film to my dad's friends, Jim Sherry of Alliance Atlantis and Michael Kennedy of the Famous Players theatre chain. They both agreed that the film showed potential, that there could be a great film in there, and that if I could find it they would give me the money I needed to finish it. If it was good enough, we'd premiere it in September 2006, at the Toronto International Film Festival, one of the biggest in the world.

I'm a big believer in self-help books and seminars. I don't turn to them for everything, but I think that hearing a new take on how to work through specific problems and toward specific goals can be extremely beneficial. With *Sharkwater* lost in a beautiful, formless limbo, I decided to attend a Robert McKee story seminar in Montreal. It was an intense three-day conference that walked all of the aspiring screenwriters through effective ways to structure a story, develop a character and just generally put together a solid piece of screenwriting that would appeal to audiences. Sitting in the auditorium listening to McKee describe traditional and archetypal story structures, I realized that I had one of those sitting in my lap.

What was missing from *Sharkwater* was the human element. It couldn't be two hours of beautiful underwater footage. My first encounter with longlining when I was twenty, setting out to do something about it, our run-in with the *Varadero I*, our exposé of the shark fin warehouse, my hospital stay in Panama: all of that drama, when strung together through my telling, formed a story structure like McKee was talking about.

After rough cut number seventy-nine, Michael was totally burnt out. We'd been working nonstop, with low-end and finicky editing equipment, killing ourselves with self-imposed deadlines, and were stuck in the framework of the piece of art we had made. Michael thought it was time to bring on another editor so a fresh set of eyes could impose the story I envisioned onto the footage. So we recruited Rick Morden, Michael's mentor. Rick was about fifty-five, an old school editor who said he liked the fire in my eyes and called me kiddo. He brought on an assistant, Hugh, to do all the button pushing so he wouldn't have to touch a computer, and the three of us went to work bringing the story of *Sharkwater* to life, with me as a central character.

Rick taught me that films should play like music, both in pace and tempo, but also in the way they bring people up and down emotionally. He wove parts of the story together that we didn't think of, and the film started coming to life. We got the film 80 percent of the way there, but the last 20 percent required something different. The pressure to come up with something good was intense; I'd raised two million dollars of other people's money, which was now resting on my creative decisions, and I'd never done any of this before. It was so stressful. Multiple award-winning filmmakers, editors and producers all told me what they thought the film needed. I didn't know who to listen to as they all had different opinions, each of which was different from my own.

At the edge of freaking out, not knowing what direction to turn, I decided the only option was to do it my way. If we lost every dollar that went into the film, at least I would know who to blame, and at least I would have tried.

When Rick and Hugh went home for the night, I started editing. I'd seen editors push the buttons for a year and, through observation, learned the basics of editing. I started cutting the scenes that weren't working, following my creative intuition. I recut the opening titles, running from Costa Rica, returning to Galapagos, and many of the wildlife scenes. Every day when Rick and Hugh showed up, I'd tell them that I'd figured out a few scenes already that they could polish if they saw fit, but that they should work on another scene. This was a nightmare. Rick didn't like what I was doing to the movie, and often changed scenes I'd worked on back to what he had cut. After a few days of this, Rick stormed out and off the project.

This was pretty scary for me. I thought what I was doing to the film was giving it a style, setting it apart, and making it much

With my parents at the Fort Lauderdale International Film Festival, where *Sharkwater* received awards for People's Choice, Best Documentary and the Spirit of the Independent Award.

cooler. But I'd lost both my filmmaking mentors, and was going it alone. I cut and recut the film.

After much hard work I thought the film was 90 percent of the way there. Hoping for some reassurance in the last three weeks before the film had to be locked if it was going to premiere at TIFF, I packed up my editing suite and flew to Santa Barbara, California, to meet with a couple of documentary filmmakers I was introduced to through contacts of my dad's at Lucasfilm, Tippy Bushkin and Jeremy Stuart. We filmed some interviews with me on the beach to tie the film together, polished the edit and persuaded another friend of theirs, Duane Trow, to cut the trailer. After two more weeks of editing with them, I came back to Toronto with a finished film.

In the week leading up to our premiere, I made a couple more last-minute changes and then resigned myself to the fact that the movie was done. It's said that you don't ever really finish a film, you abandon it.

We showed at TIFF and the rest is history.

PART THREE

REVOLUTION

Chapter Twenty-Four

It's Way Bigger Than Saving Sharks

"What's the point in stopping finning if the sharks—if all the fish—will be gone anyway?"

I'd answered the question the young woman threw at me at the Hong Kong premiere of *Sharkwater*, but it kept working away at me, demanding that I find a response that wasn't just tossed off in self-defence. And it seemed like my body was also conspiring to slow me down, and make me think.

Right after the premiere, my left eye had been bothering me. I had planned a trip to Kesennuma—a small fishing port on Japan's northeast coast—in order to film a shark-finning warehouse after finishing up in Hong Kong, but by the time I was supposed to leave, my eye had swollen so badly I couldn't see out of it. My friend Nissa, from EcoVision, the group that had organized the event in Hong Kong, took me to a hospital where I found out I had an infected tear duct likely caused by air pollution. That's what I got for riding around on the back of a motorcycle with no visor in a city so polluted some of its citizens wore masks.

Lying in the examination room waiting for a doctor to lance and drain my eyelid, it was hard not to view the infection as symbolic. I had been so focused on saving sharks for so long, it was like I had been blind to the rest of the picture. I had expected the Hong Kong premiere to feel like a triumph—it marked the movie's breakthrough into China, the country where it could have the most significant impact. Instead, I'd left the screening feeling a bit like I'd wasted ten years of my life. Making *Sharkwater* had required me to commit all-out to the idea that saving sharks was the most important mission I could ever take on, but that commitment had also caused me to ignore other pressing environmental concerns. If sharks were doomed whether or not we stopped finning, then were the arguments I'd made in *Sharkwater* useless? Had I totally missed the point? And here I was halfway blinded by one of the many environmental issues I'd been ignoring. The irony wasn't lost on me.

The doctor lanced, de-pussed, and released me. He told me that after some rest and a course of anti-bacterial eye drops, my eye would be back to normal. Over the next few days, I rearranged my travel plans, then started making my way to Japan.

The town of Kesennuma that I visited is not the one you would encounter if you went today. When the Tohoku earthquake and tsunami devastated the northeast coast of Japan in March 2011, Kesennuma was the source of some of the most dramatic and moving footage of the disaster—endless presses of charcoal grey water surging over sea walls, tossing boats like toys and washing away cars and buildings. Along with the lives of more than one thousand residents, the tsunami claimed a large portion of the city's fishing fleet. When I was there in the summer of 2010, before the disaster, Kesennuma's main claim to fame was the 6,500 or more sharks that came off fishing boats and landed in its market on a daily basis.

I had snuck in to film in one of Kesennuma's shark fin warehouses with three other filmmakers and activists I'd met on the *Sharkwater* tour—Julie Andersen, Paul Wildman and Shawn Heinrichs. We arrived early in the day, and at first tried to be very discreet, shooting undercover. I positioned myself on a gangplank that circled the warehouse about twenty feet above ground level. The interior of the building was a single open space, dark and cavernous, with a smooth concrete floor. Arranged on the concrete in lines that grew longer as the day progressed were the bodies of hundreds and hundreds of dead sharks, mostly salmon sharks, which look just like great whites only smaller, and blue sharks, which were decapitated and being moved around in giant heaps by bulldozers.

Stone-faced workers milled in near total silence. Some moved the bodies of salmon sharks still slicked with saltwater and looking so nearly alive from a conveyor belt to the lines, dragging them on the ends of large metal hooks. Others worked their way up and down the lines with curving knives, severing each fin and tossing it into the large white bins they rolled along behind them. There was blood everywhere. It coated the floor in swirling patterns made more intricate every time a shark was dragged to a new line.

It took us about an hour to realize that no one was particularly worried about what we were doing and we could shoot out in the open. I then took my Steadicam, a camera mount that keeps the picture steady as you move though a scene, and walked through the thousands of bodies of dead sharks, creating footage that is especially haunting.

Hong Kong had made it clear to me that I needed to expand my focus; Kesennuma reinforced the value of the work I'd already done. I hadn't wasted ten years of my life. I'd spent it giving everything I had to try and save an animal I loved. If going hard to save sharks themselves wasn't enough to actually save them, then I would figure out what was.

But first I needed to get back into the ocean.

The publicity tour in support of *Sharkwater* had lasted the better part of four years. Distributors were leery of putting huge promotional dollars behind the release of a feature shark documentary, so they relied on me to do press, lectures and travel with the film on an endless, makeshift media junket. In the first two years, the film made its way from Canada, through the United States, over the Atlantic to Europe and, finally, to Australia. In that grueling stretch, the longest period of time I spent consecutively in the same bed was six days—and it was a hotel bed in New Zealand.

My pace had slowed down in the lead up to the Hong Kong premiere, but getting the film shown in China had taken nearly two years of effort. To get the film released, we had to raise money, and with the help of Andre Bharti, and the Bharti Charitable Foundation, we began working with Wildaid (I'm on the international board) to use their connections to the get the film released in China. At first we planned a big star-studded opening at the Shanghai film festival, followed by a release on public television. But the Chinese government found a connection between Paul Watson and the Dalai Lama, *persona non grata* with the Chinese Communist authorities. There was a picture of the two shaking hands from some time in the 1970s that the Sea Shepherd Conservation Society proudly displayed on its website, and as a result the Shanghai festival dropped the film.

We needed another approach. *Sharkwater's* agent, Horizon Motion Pictures, had received an offer from a Chinese distributor who thought they could place the film on CCTV—Chinese government television—which had a huge audience. We also decided to edit Sea Shepherd out of the film, and add a more Chinese-friendly conservation group, Wildaid, who already had Jackie Chan and Yao Ming as spokespeople. It seemed like a small price to pay for the movie to be seen by millions of Chinese consumers. (We are just finishing the new Sea Shepherd free version, and plan on releasing it in 2012, but in the meantime our agent managed to arrange for the original version of *Sharkwater* to air on CCTV 6 twice, to a total audience of 120 million people.)

In all those years promoting the film, I hadn't had a chance to go diving or film a single animal, except when I was doing press conferences from inside an aquarium or shark tank, or taking *Entertainment Tonight* and a few other media crews diving with sharks. I was exhausted, I missed being underwater and I missed the art of filming and photography. I really needed to remind myself what I was fighting for.

After a brief stopover in Canada to see my family, I headed to Australia, to Dave Hannan's place on North Stradbroke Island. Hannan had been busy in the years since I'd last visited. He still spent as much time as he could diving and filming on reefs in Papua New Guinea for his remake of his hit DVD, *Coral Sea Dreaming*. He'd added a couple of HD cameras to his setup, and an edit suite in his garage, where he and his friend and business partner Peter Simon put together their films. He'd also acquired a new cause—ocean acidification.

I had heard about acidification before, but hadn't properly investigated what it was and what it meant for the oceans. It had been one of the auxiliary issues—as I'd seen them—that I had figured I'd look into after I put a stop to finning. Having had my limited focus rubbed in my face, I was now prepared to listen.

Hannan's all-or-nothing attitude to ocean acidification reminded me of my own toward overfishing and shark finning. He was convinced that no other environmental issue was as important for life on earth. He made wild claims: all of the world's corals could be gone in twenty years; there would be a full collapse of all ocean ecosystems by the end of the century; and so on. His passion for the subject was infectious, but I was distinctly aware during each of his orations that Dave was a filmmaker and not a scientist. If he wanted me to believe that ocean acidification was the life or death problem he made it out to be, I needed more than the strength of his convictions. I needed evidence.

Fortunately, he didn't expect to recruit me so easily. We had been planning a trip to dive and film in Papua New Guinea. As part of the trip, Dave offered to introduce me to Charlie Veron, a coral expert who regularly worked in the area. Veron had been chief scientist at the Australian Institute of Marine Sciences. Nicknamed the "Godfather of Coral," he was responsible for discovering and naming roughly a quarter of the world's coral species. "If you won't take my word for it," Hannan said. "I'll take you to meet Charlie. He'll tell you."

Papua New Guinea is a coral Eden.

Part of the coral triangle—an area demarked by Papua New Guinea, peninsular Malaysia and the Philippines—there are more species in this place than anywhere else on earth. As life rebounded after the last major extinction sixty-five million years ago, this area became the collision point for ocean currents, providing the greatest possible diversity of habitats for corals and their ecosystems. A reef in Papua New Guinea could be home to 3,500 species, compared to the Caribbean's five hundred. It was also a place I'd been dreaming of ever since I was a kid.

As I made my way from Australia to its capital, Port Moresby, and then east to the town of Alotau, it was the muck I was most excited for. Muck diving is a somewhat fanatical subcategory of scuba diving. Practitioners will travel to the other side of the globe to dive in filthy and seemingly barren industrial harbors, river mouths and shipping channels. Muck divers explore some of the most biodiverse regions on earth, but they opt for the stretches between reefs, places where there isn't enough current to sustain corals and provide a continuous supply of plankton. The sea floor is mud or rock, and there's not a lot on it besides small patches of sea grass, stones and the odd bit of coral. It's dark and dingy. All in all, it's a barren, dangerous place to live and, as a result, it's where you find all of the crazies.

People have been diving on reefs for ages. When you do a reef dive, you basically know what you're going to encounter. Because coral provides abundant hiding spots, animals move around pretty freely. They're not hard to spot and when you do see them, they're easy to understand. The environment has a set structure that makes sense and the animals you encounter fit into that structure in logical ways: for instance, branching corals provide homes for parrotfish, which eat the algae that grows on the corals, protecting the corals from algal infestations. Everything on a reef plays a role in a delicate balance.

The muck, on the other hand, is where anything too weak or weird to compete on the reef ends up; all the creatures that couldn't survive in the structured and competitive habitat of the reef come here to hide. When you muck dive, you see the most wild and wonderful animals. Animals crazier than anything you could dream up. Species people haven't yet named, photographed or written books about.

The coolest of the crazies, and the one I was most determined to find in Papua New Guinea, is the flamboyant cuttlefish. They are cephalopods—a class of animals that includes octopi and squids. They have small oval bodies and heads that sport eight tiny arms that sprout from their faces like a beard and continuously swirl and wave. They grow 2 to 5 inches long—tops—and are deeply, unbelievably toxic; almost nothing will eat them. So confident are they in their toxic splendor, they don't even bother to swim like other cuttlefish. They just rumble around the muck flashing electric reds, yellows and purples, waving their arms around like little samurai swords. They can change the pigmentation and size of each of their skin cells, and decide whether each cell reflects or absorbs light. They can go from silvery and mirror-like to bright red and roughly mottled in a fraction of a second. If they spot something they want to eat, they can turn the half of their bodies that faces their potential prey the exact colour and texture of the ground while still flashing neon on the other side to ward off predators.

When you encounter a flamboyant cuttlefish—flambo for short— on a dive, it will madly wave its arms at you. Flambos use sign language to communicate with each other. You can make hand signals at them and they'll give you a distinct and meaningful arrangement of arms and tentacles in return. They also use their bodies like banners, flashing bars, symbols and colours to communicate ideas and emotions. A study out of Australia, led by a guy named Mark Norman, catalogued sixty-eight different cuttlefish arm signs. They're trying to talk to us, we just don't know what they're saying.

The last time I had seen a flamboyant cuttlefish was on a photo assignment to Lankayan off the coast of Sabah, Malaysia. Lankayan is a tiny island paradise, and base of operations for dive trips to the surrounding reefs. It boasts a combination restaurant and dive centre and maybe fifteen private huts dotting the beach. There's also a dive jetty that stretches 60 metres into the ocean. Roughly 20 metres from the end of the jetty, the fully submerged wreck of a wooden sailboat rests on the sandy bottom, 22 metres below the surface.

Most of my dives there were at reef spots you'd get to by boat. But just before sunset, after a day of diving, I decided to check out the wreck because my dive guide had told me there was a pair of painted frogfish that lived on it. Frogfish are a muck spectacle, globular fish that are masters of camouflage. Though they shift more slowly than flambos, they can change color to almost any hue imaginable. They have tiny eyes, an enormous mouth capable of swallowing prey as large at themselves, and come equipped with their own fishing lure, which extends from their forehead. When they strike, faster than any other fish, they, open their cavernous mouths so quickly, prey is literally sucked inside. My dive guide took me down and showed the pair to me. The frogfish were sitting face to face, staring at each other, each about 2 inches long. Beside them was a coil of knotted and mud-encrusted rope. They were perfectly camouflaged except when you shone a light on them, which showed them up as a dull red with the "painted" spot near their tail that gives them their name. After pointing them out, the dive guide took off, leaving me to tool around the wreck alone. That's when I saw the flamboyant cuttlefish.

It wasn't the first one I'd seen. Earlier that year, I'd been diving off of Kapalai—another small Malaysian island—and had spotted one. It was at most an inch long and displaying the wildest colouring: swirls of dark, dark brown, bright yellow and bright red. This one was huge by comparison, about 3 inches long and an inch wide. I spotted it strutting around the mud just off the end of the wreck, doing its thing, and followed it around for almost an hour, until I had barely enough air to carefully work my way back to the surface.

I went back to the same spot first thing the next morning, but I couldn't find it. So I waited and went back again around six, the same time I'd seen it the day before, right before the sun started to dip. And there it was, in the exact same spot, trucking around the sea floor.

I dove with that cuttlefish for six straight days. At first, I couldn't help startling it in order to interact with it. I would wave my hand or splay my fingers and it would rear up and motion back at me, making patterns with its arms and flashing colours through them.

A flamboyant cuttlefish, a totally amazing creature.

Sometimes it would spread all eight arms and show me the little suction cups on the undersides of them. Then it would go back to walking around in the mud.

As it got more comfortable having me around, it startled less easily and I got a chance to watch it hunt. It would be flashing colours with no discernible pattern or purpose and waving its arms like samurai swords, and suddenly it would spot something it was interested in—a goby, a shrimp, maybe a small crab. It would briefly flash a bit of bright colour, like it was unable to deny itself a short burst of surprise and delight, and then it would spread out its two lowest arms and flatten them to the ground like blades, either to stabilize itself or eliminate a pathway of escape for its prey. In addition to their eight arms, flambos have a pair of clear tentacles with suckers and spikes on the end that shoot out like lasers to catch their prey. As it got ready to strike, its body would change to match the exact colour and texture of the ground. Then it would shift its head subtly back and forth, fine tuning its aim, and point its other six arms like arrows at its prey. One of its tentacles would slowly start to creep out from beneath the arms and then rocket forward so fast you couldn't tell what had happened really, except that there was no more goby or shrimp or crab and the flambo was back to proudly blazing its colours in delight.

On the sixth day, I had been following it around as per usual—struggling to stay in front of it to try and get the best shots—when it headed over to the wreck and went inside. I was low on air again, but I followed it, maneuvering myself around a broken section of hull so I could see what it was up to. On the other side there was a small nook about 8 inches high, below a ledge created by a heavy wooden crossbeam. The cuttlefish got close to the nook and then, for the first time in six days, began to swim. It hovered just above the ground and then brought its whole body vertical and raised itself up to the ledge. It stretched its face up and out of sight and then floated back down and sat still for a moment. While it rested, I got as low as I could so I could look underneath the lip of the ledge. I saw one white tear drop-shaped egg. It had gotten so used to me it was laying its eggs before my eyes!

I watched the cuttlefish make six or seven more trips to the underside of the ledge. Then it drifted down to a small depression in the sand and sat there. It started turning the colour of the sea floor, but not as precisely as it normally would have—it was more like it was losing its colour rather than camouflaging itself. It was the first time I'd ever seen it stay still. Almost completely out of air, I had to leave it. The next day I turned up at the usual spot just before sunset. I knew it wouldn't be there and it wasn't. After a week of putting up with me following it around and falling in love with it, it had died right in front of me.

In Alotau, Hannan and I boarded the M.V. Chertan, a 65-foot dive boat captained by Rob van der Loos. Dive trips around Papua New Guinea tend to offer a pretty even split between reef spots and muck diving. We were fortunate enough to be a mucker-heavy boat, so over the course of our 15-day trip, we managed to hit somewhere in the ballpark of thirty muck diving spots.

Most of the animals you'll encounter at the mouth of a river or on the bottom of a filthy harbor don't do you the favour of advertising their presence to the degree the flamboyant cuttlefish does. There are few hiding spots in the muck, so everything is camouflaged. It takes a while to train your eye to look for the features that make some line, ridge or bump an animal and not mud.

You learn to recognize eyes. You start to notice that you're magnetically drawn to anything circular. Once you catch an eye, you try to figure out where its body is. You learn to appreciate the lay of the mud on the bottom and recognize when its regular patterns are interrupted. Every now and then you spot an edge and you know there has to be something there. You delicately brush it off and an animal leaps up and goes careening off.

I didn't see a flamboyant cuttlefish in the muck of Papua New Guinea. The creatures I seemed to encounter most were stinging sea feathers. Rising about 5 inches out of the mud, they have a central stalk with a few diaphanous, featherlike branches reaching an inch and a half to either side. Brushing one just the tiniest little bit caused it to disintegrate into my hand, where each delicate shard would embed itself and start releasing poison. It would eat away at my skin like acid and I wondered how far into my body it would go. I tried to avoid them as best I could, but I would become so engrossed trying to spot eyes that the sea feather stings were an occupational hazard. I still have marks on both hands that look like bad acne scarring.

I also saw coconut octopi, who scavenge two sections of coconut—halved, eaten and tossed into the water by people—as a shell. If I startled one, it would close its coconut around itself, wait for a bit and then separate the halves a crack. One little eye would pop out, then another. When it decided I probably wasn't going to try and eat it, it would open up its adopted shell and go walking off. A couple I saw used Coke bottles instead of coconut shells.

Spotting a mimic octopus was rarer, but infinitely cooler—if you could figure out what you were looking at. Mimic octopi imitate a handful of other creatures that live in the muck. They'll flatten themselves on the ground and trail a tail to look like flounder or stingray. They'll stretch their body out into a long line with their head at one end and swim like a sea snake. They'll hide in a hole in the ground and put up a fake pair of claws to look like a mantis shrimp. Seriously cool critters.

I had a hell of a time trying to film Bobbitt worms, a nocturnal worm growing over 9 feet in length. I'd spot them stretched about 3 feet out of holes in the mud, waiting in perfect stillness for their next victim to swim overhead. They've got sense organs in their faces that can detect when water is moving above them and a set of serrated blade-like mandibles twice the size of their heads. When they feel the water move, the mandibles (which hang open waiting for a meal) scissor shut and the fish—or whatever else strays near enough—is immobilized, often sliced in two and then pulled back into the Bobbitt worm's hole to be eaten. Every time I spotted one, I would raise the camera, turn the lights on, press record and bring the worm into focus just in time to see it disappear back into its hole. They do not like the lights.

It was against this backdrop of mud and weirdness, about halfway through our dive trip, that I finally met Charlie Veron.

Clean shaven with a head of thin, white hair and an easy smile, Veron has been working on coral reefs for nearly forty years. In that time he's been a part of sixty-six different scientific expeditions, studied every major coral reef region in the world, discovered and described all those coral species I mentioned, won a boatload of prestigious awards and citations; and logged more than seven thousand hours underwater. Veron resigned his position at the Australian Institute of Marine Sciences after he failed to convince his employers to take a public stand against ocean acidification and climate change. Now, he works with a handful of activist organizations, including the Ocean Ark Alliance, to spread the word about the threats to ocean ecosystems posed by unchecked carbon emissions, and the consequences our continued failure to properly address those threats hold for all life on earth.

In between dives, Charlie and I found a quiet spot on a beach in the shade of some palm trees. There we talked for some hours about overfishing and the devastation it has already inflicted on marine life; about ocean acidification and the interconnected problem of mass coral bleaching; and about the beauty of the oceans and their importance to all life on earth. By the end of our conversation I felt terrified, but also inspired to act.

I knew a lot about what's going on in our oceans, but had never stopped to arrange it in my mind into the complete picture. First, the oceans are not an inexhaustible resource, nor are they indestructible. In line with the nature of all life on earth, ocean ecosystems are beautiful accidents. They are fluke assemblies of the exact right circumstances necessary to nurture and sustain life—webs of interconnectedness and interdependence so complex that brilliant minds like Charlie Veron have labored their entire lives to describe just one or two of the connections.

For the bulk of human history, when there was a sustainable human population, we got away with treating the oceans as though they were endless and unchanging: Our fishing techniques were relatively ineffective, our carbon footprint was relatively small and the demands we made of the ocean, as significant as they were to us, were sustainable ones. That is no longer the case. It hasn't been for some time. And yet, somehow, as we've dreamed up increasingly effective industrial fishing techniques like trawling, purse-netting, gill-netting and longlining and implemented them on an unimaginably massive scale, we've maintained the illusion that our actions still have little impact on ocean ecosystems.

Overfishing and illegal and unsustainable fishing practices have depleted large predator populations in the ocean by an average of 90 percent. Sharks, tuna, billfish, larger ground fish like cod and halibut, whales, seals, sea lions, walruses, manatees, even sea turtles—everything large that can be found in the ocean has been depleted, on average, by *90 percent*. The devastation, which so captured my attention while making *Sharkwater*, is unequally distributed across species and locations—some species have only declined by 50 or 60 percent, while coastal populations of tuna and billfish have dropped by as much as 99.9 percent in some places and sharks have completely disappeared from large parts of the Mediterranean and Caribbean. (We also waste about fifty-four billion pounds of fish every year as bycatch, fish that are caught and killed then thrown back because they aren't the target fish.)

The assault on the top of the food chain has serious consequences for even the smallest marine animals. Without large predators to keep their numbers in check, populations of smaller fish have ballooned grotesquely. This manmade imbalance poses a serious problem for the tiny planktonic plants and animals that make up

Illegal and unsustainable fishing practices have depleted the ocean's large predator population by an average of 90 percent. This assault affects the whole food chain, and us too.

the base of the ocean food chain. At the same time as we exert top-down pressure by wiping out large predators, we are also attacking ocean ecosystems at their base. As the name suggests, ocean acidification is a lowering of the pH balance of ocean waters, making them more acidic and less hospitable to life; the oceans are already 30 percent more acidic than they were one hundred years ago.

Acidification is caused by the ocean's constant absorption of airborne carbon emissions. As carbon dioxide dissolves into the surface of the ocean, it forms an acid—carbonic acid. Under normal circumstances, that acid would be circulated from the surface waters into limestone-rich deeper waters and gradually neutralized. Unfortunately, we are not dealing with normal circumstances. Our constant, feverish consumption of fossil fuels means that we are releasing carbon dioxide into the atmosphere in a quantity and at a speed that the oceans cannot process. If we were to completely stop burning fossil fuels today, it would take thousands of years for the oceans to balance out.

The increasing acidity of ocean waters has disastrous consequences for any organism that builds a skeleton or shell. Carbonic acid destroys the carbonates that corals, plankton and other creatures use to build skeletons. The growing scarcity of carbonates means that skeletons and shells are becoming softer and more prone to damage. Carbon emissions absorbed by the surface waters of the ocean are literally dissolving the animals that are most fundamental to the continued operation of ocean ecosystems.

In the last fifty years, the combined impact of overfishing, ocean acidification and climate change has caused a 40 percent drop in the overall quantity of phytoplankton in eight of ten major ocean regions. In many ways, that 40 percent drop is scarier than the 90 percent drop in large predator populations. Through massive-scale photosynthesis, phytoplankton are the driving force behind the oceans' ability to absorb carbon dioxide and produce oxygen. For at least the last two decades, we've been led to believe that deforestation poses the greatest threat to our oxygen supply. It doesn't. In the course of human history, the oceans have taken in about 30 percent of the entire amount of carbon we've emitted. In addition, half of the oxygen on earth is produced in the oceans.

Every second breath you take comes from the ocean.

We have destroyed almost half of the phytoplankton responsible for controlling the balance between carbon dioxide and oxygen on earth.

At some point, our behaviour will render the oceans incapable of absorbing any more carbon dioxide: they'll be saturated, like a sponge that can't absorb any more water. When that happens, we'll force the earth into a state of runaway climate change. Sea levels will rise displacing hundreds of millions of people, agricultural production will drop off dramatically, conflicts will break out over the most basic necessities—food, water and space—and ecosystems will collapse.

According to Charlie Veron, coral is already predicting this future. To understand how, though, requires a brief explanation of what a coral is and how reefs are formed and sustained. Corals are tiny animals—called polyps—that take in nutrients and secrete calcium carbonate, which forms the base or skeleton of the animal. Despite being animals and obtaining a small amount of their energy by eating plankton, coral polyps are sustained by single-celled algae (called zooxanthellae) that live within each polyp and provide as much as 90 percent of its energy by photosynthesizing sunlight and carbon dioxide. Millions of these coral polyps, striving for sunlight for thousands of years, build reefs.

The symbiotic relationship shared by polyps and their algae is a delicate one that requires the pairing to live in shallow, sun-drenched waters that are, ideally, just shy of the maximum temperature the polyps can bear. The abundant sunlight allows the algae to pump out peak amounts of energy. This allows the corals to secrete calcium carbonate as fast as they can, creating the beautiful, branching corals that are so appealing to fish. The fish are lured in by the safety of the branching corals and help to keep down larger algae, such as the big kelps, which might otherwise threaten the growth of the reefs. Everybody wins.

Because they live in such a delicate temperature range and depend on an equally delicate relationship with their algae, corals are particularly acute gauges of shifts in carbon concentrations. As carbon emissions enter the atmosphere, they cause the greenhouse effect, raising the temperature of the atmosphere and the ocean. As the ocean temperature rises, the zooxanthellae respond by producing greater amounts of oxygen. Eventually, they produce too much, and it becomes toxic to the coral polyps. Many are killed and those that survive have to purge themselves of algae to avoid being poisoned. But when they sacrifice their primary energy source, the remaining polyps wither and die, leaving behind nothing but their gleaming white calcium carbonate skeleton. Without vibrant, electrically coloured branching corals, reefs no longer provide adequate protection for the species that live on them. The fish leave and the reef ecosystem collapses. This is coral bleaching and it has already claimed a quarter of all the world's corals.

At the same time as corals are being wiped out by mass bleaching, ocean acidification is also weakening their calcium carbonate skeletons, rendering them more susceptible to disease and fracture—especially when buffeted by heavy weather—and making it harder and harder for them to grow. Unless we take immediate action, the chemistry of the oceans will become hostile for corals by the mid-point of this century—about the time scientists predict we will lose the last of earth's shallow water corals to mass bleaching. Yes, they have a date in mind: coral's limestone skeletons will literally start dissolving in 2070.

There are children alive today who will live to see the end of coral reefs on this planet, unless we act now. The science says so. As reefs are home to somewhere between a quarter and a half of all the species of the ocean, losing the reefs will have effects that are so far-reaching as to be unimaginable. Most of us certainly aren't spending our time trying to imagine those consequences. Corals are the canary in the coal mine. Though we weren't around to take note, they offered similar warnings before each of earth's mass extinctions. Those big die-offs were all preceded by a major change in ocean chemistry—an increase in acidity, much like the one we are causing today, that eventually killed all the corals. At the moment, our canary is at least a quarter dead, and of the three quarters that remain, about 70 percent are severely degraded. In the Caribbean, where I learned to dive and fell in love with reefs, 75 percent of the corals are dead. The Great Barrier Reef has lost 36 percent of its coral in the last forty years.

All mass extinctions, and most of the minor ones, have been caused—in part or in whole—by a disruption of the carbon cycle. Sixty-five million years ago, an asteroid hit earth. The force of its impact set off every volcano on the planet that was anywhere close to erupting. This all-encompassing blast launched huge amounts of carbon dioxide, sulphur dioxide and dust into the atmosphere, plunging the earth into darkness and drastically altering the chemistry of the oceans, which became acidic, oxygen-starved and rotten. They lost their capacity to regulate the atmosphere, provide food and control the earth's climate. Very, very few major groups of organisms survived. Today, there are already four hundred dead zones in the ocean—areas of no life, no oxygen and no productivity.

We are our own asteroid. Our consumption of fossil fuels has released—is releasing—a store of carbon into the atmosphere that has been accumulating for hundreds of millions of years. Corals, plankton, predators: everything in the ocean is screaming at us to stop. If we don't listen and take action right now, we could be witnesses to the death of most life on earth. We will be the cause of that death. What will survive are the hangers on, the muck dwellers. The ocean—dark, barren and unproductive—will remain much the same for them. Over time they will evolve and very gradually repopulate. In millions of years, new animals will once again develop the capacity to build reefs, the oceans will neutralize themselves and life will return to normal.

We will have erased ourselves in a blink of geologic time.

Chapter Twenty-Five

Saving the Humans

I'd made a movie about sharks in hope that if the public knew that for the sake of soup we were destroying one of the oldest, most important predators on the planet, they would do something about it. *Sharkwater* had inspired a lot of people to act, to join or start conservation efforts, to get laws changed and reform fishing practices, to let go of their fear of these ocean predators. It wasn't a big leap for me to think that the way I could have an impact on ocean acidification was to make a movie about it. But what sort of movie? The death of coral is hard to bring home to people, and I wasn't sure anyone would want to see the sludgy world of the flamboyant cuttlefish.

It was clear that people were at risk in ways I'd never understood. To do my part, I felt I had to expand my efforts, my message, my whole outlook, really. But I still didn't really know how I was going to make a movie about this. I decided that first I needed to find out what people were already doing to combat carbon emissions and climate change in order to figure out what I could contribute. I needed a new Sea Shepherd, a group devoted to radical action in the name of stopping carbon emitters. Back in Toronto, I started looking for options with the help of a few researchers and the Internet. It didn't take us long to find out about Power Shift, an annual youth-oriented climate conference.

Taking place in Washington, D.C., it was promoted as the largest youth initiative on climate change in the history of the United States and expected to attract twelve thousand young people from around the world. Jen Zabawa, our team's production manager, got in touch with the Energy Action Coalition (the group that was putting on the event) and arranged passes. Then we packed me, a small film crew and all our equipment into a truck and set off for D.C.

Power Shift did indeed attract as many as twelve thousand people. Among them were some of America's most prominent environmental activists and policy makers: the actor Darryl Hannah; Nancy Pelosi, the Speaker of the House; John Sellers and Andrew Boyd of Agit-Pop; Adrienne Maree Brown from the Ruckus Society; Lisa Jackson of the Environmental Protection Agency; and Robert Kennedy Jr., to name a few. My crew and I stayed on a boat owned by Ann Luskey, a friend and fellow environmentalist, docked in National Harbor, and filmed day and night. It was like a crash course in activism and the approaches various groups are taking to tackle these issues.

In the 1970s, the environmental movement got a huge boost when some brave activists brought back footage of Greenpeace trying to stop whalers and used it to attract international news coverage. No one had seen modern whaling before, with its speedboats and grenade-tipped harpoons, nor had they seen people willing to risk their own lives to put a stop to it by putting themselves between the whale and the harpoon. It was revelatory and brought an unheard of level of attention to a variety of environmental issues.

The problem now, however, is far bigger than saving whales, and the enemy is all of us. It's no wonder the environmental movement feels like it has been treading water—maybe even sinking. Most environmental issues have gotten worse since those early days of Greenpeace actions—pollution, climate change, overfishing, soil erosion, deforestation—on par with our population growth and energy consumption. I know there are still awesome and dedicated individuals fighting for a variety of causes all over the world—I've met some of them—but the popular environmental movement is in serious need of a rethink if it's going to save us. Seeding environmental issues deep into the public consciousness requires actions and approaches that ordinary people will pay attention to, not just those who are already aware. By and large, the strategies activists are using to attract that attention nowadays are forms of "non-violent direct action" (NVDA).

Anything you do to impede, prevent or draw attention to an act that is destructive to the environment without hurting or damaging people or property is a non-violent direct action. Sitting in a tree someone intends to cut down, chaining yourself to a bulldozer, picketing a corporate headquarters, you name it. Power Shift was crawling with individuals and organizations for whom NVDA was and is a way of life, and they had plans to temporarily shut down the coal-fired power plant that powered the White House. The conference organizers actually held seminars on NVDA and I fully participated, joining the coal-fired power plant "action."

On the day of the "Capitol Climate Action," thousands of activists marched on the plant carrying flags and signs, chanting and singing, some decked out in elaborate costumes—but many wearing their Sunday best—to show the world that it's not just hippies and youth who are concerned about coal. We made our way on foot from Power Shift's base of operations in a huge conference centre to the gates of the plant. There we set up shop, with groups of activists surrounding the plant and blocking all the entrances. People marched and picketed, several speakers addressed the crowd and not a single car or truck was allowed to enter or exit the plant. Many of the activists planned to try to get arrested at the plant, the arrests themselves considered the acts of NVDA they hoped would attract further attention to the cause. Darryl Hannah was willing to leave in the back of a cop car. I wasn't. As a Canadian, moving around tons of gear without permits, I already had enough trouble getting into the United States.

My experience at Power Shift got me thinking in a much bigger way. Twelve thousand committed people, mostly youth, gathered in Washington. They marched on and blockaded the power plant that fuels the White House, and there was little press coverage. It seemed like the only people who cared were the ones who were already involved. Yes, we successfully blockaded the plant, but coal-fired power plants have enough fuel on reserve to run for days. No less coal was burned and no environmental policy was enacted, though as a result of actions like these proposals for new coal-fired plants have been shelved in the United States. The trouble is we're still building them elsewhere; China is building one a week.

Power Shift didn't fail in the sense that new activists were created, community was built, and people felt like they were changing the world—and they were, just not enough of it. NVDA can work, but it's hard to scale it up to the point where it will save humanity.

One hundred thousand protestors took to the streets of Copenhagen when Denmark hosted the fifteenth UN Climate Change Conference in 2009, in one of the biggest protests on the environment in history. But the Copenhagen conference failed to create policy to ensure our future. Imagine instead one million people gathered in Washington around that coal power plant who wouldn't leave until coal power plants were banned outright: that could work. If millions gathered in the streets in Copenhagen or other cities, and world leaders received millions of messages from their own citizens, maybe something would change. But to mobilize on that scale we need a hell of a lot more people who know what's going on, who care, who want to act.

Traditional activism hasn't scaled up to match the scale of our problem. We need to think of something new and stronger. The environmental movement itself has to become a lot more unified. At Power Shift it was glaringly apparent that nearly everyone involved represented a different group, organization or interest. Right now, if by force or by some incredible miracle, a government or business actually came to the environmental movement looking for information, a solution or a directive on a particular issue, they'd get fifty different reports, solutions or directives in return. That inconsistency hands them an excuse for inaction on a silver platter. They can waffle over which recommendation to follow for years while continuing to do nothing. On climate for example, many scientists believe we need 100 percent decarbonization *now*. Some environmentalists, particularly those who work with big corporations, believe this to be too big a jump for their clients (and people in general) to make, and temper their versions of necessity to suit their clients. Yes, let's all buy solar panels and hybrid cars, and aim instead for a 30, 25, 20 or even smaller percentage reduction in emissions. That the corporate world can handle.

Division on that scale makes significant change impossible. The enemies of the environmental movement, of course, are also subdivided—thousands of businesses, hundreds of complicit governments, and so on. They are, however, united by one thing: the pursuit of profit. It's a motivating force more powerful than any other the human race has yet dreamed up. We need to face it with a motivating unity of our own. If we come with a strong, clear message, we'll be way harder to resist!

No anti-slavery crusader aimed for a partial solution or settled on a regimen of interim targets. The fight to end slavery was a fight to end 100 percent of slavery for all time. In just that way, we can't settle for partial measures if we are going to win the war for our world. We need to fight for 100 percent sustainability, now.

Chapter Twenty-Six

Money and Madagascar

In the months following Power Shift, I continued my search for people and organizations I could partner with. Topping my list was Romuald Vaudry. Vaudry is a project manager with GoodPlanet, the activist foundation headed up by French photographer, film-maker and journalist Yann Arthus-Bertrand, a hero of mine. Vaudry is a part of GoodPlanet's Action Carbone initiative to tackle carbon emissions and climate change. Specifically, his focus is deforestation and carbon sequestration and the majority of his work takes place in Madagascar, which by many estimates is about 85 percent deforested.

I had originally met Vaudry at a UN climate conference. I'd interviewed him there and at some point in the conversation we'd begun to talk about Madagascar. I told him about my trip there as a university student, shooting photos in some of the country's amazing wildlife parks, and said I'd love to go back and film there. It seemed to me that the story of Madagascar, what humans had done to the astonishing and unique life there, and what had happened to its beneficent natural resources, could form a vivid part of the film I was struggling to conceive. He promised to show me around the country. In the spring of 2010, I once again landed in Antananarivo, a city natives nickname Tana.

The ten years since my last visit to Madagascar had been tumultuous ones for the island. In March 2009, after serving as the mayor of Tana for less than two years, a thirty-five-year-old radio personality named Andry Rajoelina seized control of the country in a popular uprising. Though he seemed to have the will of the people behind him, Rajoelina couldn't be recognized under the Malagasy constitution, which required presidents to be at least forty years of age. Within days of establishing an interim government, his party faced large-scale condemnation from the international community, including the African Union, the European Union and the United States. Humanitarian aid dried up, sanctions were threatened and all hell broke loose.

Already faced with the challenge of running one of the poorest nations on earth, the interim government's resources were stretched so thin without international support that the door was opened to horrendous environmental abuses. The booming trade in illegal teak and rosewood is one distressing example. Taking advantage of the confusion brought on by the chaotic political climate, corporations have established logging operations in national parks and other protected areas. More than three quarters of the species found in Madagascar exist nowhere else on earth. Logging within protected areas is destroying the habitats of some of the most endangered animals on the planet, all so consumers in more affluent parts of the world can have the opportunity to blow their money on a teak bedframe.

Even scarier is the fact that Madagascar possesses the third largest tar sands reserves in the world. If the Malagasy government allows companies to start exploiting those reserves, the potential for Madagascar to become the site of one of the largest environmental atrocities in history is enormous. In my home country of Canada, at the peak of the first world, tar sands are a devastating environmental catastrophe. Unsupervised exploitation of them at the infrastructureless bottom of the third world is an absolute worst-case scenario.

I hoped that with Vaudry's help, I'd be able to get a sense of how such an environmental shitstorm could have ever happened in place as close to paradise as Madagascar.

My decision to go had been a bit spur of the moment. It didn't take too long for the lack of long-term planning to bite me in the ass: I arrived in the middle of the monsoon season, a horrible thing for delicate cameras. After landing in Tana, I was picked up by Romuald to begin our trek overland to Andasibe-Mantadia National Park. He managed to wrangle a small SUV across roads that didn't exist during monsoon season—they were washed out by floods or buried in mudslides. The drive took us six hours.

A day of nice weather was waiting for us at Andasibe. I spent all of it—sun up to sun down—in the jungle filming beautiful black and white indris, the largest species of lemur in Madagascar. About 3 feet tall if you stand them up on their hind legs, they look like stretched-out, very thin pandas. They lounged in the trees above my head and every now and then one of them let out a trademark howl. Lemurs are some of the earliest primates, and were once widespread throughout the world. Then monkeys evolved, and were smarter, faster, meaner and hardier; they out-competed lemurs in every environment. But about 75 millon years ago, Madagascar started drifting away from Africa, creating a lifeboat for lemurs: the monkeys didn't make it onto the island. There were once seventeen species of lemurs larger than the indri, some as big as gorillas, but they were easy hunting, and were wiped out early into man's inhabitation.

In Andasibe I started a pattern of reverse storm chasing. Not only was it monsoon season, a hurricane was headed for the island. I boarded a plane from Andasibe to Berenty in the desert south, just in time to miss it.

All of my flights around the country were pretty stressful. Madagascar is so removed from the rest of the world, you often can't use a credit card to pay for a plane ticket. Instead, you have to arrive at the airport cash in hand; a flight costs something like two million Malagasy dollars. Once you're in the air, the plane makes questionable (and sometimes seriously questionable) noises and feels like it might fall apart at any second. Before one of my departures on that trip, I watched the plane's repair staff out the cabin window as we sat on the runway preparing for takeoff. Each man had a small handful of bolts and they were all holding them up for inspection and comparison. They seemed to be debating whether they had one that might fit whatever it was on our plane that was missing a bolt. This was minutes before takeoff.

In Berenty, I spent a day filming another species of lemur, sifakas. Like many lemurs, sifakas are almost entirely arboreal. They have four hands, instead of two feet and two hands, to better suit life in the trees. When they have to cross the ground from sleeping trees to food trees, they do so in an enormously comical sideways dance—long white limbs flailing their way across the red sand. I filmed the sifakas crossing deforested areas to try and bring emotional elements to our new film's deforestation scene. As the second biggest contributor to climate change, deforestation releases massive amounts of carbon into the atmosphere, as well as destroying nature's most perfect carbon sequestration devices, the ones responsible for the other half of the oxygen we breathe. It's estimated we've lost about half of the world's tropical forests already, and will have just 10 percent by 2030, and none by 2050.

After filming dancing sifakas, I set out in search of the World Food Program. Romuald had told me the WFP had a headquarters just outside of the Berenty wildlife reserve and he'd given me a contact number for them. I'd called and asked if I could visit and film their compound. They'd agreed, but now I had to find the place.

I hired a driver to take me into the nearest town. It had recently flooded and looked out and out apocalyptic. Townspeople lined the sides of the road, watching what little traffic passed as though they were waiting for something. It wasn't clear to me what that might be. I got out and shot footage for about ten minutes before a pristine white Toyota Land Cruiser passed by with the letters WFP emblazoned across its side. I didn't bother packing up the camera, just ran back to where my driver was waiting and told him to follow the shiny white SUV.

The Toyota led us to a squat one-storey building in the centre of a fenced-in compound: the headquarters of the World Food Program. Once we were let through the gate, I was greeted by a staffer named Enrique. He gave me a brief tour of the compound and then agreed to be interviewed.

I had been an animal person my whole life, decidedly and completely. As a kid, I had always turned off the TV or changed the channel when one of those sponsor-a-child charity infomercials came on with the starving kids and their swollen bellies. I'm ashamed to admit it now, but it never really occurred to me to ask why there are people in the world who don't have any food. There just were.

But in Madagascar that question took on a profound and troubling weight.

There are twenty million people on the island. That's a lot, but Madagascar is one of the biggest islands on earth and possesses one of the most productive ecosystems. It has an enormous wealth of natural resources in the ocean and on land. Why are people starving here?

Enrique explained that it's not that there isn't enough food to feed everyone, it's that access to that food is unequally distributed. The Malagasy may live in a place that should easily provide for their needs, but they also live within a system that denies them access to those means. With no money to buy food and no land to grow it on, they are left to starve while watching the natural wealth of their country drain north toward the first world. It's the logic of global capitalism. What hit me was how far reaching this faulty system was—capitalism, commerce, the imperative of growth—it was everywhere, even in Madagascar. I had somehow imagined that there were still places on earth where people weren't part of that system: they could live, hunt and grow food as people have for hundreds of thousands of years. Not so. Most land is now privately owned by someone or something that wants to profit from it. It's more profitable to exploit that land to its fullest extent, whether that's farming crops for foreign markets or other uses, than it is to use it to grow food for the hungry—even if they are people who have lived off that land for centuries. With the world's population at seven billion people and climbing, hunger is becoming an even more serious issue. Already one billion people don't have enough food.

When our interview was over, Enrique invited me to come back the next day and help the WFP hand out food at a small school they operated. Driving back to the wildlife reserve that evening, the sisal plantations that seemed an ever-present feature of the landscape around Berenty, became glaring symbols of local hunger. Sisal is a type of cactus. It looks like the top of a giant pineapple and is used in the production of rope and heavy-duty fabrics. All of the sisal plantations that stretched away from the road in either direction as far as I could see were French-owned. French companies growing French cactuses to export to French manufacturers for use in French goods. It didn't take a genius to recognize that if you didn't have so much sisal occupying all of the available agricultural land, the Malagasy might be able to grow themselves some food, or forests that would sustain life that would sustain them.

Meeting Enrique and a host of WFP staff at their schoolhouse the next day, I immediately encountered an even less palatable symbol of the logic of globalization: U.S. corn. Malagasy kids ranging in age from four or five into their early teens were arrayed on either side of a pair of long wooden tables, eating what for many of them would be their only meal of the day: U.S. corn hydrated in water. U.S. corn shipped from America, all the way around Africa, to end up in the bellies of starving kids in Madagascar. Genetically modified, lacking in nutrients, hard on their digestive systems and sporting an insane carbon footprint after a journey across half the world. I filmed the kids as they ate and continued when they started the day's lessons. They played games and sang in Malagasy and just generally made the most of what little energy the corn had provided. I left when the lessons ended and made my way back to the wildlife reserve where I packed and hopped on a plane to Tana. From there, I flew north to Ankarana and spent a few days filming chameleons and crown lemurs against the backdrop of Madagascar's mind-blowing limestone forests before catching my flight out. Through it all, though, I couldn't stop thinking about those kids and their bowls of U.S. corn.

Chapter Twenty-Seven

Surrounded by COPs

In December of 2009, I'd watched on my computer screen as 100,000 protestors took to the streets of Copenhagen to demand that representatives of major governments at the 15th Conference of the Parties to the United Nations Framework Convention on Climate Change (COP 15) agree on policy to control carbon emissions and prevent catastrophic climate change. It was the largest environmental protest in history—three times the turnout anyone expected—and was accompanied by sister rallies that attracted tens of thousands of people in several countries around the world. As I mentioned earlier, it had seemed like a massive coup for the environmental movement, but when the conference came to an end on December 18, no new policy had been enacted. As they had 14 times before, the delegates agreed to meet the next year and try again.

After witnessing the failure of so large a movement to spur any kind of change, like a lot of people, I wrote off the COP process. So, the following year, when I was invited to join Canada's youth delegation to COP 16 in Cancun, Mexico, I accepted with the intention of doing whatever I could to disrupt the process from the inside. I also got a media pass for my buddy, filmmaker and activist Tristan Bayer, and set out to shoot scenes for *REvolution*.

Climate change, despite being considered the largest environmental issue we face, is a symptom of the problem, not the problem itself. If you were sick and had a cough, you would try to treat the illness, not tape your mouth shut. Our climate is changing because there are too many people consuming too much. Our consumption is destroying our forests, biodiversity, soil, fisheries and oceans—our life support system. It's also literally burning hundreds of millions of years of sequestered carbon in the form of fossil fuels—decayed plant and animal matter. One big and measurable by-product of this consumption is climate change and atmospheric CO_2 concentrations, an issue Al Gore's *An Inconvenient Truth* brought to a wide audience. Despite it being a symptom of the problem, climate change is a relatively easily measurable one, and the biggest and most publicized environmental conferences in the world are still climate change conferences.

Driving from our hotel to the conference centre on the first day, I found it obvious that the Mexican government had done its best to eliminate the possibility of protests on the scale of those seen in Denmark. Not only was the conference held in a remote location well outside the city—making it extremely difficult for protestors to get to—the complex was fenced. Any protestors organized enough to have made the trek were still 7 kilometres out of sight and earshot of the official delegates. With mass demonstrations effectively neutralized, the burden of voicing dissent at the conference fell to youth delegations like the one I was part of. Working in our own groups or teamed with delegations from other countries, we staged protests and skits, gave speeches, sang songs, screamed ourselves hoarse and did pretty much anything else we could think of to pressure the delegates. Though it was inspiring to see the energy, urgency and passion with which the youth delegations attacked their role, I could tell that most of our words fell on deaf ears.

The other dissenting voices I found really profound were those of the indigenous peoples of the world, most movingly conveyed by Evo Morales, Bolivia's first indigenous president. He took the podium on the second last day of the conference and delivered a speech urging world leaders to ignore the air-conditioned comfort of the conference hall and, for once, imagine themselves in the shoes of one of the 300,000 people who die each year as a result of climate change. He identified the global climate crisis as one of the many crises of capitalism and urged his fellow world leaders to begin talking about the causes of climate change rather than just its effects.

He also made a powerful point about carbon markets. Carbon markets and emissions trading are initiatives that seek to control pollution and deforestation by creating economies out of clean air and trees. They assign dollar values to natural resources in an effort to create financial incentives for companies and governments to reduce pollution. The World Bank has even announced a trading scheme for animals that would allow countries with beautiful and abundant wildlife to sell it off to foreign interests. Morales argued that the goal of the conference should be to save the natural world rather than turn it into a commodity. His arguments struck a particular chord with me.

In its current incarnation, it seems the COP conferences are over before the delegates even walk in the door. Those looking at the process from the outside see the environment as the most important issue—the very reason for the conference's existence—but to the world leaders and other delegates involved in the actual negotiations, the environment is just one item on a long list of priorities, nestled in at number 37 or 72 or 115. The other 36 or 71 or 114 items on that list are, by and large, issues pertaining to economic growth. We haven't even reached the stage at which we can argue whether environmental collapse is a scarier prospect than economic collapse. We haven't even begun to acknowledge that environmental collapse will make economic collapse a foregone conclusion.

Instead, the assumption of every delegate present is that the economy of the territory they represent is the most important thing in the world. They will only agree to a change that benefits the environment if it has little or no negative consequences for their economic growth. Their country will be wealthier if they give up less; if they are allowed more emissions, their country will prosper, which reflects a fundamental flaw in our economic system: progress currently comes at the cost of our life support system. If the developed world, mostly restricted to the northern hemisphere, has warmer climates and longer summers, it could mean a longer and more fruitful growing season and less harsh winters; if the developed world continues to exploit the third world, driving poorer nations further and further into debt, they will be able to buy the resources of those nations even cheaper than they do today; if they have to pollute, poison some people and destroy some resources for their economies to grow, so be it. Some delegations are so stuck in their ways that they announce on the first day of the conference that they are not willing to commit to a binding treaty. Japan did it in Cancun on day one! Why even bother to show up at all? The whole premise on which the negotiations are based just sucks. There is no other word for it. Countries protect their interests, which they define as their future economic growth. With representatives at the negotiating table with a political lifespan of a couple of terms in office, the issue of whether we'll have a future is an afterthought.

But at the moment this process is all we've got.

I went to COP wanting to dismantle it. I wanted to help stir up so much shit that the process would fall apart, completely disintegrate. I thought that only with a clean slate could we really start to change things. But once I got there, I realized that none of that was really an option. The environmental problems threatening life on this planet demand action right now—yesterday even. To set up another system like COP to try to get governments together to commit to binding environmental policies would take years, maybe decades. And, when it was all said and done, you'd still run the risk of ending up with exactly the same injustice and self-interested bullshit. I believe the indigenous movement is right in advising against carbon markets. Turning the environment into yet another economic instrument and then handing it over to the financial powers that have gotten us into this mess in the first place would be beyond foolish. But the idea at the heart of carbon markets—using the financial incentives and penalties that seem to be the only thing governments and corporations can understand to convince them to stop polluting—is a useful one. Maybe it just needs to be pushed to a greater extreme.

Since the COP process provides our best means of getting governments to take concrete steps to stop carbon emissions and climate change, we have to force those involved in that process to better represent our interests and goals. Since the only arguments delegates to COP seem to understand are economic ones, we should make it financially unthinkable for them to continue to put off acting to save the environment. In a poll taken a few months before COP 16, 66 percent of Canadians said that they didn't feel their government was doing enough for the environment. If that same two-thirds of the Canadian public had written their elected officials and expressed their desire to see Canada sign on to an international climate change treaty, they may have gotten their wish. If that two-thirds of the Canadian people had refused to buy anything or go to work until those same desires were met, it would've brought the entire economy to a halt and you can bet the Canadian government would've signed on the dotted line.

But, as nice as it is to imagine that great mass of people rising up in defence of the earth, none of those things happened and there's no guarantee that they will, unless everyone recognizes what's going on and finds the will to act.

The only thing any of us can know for certain about this fight is that somewhere inside us, whether deep down or blasting out of every pore, a voice is telling us that it's wrong for us to ruin the world for our children; that it's wrong for us to live in comfort while so many people starve and struggle for survival; and that it's wrong for one species to destroy the lives of every other.

I entered COP 16 as a filmmaker and delegate. I spent the conference singing and acting and chanting and screaming and dressing up in a giant shark costume to try to draw attention to the oceans. I interviewed protestors, scientists, activists, diplomats and world leaders. And I left COP 16 most affected by a kid, Felix Finkbeiner, who had decided to plant a tree on the conference centre lawn for every country in attendance because he felt that it was the right thing to do. He told me his organization—Plant for the Planet—intended to plant one million trees in every country of the world, and I believed him.

Chapter Twenty-Eight

Children Know Best

About a month before I left for COP 16, I received an email from Kathy Pagapular, a grade six teacher at San Vicente Elementary School on Saipan, a tiny 19 by 9 kilometre island in the Northern Marianas in Micronesia, which is home to eighty thousand people. Kathy had written to tell me that she had shown *Sharkwater* to her class and it had struck a chord with the kids. They were pissed. They wanted to do something to save sharks and they wondered whether I was willing to help.

I wrote them back to tell them I would love to be involved and ask what they wanted me to do. Along with my letter, I sent a few copies of the film and some *Sharkwater* photo books. Then I got swept up in the preparations for COP 16 and, for a while, forgot about the tiny island of Saipan.

But soon after I got back from Cancun, a second email arrived. In it, Kathy and the kids brought me up to speed on their efforts to save sharks. The kids had begun by dividing into groups, each one assigned a specific task. They organized public screenings of *Sharkwater*; gave talks about the shark fin industry; handed out surveys to raise awareness and gauge public opinion; and called or visited local restaurants to figure out which ones served shark fin soup. They also managed to get a bill introduced into the legislature to entirely ban shark fins from the island, and with their campaign to change the public perception of sharks gaining momentum, the bill had passed through both the House and Senate. The kids only needed one signature—that of the governor of the island—to bring into effect a law that would make Saipan the second place on earth to completely ban shark fin. I wrote them back to tell them I was coming to Saipan, bringing cameras with me, to personally congratulate them for all their hard work and try to help them sway the governor's decision.

I got in touch with the Pew Environment Group, which had done a lot of work on marine conservation in Australia, New Zealand and Micronesia and asked them to help me and another cameraman, Sean Heinrichs, get to Saipan and then around the island. They put us in touch with a local woman named Laurie Pterka, who would show us around and, if necessary, set up meetings with government officials who might have a say in getting the bill signed. In advance of my arrival, Pew also sent out a press release announcing that I was coming to Saipan to film for my next movie and that Kathy's grade six students were going to be part of it. The announcement caused a stir and, before I'd even set foot on the island, officials announced that the governor would sign the bill into law while I was there.

My first stop was, of course, San Vicente Elementary. The kids were riding high off the news that the bill was actually going to become law and were incredibly excited for my arrival. I walked into their class to screams and applause, and they made me a gift of a crown of flowers. They showed me their classroom and walked me through all the different projects they'd been working on with pride. I talked to them about sharks and told them that what they were doing was awesome, that they were going to make history and change the world, and that I was incredibly proud to know them.

I spent the next couple of days filming around the island and interviewing Kathy and the kids about how they had gone about trying to save sharks and what had made them want to do it in the first place. Each of the kids, in his or her own way, told me that once they'd found out what was happening to sharks—that many were killed cruelly, wasting most of the animal, threatening the balance of the oceans just for the sake of profit—they started trying to do something about it. We had planned a celebratory screening in the evening a couple of days into my visit, but on the day the screening was to take place, I got word that the governor had decided not to sign. With the possibility of precedent-setting legislation coming into law, the fishing lobby had thrown its weight around, claiming the bill violated the rights of fisherman. The governor had apparently caved under the pressure.

Before the no-longer-celebratory screening that night, I addressed the audience. I told them that I'd come all the way to Saipan to film for my next movie because they had a very real chance to become world leaders in the protection of both sharks and the invaluable marine resources that surround their island. I reminded them that their entire infrastructure was based on those resources and it would be insanity to pass up the chance to institute a law that might better protect their future. I promised them that the fight to get the governor to sign the bill was not over, and then we screened the film. During the question and answer period afterward, the audience promised me they would do anything they could to get the bill back on track.

The next day brought a brief ray of hope. I was doing a radio show at 7:30 in the morning when one of the producers, who had a relative in government, was tipped off that the signing was back on. I found out on the air and couldn't hide my excitement.

Then Kitty Simonds, the executive director of the Western Pacific Regional Fishery Management Council, showed up on the island. Simonds is one of the most effective fishing lobbyists in the world. It took her less than twenty-four hours to get the signing cancelled again.

The next few days were a blur. I went back to visit Kathy's class at San Vicente and told the kids that the governor had decided not to sign the bill. In response, they began a letter writing campaign, bombarding his office with pleas to stop the slaughter of sharks. While the kids were busy writing, Laurie set up a series of meetings for me with ranking members of Saipan's government. I met the ministers in charge of the environment and tourism and made the case for a shark fin ban, but it felt like Simonds was right on my heels everywhere I went. Still, I could tell as I left my meetings with various politicians that they were excited by the possibility of positive change, and by the publicity that would result. With the kids, the public and many of the politicians on our side, I knew that the only thing that could sink the bill was effective pressure from Simonds and her lobby. The same old money talk.

In the two days left before the original signing date, Simonds and I did back-to-back interviews on Saipan's biggest TV station. I went first and, despite the fact that the interview went well, couldn't shake the feeling that no matter what I said, Simonds would have the last word. But by the time she arrived for her interview, the island was of one mind to such a degree that the station ran footage of sharks being finned, hacked up and thrown back into the ocean behind her comments about shark fishing being a sustainable right to be enjoyed by fishermen. We had won. I was there the next day when governor Benigno Fitial signed the second shark fin ban on earth into law. (Hawaii passed the first ban.)

After the signing, a few of the kids told me they hoped the movement they had started would spread from their island to the next island and then on to countries around the world. It didn't take long for them to get their wish. While I was still in Saipan, a class of grade seven kids in Guam heard what was happening on Saipan, and thought if a grade six class could do it, they could too. I took a detour to Guam to meet them, and found out two schools had taken on the cause. They had watched *Sharkwater*, done class projects, and with the help of Pew and local politicians, got a bill to ban shark fins proposed for the island. I promised to come back to Guam and teach the kids how to scuba dive if they managed to get their bill passed into law.

When the hearing came, the kids filled the senate halls in such numbers that the fishing lobbyists could barely get in to make their case. Many of the kids testified at the hearing, and spoke for so long that it ran until two in the morning, when the bill was finally passed. In March 2011, the governor of Guam signed that bill into law.

The kids in Guam coined the term "Shark Tsunami" to describe the wave of environmental action they imagined would sweep the world. Their reasoning was simple: if kids in Saipan and Guam could do it, kids all over the world could do it too. Their prophecy is coming true right now, as groups of kids in Maryland, Washington, Oregon and California helped get similar bills introduced into their respective state legislatures. Kids testifying at city hall in Toronto helped push councillors to ban shark fin in Canada's biggest city. It's a global movement to save sharks and kids are leading the way.

Kids are such effective activists because they don't try to reason their way out of what they know to be the right thing to do. Adults look at the exact same problems, but for them things are "complicated." They've got mouths to feed, mortgages, jobs and lifestyles that depend on an unsustainable level of consumption. We fly, drive, buy food and goods we rarely know the origins of, and work within an economic system whose imperatives trump all other concerns. The economy is viewed as the most important thing ever. We think we can only protect the environment if it doesn't affect our economy.

But kids aren't in the system yet. They don't have debt and dead-end jobs or the fear of losing their livelihoods. They haven't lost the fascination with and love of the natural world that we're all born with. When they find out about an environmental injustice, they say, "Okay, we've just got to save that stuff? Let's do it!" I bet if you asked kids what we should do to protect the environment, they'd tell you in pretty commonsense terms. Stop polluting, stop destroying habitats and stop killing stuff. Simple, right? So why is it so difficult?

A hundred years ago there were two billion people on earth, and modes of transport were sustainable. Now we have seven billion people, either flying and driving around the world with multiple gadgets to keep them connected, or wishing they could. The systems we built when there were far fewer of us are out of date, and need a redesign. Our economy is addicted to infinite growth, yet we live on a planet with finite resources. Which makes for a zero-sum game where there are big winners and big losers, and an enormous cost borne by our environment, our health and happiness.

Our living world has no rights in this zero sum game, even though it's the basis of our civilization and we cannot survive without it. Legal systems rarely punish those that pollute and destroy the environment, and governments often reward them with tax breaks and subsidies, on the theory that they generate tax revenues. Our governments are corruptible by financial interests,

Kids don't try to reason their way out of what they know to be the right thing to do, which makes them really effective activists.

and by the strong belief that the only way they can get out of the current economic shakiness is to grow their way out, using tax revenues to service their huge debt loads. Our corporations operate with no moral or social conscience, and certainly no devotion to paying taxes. They can destroy the world and profit from it, and those in charge aren't liable for the damage.

Inside every one of us is a voice saying the same thing as those kids said in Saipan and Guam, California and Ontario. Everyone can change the world, and indeed everyone does. Saving the world doesn't have to be complicated. Just take what you love and what you're best at and slam them together into a life of purpose and meaning, and your choice will inspire others to do the same.

The biggest hurdle we have to overcome is the fear and conditioning that drowns that child's voice out. The fear of change, the fear of not being enough, of not having enough, of not counting for enough. All of us fear living a life without purpose and yet many of us struggle to find one, to stay focused. There's no surer way to have purpose than to fight for something you love. There's also no surer way to find people you'll end up loving than by joining in that fight.

Forget what everyone's told you about the economy, the system, the way things are and the way you should be. That's what's gotten us into this mess. It's going to take some revolutionary thinking to get us out of it. The problems we face are immense, and they are not outside us but within us. Our need to consume has driven this disposable, superficial society. Our lack of awareness has allowed corporations to pillage the earth and pay nothing for it. Our lack of involvement in our government and its structures has led democracies to become corporatocracies that serve the best interests of the economy over the long-term health and happiness of citizens.

Evolution is the cure for this and awareness is its fuel.

When everyone understands how ecosystems work and why they're being destroyed, and by whom—the 1 percent minority, the rich few who are ripping around the world destroying everything and profiting from it—that 1 percent will be the ones considered the dangerous radicals. Our majority will change the world. The environment and human welfare into the future will be our sacred trust. Our growth-centred economy and civilization will shift focus from generating wealth to regenerating ecosystems, which will secure the survival of humans too.

This may seem like a giant task, and it is, but we can do it. It was ordinary people acting together against special interests and even cultural norms who succeeded in banning slavery, fought for civil rights, the rights of women, the lives of whales, to fix the holes in the ozone. Enough people took action and forced changes in the world. And now we have to do it again. We need to take a stand and fight for our world.

I don't think we want to just scrape by as a species, surviving with a degraded natural world, suffering ecosystem and societal collapse, and mass human suffering on a scale that dwarfs anything we've experienced as a species. I think we all want to see what we're capable of, and make this world of ours the best it can be. I think we should be aiming at paradise on earth, but at the very least we should strive to bring the earth into balance again. Sustainability should be the bottom line. Anything that is not sustainable needs a revamp, and in retrofitting our world we'll find jobs and economic growth that is sustainable too.

The vision of the ideal life that we've been taught in the West, which is gaining ever more purchase in China and India and elsewhere, feeds the system we need to undo. Go to school in order to get a degree in order to get a job in order to earn money so you can try to buy happiness because your life sucks, then retire and die: this is not meaningful living. What's truly meaningful, and cool, is changing things. Martin Luther King, Jr. is cooler than Kanye West. Nelson Mandela is cooler than A-Rod. Mother Teresa is cooler than Paris Hilton. These icons of change are all people who showed us what's possible, who took us to a higher level as a species. Fighting for something other than your own wealth, working for someone else's happiness, saving species, pulling people out of poverty, conserving instead of wasting—this is what really matters, and this is what's cool.

What you buy doesn't make you cool, it makes you the opposite. Stop buying stuff just to have more stuff. Most of us have enough of everything already. Let's care for what we've got, instead, and dispose of our disposable society.

We do need a new paradigm, though, and one is upon us, whether we like it or not. The battle ahead is the largest ever waged by humanity, against the greatest of adversaries. Fifty-one of the biggest economies in the world belong to corporations. The trillions of dollars spent bailing out failing companies through our most recent financial crisis could have solved many of our environmental problems. In fact, Lester Brown of the Earth Policy Institute has worked out what it would cost to save our environment and civilization: $200 billion a year. That's a quarter of the United States' annual military budget.

Our species has been here on this earth for 200,000 years, and in the last thousand, we've grown from 100 million people, to more than seven billion. We've created enormous advances, and lifted our species higher than anyone dreamed possible. But in the next hundred years, we face a problem so large it threatens our species as well as every other. Biologists predict that we're now in the midst of the sixth mass extinction, with potential consequences as catastrophic as the one that ended the reign of the dinosaurs sixty-five million years ago. Except in this case we as a species are to blame, and we will be part of it.

The major extinctions of the past have wiped out innumerable species, but became opportunities for other species who evolved in the face of adversity. Without these earlier extinctions, there would be no mammals, no bird flight, no humans. If we choose to evolve in the face of the coming extinction, imagine what we'll be capable of in a hundred years, a thousand years, a million years or even a billion years. Imagine what we could do, what we could be, what we could see?

Now is our opportunity, as a species, to take this challenge, and use it as a driver to evolve. We need to evolve our systems, our communities, our thoughts and ourselves to cope with this problem and usher in a new era of humanity. We need to save the humans, and along with the humans, our fascinating, complex, glorious, life-enhancing, subtle, startling, totally amazing natural world.

Back underwater in Papua New Guinea, I was reminded of life's ability to find a way. Dave Hannan and I had spotted another flamboyant cuttlefish. This one, the largest I've ever seen, dominated the sea floor next to the jetty at Samarai Island in Milne Bay.

I spent a day following her around with our giant camera as she devastated tiny sea creatures. Then, at sunset, she started laying eggs. First in a coconut shell, cracked open by some human intent on drinking the delicious water inside. Then in a Coke can also discarded under the jetty. A rare and supposedly delicate creature, the flambo had found a way to adapt, taking advantage of the situation by depositing twelve teardrop-shaped eggs in a tiny aluminum fortress perfect for its young.

Life in general, the oceans and the planet will survive, as they have for billions of years. It's our fate that's at stake. It's our opportunity to evolve.

Conclusion

My Own Action Plan

I'm confident we're going to get there. And to help make it happen, I've started two organizations dedicated to saving humanity.

United Conservationists is a non-profit conservation group which hopes to help guide humanity towards "paradise" on earth. Here's our mission statement:

> We're realists, dreamers, and revolutionaries. We believe in the earth, life and that 3.5 billion years of evolution created a world of unmatched productivity and diversity, perfect for humans, and that by undoing the damage wrought by short-sighted human expansion and greed, earth can be paradise for humans and millions of other species.
>
> We believe the health of our life support system to be of paramount importance, and that the design flaws of pre-*REvolutionary* civilization can be undone by an active and aware population, restoring ecosystems and achieving balance between human ambitions and our living world.

(Balance includes not artificially increasing the earth's carrying capacity at the expense of future ecosystem health with devices such as fossil fuels, fish farms and chemical fertilizers.) We believe capitalism has subverted democracy and the unfulfilling path of growth sold to us in the modern world will lead to environmental and societal collapse.

United Conservationists won't stop until a sustainable and equitable human population is reached, human consumption is in balance with the natural world, and the world's ecosystems are restored to full capacity—meaning lakes and rivers are unpolluted and teeming with fish, and diversely thriving forested ecosystems cover most of the land.

We believe this to be humanity's greatest challenge, and that the size of this adversary will call the best in humanity to the height of their potential, ushering in a new era of human evolution.

We believe all this to be achievable and probable within our lifetimes. United Conservationists are backed by 3.5 billion years of evolution, love and humanity. Even if you can't envision this future yet, your children can, and instead of shrinking in the face of such a challenge, this new generation of heroes will grow to defeat it, and achieve paradise on earth.

In 2013, United Conservationists will begin releasing the Collapse Prevention Report (CPR), giving each country of the world its very own outlook on its birthday, starting with Canada on July 1. The CPR will be a constantly updated graphical representation of where a country is at concerning its resources: a report card on its agricultural capacity, its soil fertility, its water quality, its population growth, and its consumption rates, that calculates when and why the country will collapse.

Every citizen in the country will be able to see the state of their country and its environment, put together by unbiased experts.

With this information in their hands, they'll be able to hold their governments and corporations accountable for their future.

The second initiative is Sharkwater Studios. *Sharkwater* proved to me that humanity is good. That people will take action against an atrocity when they're made aware of it—they just need the information.

To that end, Sharkwater Studios will design and release groundbreaking entertainment across all mass media, reaching the widest possible audiences with the information necessary to save humanity: what's happening to the planet, who's doing it, and what we can do about it, including how to influence government. We're going to give you what you need to know, every way we can give it to you: that's our promise.

In late 2012, Sharkwater Studios will release *REvolution* free with a marketing strategy to reach one billion people. I believe that if one billion people knew what you know now, the world would change.

To activate the public, bring them together and show them what to do, we're also releasing the REVOLUTION MOBILE—a mobile phone app that will play all of the content we think you need to see, including our own; contain interactive textbooks of information, serving as an open source for conservation education and a curriculum tool; connect activists, scientists and conservationists, show them what to do and how to change the world; allow people to track the progress of legislation in real time; and eventually, if we do our job correctly, to enable democracy within your hand so you can vote through the app on government policy susceptible to public opinion.

These are some of the ways I'm going to change the world, making best use of my talents and having an incredible time doing it with people that I love. If the making of *Sharkwater* and the last ten years are any indication of what's ahead, I'm going to fail more than I'm going to succeed. But I'm going to have a blast, live a life beyond my wildest dreams, and never feel alone a day in my life, because every day, more people will get educated and join our cause. The cause.

Thank you for reading this. You're now morally bound to me and everyone else who knows this stuff. Please share this book and these ideas with everyone you know by any means possible. I hope to meet you someday on the path of REvolution, and I hope you're as excited as I am to see what you're capable of.

Love and REvolution,
Rob

April 2012

Acknowledgements

This book wouldn't have been possible without the incredible love and support of my parents and sister, who nurtured my passions, however ambitious or different. Or without Evan Rosser, the great writer who helped put this story into words, and Anne Collins, publisher at Random House Canada, who helped me believe this is a story worthy of being told.

Tyler MacLeod, Julie Andersen, Jen Zabawa, Douglas Braun, Geordie Gregg, Tristan Bayer, Vanessa Pereira and Dave Hannan: thanks for helping bring this adventure to light.

Index

Oviedo, Fabian, 175–76
oxygen
    –nitrogen mix (tank), 148
    concentration of, 152
    excess. *See* hyperoxia
    insufficient. *See* hypoxia
    oceans, 141, 228, 229, 231, 240
    scuba tanks, 148–49, 151, 152
ozone layer depletion, 257

PADI. *See* Professional Association
    of Diving Instructors
Pagapular, Kathy, 250–51, 252, 253
Panama City, 165
Panama, 162–73
Panasonic VariCam. *See* VariCam
Papua New Guinea, 36, 37, 63,
    217–23, 259
"paradise on earth" concept, 257,
    261, 262
parrotfish, 219
PBS, 202
Pelican cases, 98, 123, 188, 189
pelicans, 34
Pelosi, Nancy, 233
penguins, 81, 180
Pew Environmental Group, 251,
    253
pH balance, 227, 228
Philippines, 218
photography, 67–68
photosynthesis, 228
phytoplankton, 141, 228
pirate treasure, 143

pirates, 84
PJ's Pets, 10
plankton, 91, 218, 226–27, 228,
    229, 231
Plant for the Planet, 249
plecostomus, 37, 38
polyps (coral), 229
pony bottle, 152, 181, 182
population growth, 234, 242,
    255, 258
Port Credit Pets, 46–47
Port Moresby (PNG), 218
Portuguese man o' war, 51–52
Power Shift (conference), 233,
    234–35, 236
predator populations, drop in,
    226, 228
Predators and Prey (*Wild*
    magazine), 70
proboscis monkeys, 111–13
ProCam (post-production house),
    204–5
Professional Association of Diving
    Instructors (PADI), 61, 64–65
    progression of levels, 66
profit motive, 236, 242, 255–56
    (*See also* economic growth;
    globalization)
Pterka, Laurie, 251, 253
Puerto Ayora (Santa Cruz Island),
    174, 190
Puntarenas (Costa Rica), 136–40,
    141, 197, 198
purpose, sense of, 256, 257

predator behaviour, 146

size, 145

Wild (magazine), 69–70, 71, 96

Wildaid, xvi, 216

wildlife films, new approach, 201–2

Wildman, Paul, 214

Wildscreen Festival, 201–2, 205

Wolf Island (Galapagos), 81, 82, 90–93, 114, 171, 190, 191, 192

women's rights movement, 257

World Bank, 246

World Food Program (WFP), 240–43

wrist computer, 151, 182, 184, 186

Wu, Daniel, xvii

Yao Ming, 216

Zabawa, Jen, 233

Zambia, 101

Zithromax, 181

Zodiac (boats), 129, 134, 137, 142–44, 146, 149, 154, 162, 178

Zooxanthellae (algae), 229

Born and raised in Toronto, ROB STEWART started his journey to becoming an award-winning filmmaker at the age of thirteen when he began photographing the underwater world. By the age of eighteen he became a scuba instructor trainer and then moved on to earn a Bachelor of Science degree in Biology, studying in Ontario, Jamaica and Kenya. Before making *Sharkwater*, Stewart spent four years traveling the world as chief photographer for the Canadian Wildlife Federation's magazines and as an award-winning freelance photojournalist. Leading expeditions to the most remote areas of the world, Stewart has logged thousands of hours underwater, using the latest in rebreather and camera technologies. At the age of twenty-two, he left his photography career behind and embarked on a remarkable journey over four years and through fifteen different countries, resulting in the multi award-winning documentary film: *Sharkwater*.